Icons of War and Terror

This book explores the ideas of key thinkers and media practitioners who have examined images and icons of war and terror.

Icons of War and Terror explores theories of iconic images of war and terror, not as received pieties but as challenging uncertainties; in doing so, it engages with both critical discourse and conventional image-making. The authors draw on these theories to re-investigate the media/global context of some of the most iconic representations of war and terror in the international 'risk society'. Among these photojournalistic images are:

*   Nick Ut's Pulitzer Prize-winning photograph of a naked girl, Kim Phuc, running burned from a napalm attack in Vietnam in June 1972;
*   a quintessential 'ethnic cleansing' image of massacred Kosovar Albanian villagers at Račak on 15 January 1999, which finally propelled a hesitant Western alliance into the first of the 'new humanitarian wars';
*   Luis Simco's photograph of marine James Blake Miller, 'the Marlboro Marine', at Fallujah, Iraq, 2004;
*   the iconic toppling of the World Trade Center towers in New York by planes on 11 September 2001, and the 'Falling Man' icon, one of the most controversial images of 9/11;
*   the image of one of the authors of this book as close-up victim of the 7/7 terrorist attack on London, which the media quickly labelled iconic.

This book will be of great interest to students of media and war, sociology, communications studies, cultural studies, terrorism studies and security studies in general.

John Tulloch is Professor of Communications, University of Newcastle, Australia. He is the author of 18 books in media and television studies, film history and theory, literary and theatre studies, and the sociology of risk. His books include the widely cited *Risk and Everyday Life* (with Deborah Lupton, Routledge, 2003) and monographs on *Doctor Who* (1984), *A Country Practice* (1986) and *Trevor Griffiths* (2007).

R. Warwick Blood is Professor of Communication, Faculty of Arts and Design, University of Canberra, Australia. Previously, he was a reporter, foreign correspondent and producer for the Australian Broadcasting Corporation. He has published on risk, news reporting and portrayal of health issues.

Media, War and Security
Series Editors: Andrew Hoskins, University of Nottingham
and Oliver Boyd-Barrett, Bowling Green State University

This series interrogates and illuminates the mutually shaping relationship between
war and media as transformative of contemporary society, politics and culture.

Global Terrorism and New Media
The post Al-Qaeda generation
Philip Seib and Dana M. Janabek

Radicalisation and the Media
Legitimising violence in the new media
Akil N. Awan, Andrew Hoskins and Ben O'Loughlin

Hollywood and the CIA
Cinema, defense and subversion
Oliver Boyd-Barrett, David Herrera and Jim Baumann

Violence and War in Culture and the Media
Athina Karatzogianni

Military Media Management
Negotiating the 'front' line in mediatized war
Sarah Maltby

Icons of War and Terror
Media images in an age of international risk
Edited by John Tulloch and R. Warwick Blood

Icons of War and Terror

Media images in an age of
international risk

**John Tulloch and
R. Warwick Blood**

Routledge
Taylor & Francis Group

LONDON AND NEW YORK

First published 2012
by Routledge
2 Park Square, Milton Park, Abingdon, Oxon, OX14 4RN

Simultaneously published in the USA and Canada
by Routledge
711 Third Avenue, New York, NY 10017

Routledge is an imprint of the Taylor & Francis Group, an informa business

© 2012 John Tulloch and R. Warwick Blood

British Library Cataloguing in Publication Data
A catalogue record for this book is available from the British Library

Library of Congress Cataloging-in-Publication Data
Tulloch, John.
  Icons of war and terror : media images in an age of international risk /
John Tulloch and R. Warwick Blood.
  p. cm. — (Media, war and security)
  Includes bibliographical references and index.
  1. War in mass media. 2. Terrorism in mass media. 3. Violence in mass media.
  4. Visual communication—Political aspects. I. Blood, Richard Warwick, 1947–
  II. Title.
  P96.W35T85 2012
  303.6—dc23
  2011052094

ISBN13: 978–0–415–69804–7 (hbk)
ISBN13: 978–0–415–69805–4 (pbk)
ISBN13: 978–0–203–11309–7 (ebk)

Typeset in Baskerville by
by Swales & Willis Ltd, Exeter, Devon

Printed and bound by CPI Group (UK) Ltd, Croydon, CR0 4YY

Contents

Acknowledgments

The authors would like to thank Stuart Allan, Anton Tulloch and Janet Andrew for their meticulous and creative advice in terms of the book's stylistic and conceptual presentation, Associate Professor Kerry McCallum and Dr Kate Holland for their support in completing the text, Dr Sonja Chandler for her help with references and style, and Janet Andrew for compiling the index. We have been given ongoing advice and support by the series editors, Professors Andrew Hoskins and Oliver Boyd-Barrett, who have been important in the final edits of this book, while Brunel University was generous in providing John Tulloch with six months research leave to compile the first draft. Our thanks also go to Andrew Humphrys and Annabelle Harris of Routledge for their ongoing professional support and advice on all areas of the book's development.

Excerpts from Hariman, R. and Lucaites, J.L. (2007) *No Caption Needed: Iconic Photographs, Public Culture, and Liberal Democracy* courtesy the University of Chicago Press.

Excerpts from Schama, S. (2006) *The Power of Art* [TV programme] BBC, BBC2; [DVD] courtesy BBC, London.

Members of Aboriginal, Torres Strait Islander and Maori communities are advised that this text contains names and images of deceased people.

Introduction

Said to be Neda Soltan, fatally wounded in Tehran, on a video posted on YouTube, June 21, 2009. © AAP

On 23 June 2009, SBS television news in Australia showed an image caught on a mobile telephone camera, which, the newsreader said, was 'rapidly becoming iconic'. It was the death scene of the 27-year-old music student Neda Agha Soltan. She had been shot in the chest during the Tehran street protests against the reportedly rigged election results returning Iranian President Mahmoud Ahmadinejad to power.

The following morning the *Canberra Times* headed its world news page with 'Dying Neda icon of Iran unrest' (24 June 2009: 8). Beneath this headline is the photo-image of a prostrate young woman, her panicking eyes wide open, looking sideways towards the camera. Her arms are sprawled on either side of her ashen face, while male bystanders lay their hands on her chest, trying to preserve her failing breath. Inset in this image is the photograph of an attractive young woman smiling at camera with her head whimsically tilted to the side, her hair-style and make-up instantly recognizable as 'Western'. On the same day *The Australian* newspaper headlined its front-page piece, 'Death on video grips world' (Lyons 2009: 1). Its photograph of Neda is of an entirely different young woman. But again, her long hair framing the face, without headscarf, signifies 'Western'. The *Sydney Morning Herald* led its world news piece with 'A martyr emerges from the bloodshed' (Erdbrink 2009: 9), in this case accompanied by a photo of Iranian women lighting candles in memory of Neda Soltan 'whose death in Tehran last Saturday has sparked world anger'. We can see a framed photograph of Neda in this 'shrine to a martyred victim', positioned at the apex of the triangle formed by the burning candles. She is dignified, slightly smiling to camera, and in a head-scarf this time, as befits this impromptu spiritual memorial.

What we are observing here is the international news media's part in constructing photojournalism's icons. Newspapers are aware of their part in this. Indeed, the same *Canberra Times* photo of Neda, now carried large on *The Australian*'s world page, is anchored by words specifying that this image was taken by her boyfriend who is also a photojournalist. Part of the accompanying article relies on the gap the newspaper recognizes between the boyfriend as worldly journalist and Neda as innocent victim.

The Australian's John Lyons comments on Iranian people clustering in internet cafes, comparing their images of state brutality, and especially keen to show them to Western journalists. 'What is happening in Iran at the moment is an uprising by the internet generation' (Lyons, 2009: 8). The Associated Press/Agence France-Presse article in the *Canberra Times* says that 'Poems, tributes and angry denunciations of Iran's Government have multiplied online. In some, she is compared to the lone man standing with shopping bags in front of the column of tanks in Tiananmen Square' (*Canberra Times* 2009: 8).

In this description of icon-making, old media (the foreign journalist) and new media (local people using the internet) are portrayed conducting together the democratic process of spreading the news of state terror. Lyons of *The Australian* says 'In this strange civil war, internet cafes have become the command-and-control centres of the opposition' (2009). The *Canberra Times* also describes how the image of Neda, 'Angel of Iran', has been circulating inside Iran via bloggers and Twitter despite official blocking of websites and jamming of satellite television signals.

In their own discussion of the Neda icon, Aleida and Corinna Assmann argue that these different professional and amateur communication systems are usually kept separate because the role of journalists is to provide verifiable information for which they are accountable, whereas social network systems exchange information that is unverified opinion (2010). But in the Neda case, the Iranian government had blocked foreign news reporting, so the amateur communication system took over its function.

Assmann and Assmann discuss four stages in this process. The first level relied on an on-the-spot witness, in this case a trained doctor and publisher, who tried to help the fatally injured Neda and spoke out about the shooting as having truly happened. At the same time another witness captured her image on a 40-second video-clip on his mobile phone camera. The second level of the making, multiplication and communicating of the Neda image was that the video-clip, together with the oral testimony of the witness, was uploaded to the internet where it was sent around the world by social networking:

> The news spread as quickly as it did because many people around the world were watching the events in Iran closely and minute by minute. Thus, within hours, the discussion about her death, marked with the hashing #neda, was among the first on the list of 'trending topics' on Twitter.
>
> (Assmann and Assmann 2010: 227)

Thus, as CBS television put it, Neda became a world-wide cyber icon and images from the amateur video-clip were broadcast on TV channels and printed in newspapers internationally.

The third level Assmann and Assmann describe is the turn from private and public communication to political action in Paris:

> Stills from the clip were printed out and transferred to placards used during new protests in Iran and in other countries around the globe. Images of her death, contrasted with pictures of Neda alive, smiling into the camera, sent a highly emotional statement to the world, serving a powerful indictment of the Iranian regime.
>
> (p. 228)

At the fourth level, further videos and photos of local street demonstrators followed those of Neda into global observation. 'In this process of reproducing and recycling her picture on multiple levels, Neda's image supports a living memory that is kept alive' (p. 228).

Yet Assmann and Assmann note that although 'this new technology system offered an alternative of democratic empowerment against censorship' (p.229), it also had pitfalls, since in the early stages of constructing her story the urge for pictures led to a search of the internet which turned up another image of a different woman, Neda Soltani, being downloaded from her Facebook profile. The image was circulated on the web and taken up by international newspapers (as we noted ourselves in the Australian press). This had tragic consequences for the second Neda who felt the need to flee from Iran (Mekhennet 2010).

However, there is another downside in the circulation of the Neda image that Assmann and Assmann do not mention, which is to do with newspaper professional ideology. This making of icons is seen as legitimate in newspaper narratives because of their high valuation of Western democracy and the role of the news media within it. Neda herself is defined as icon in each newspaper in that self-same context. Each newspaper finds in Neda's own name a circulating voice on behalf of democracy, even as her personal light is turned off. *The Australian*, printing a piece from within the Murdoch stable, *The Times*, says 'Soltan, whose first name means "voice", has become a martyr for freedom' (Lyons 2009: 8), while the *Sydney Morning Herald* says her 'first name means "the calling" in Farsi' (Erdbrink 2009: 9). This voice, calling powerfully to her own people and to the world via new media, is contrasted poignantly with the helpless local words of a fatherly old man seen in the video image bending over her dying body. He is said to be her music teacher, calling 'Neda, don't be afraid . . . Neda stay with me, stay with me' as blood gushes from her nose and mouth (Lyons 2009: 8). His lone voice is futile; but her ringing voice to the world is pictured in contrast to the Iran government's failing 'attempt to suppress details surrounding election protests' (*Canberra Times* 2009: 8).

This contrast of the voices of 'the people' against 'the government' is symbolic at three levels. First, it is the voice of Western-style democracy; as both in images and words Neda is constructed as 'Western' in spirit. The video clip 'shows her sinking backwards to the ground as two men rush to her side. Her long black cloak falls open to reveal Western jeans and sneakers' (Lyons 2009: 8).

Second, though, this icon-in-the making is revealed as embedded in a historical 'Eastern' religious consciousness. All three of the newspapers we mentioned emphasize that Neda's

> bloody imagery could have an important impact on public opinion inside Iran, where the idea of martyrdom resonates deeply among a populace steeped in the stories and imagery of Shi'ite Islam, a faith founded on the idea of self-sacrifice in the cause of justice.
>
> (*Canberra Times* 2009: 8)

This is why the newspaper headlines mix the terms 'icon' and 'martyr'.

Third, the newspapers contextualized Neda's 'voice' and 'calling' via immediate reference to the reaction of US President Obama. *The Australian*, for example, quotes a White House advisor saying that the President 'has been moved by what we've seen on television . . . particularly so by images of women in Iran, who have stood up for their right to demonstrate, to speak out and to be heard' (Lyons 2009: 8). Neda's image thus enters the symbolic realm of US real-politik, representing the shift from George W. Bush's 'Axis of Evil' confrontation with the Iranian state to Barack Obama's preferred negotiation. His reported comments at the time of the shooting were that 'the last thing' the West needed was for Iran's people to see the election demonstrations as events manipulated by the US. *The Australian* article 'Footage of woman's death gives protestors a martyr' (24 June 2009: 8), placed just below their large 'Western' photo of Neda, is near another article 'Obama still keen to talk to regime – Revolution in Iran' (p. 8).

But *The Australian*'s editorial on the same day concludes that 'Barack Obama is being overly cautious in responding to Iran' and draws on one of the neo-liberal heroes of the Murdoch press to offer him guidance:

> Like the protestors mown down in Tiananmen Square 20 years ago, Iranian student Neda Salehi Agha Soltan, 26, has become a powerful symbol . . . The

US President wants to avoid being accused of 'meddling'. As the leader of the free world, however, he would erode his credibility, and that of the US, if he remains on the fence between the Iranian regime and protestors whose principal crime is battling for democracy . . . Ronald Reagan proved how effective a hardline approach could be in dealing with the former Soviet Union . . . Being too timid will not advance democracy and peace.

(*The Australian*, 24 June 2009: 13)

Reflexivity and the making of icons

We have opened our book with the death images of Neda Soltan for two reasons which are central to our argument throughout the chapters that follow. First, this imaged event clearly illustrates how the media are active in constructing icons. In particular, the editorial from Rupert Murdoch's *Australian* shows how the making and reporting of 'a martyr' is embedded in icon history (the Tiananmen Square image), political history (President Reagan) and current politics as defined using jargon words from Cold War days ('leader of the free world'). This newspaper welcomes current heroes (the Iranian people) into a world 'battling for democracy', a battle which *The Australian* and *The Times* have been waging for many years. These new 'icons' and 'martyrs' are described in the same term, 'battling for democracy', which the Murdoch press similarly trumpeted in relation to the (now old and publicly discredited) Iraq War. Further, as we will illustrate in chapters that follow, the Murdoch media narrative about 'the free world' and 'democracy' will be a haunting theme of other iconic images we describe. Both in words and images the notion of 'Western lifestyle', as invoked graphically by the detail of Neda's black cloak falling open to 'reveal Western jeans and sneakers', is symptomatically part of a neo-liberal concatenation of 'freedom' with 'democracy', and of 'democracy' with 'capitalism'.

Second, the reporting of the circulation of the death images of Neda Soltan displays a degree of media reflexivity. The newspaper stories have at their heart the role of the old and (especially in this story) the new media in circulating ideas of freedom and democracy. In an important sense this story promotes the media itself. New media, in the hands of 'the people' against an oppressive government, is 'the story' itself. It is the underpinning 'new angle' of this tragic tale. Through this new media the 'voice' and the 'calling' of the dead woman–martyr–icon supposedly offers us all hope from beyond her isolated grave.

Yet this making of an icon in and through the media is only reflexive to a limited degree. It is reflexive in the 'news' content of the story; but not in its own critical assumptions which are in fact the underlying context of this reflexivity. The 'free world' of *The Australian* editorial and journalistic narratives about Neda is the selfsame neo-liberal (Reaganite) 'free world' which former Australian Prime Minister Kevin Rudd denounced not long before in February 2009. In a long article entitled 'The End of Neo-Liberalism' in *The Monthly* magazine, he said:

The time has come to proclaim that the great neo-liberal experiment of the past 30 years has failed, that the emperor has no clothes. Neo-liberalism, and the free-market fundamentalism it has produced, has been revealed as little more than personal greed dressed up as an economic philosophy.

(Rudd 2009: 25)

The 'free world' of neo-liberalism, which *The Australian* was still proclaiming in its editorials, was itself experiencing an acute loss of credibility at the very time that its editor was warning Obama of the erosion of his credibility. Rudd describes the current global economic crisis, employment crisis and ensuing social crisis as the result of the triumphant ideology of 'neo-liberalism – that particular brand of free-market fundamentalism, extreme capitalism and excessive greed which became the economic orthodoxy of our time' (p. 20). On the twentieth anniversary of the fall of the Berlin Wall, former Soviet President Mikhail Gorbachev expressed similar concerns as Rudd.

Today's global economic crisis was needed to reveal the organic defects of the present model of western development that was imposed on the rest of the world as the only one possible; it also revealed that not only bureaucratic socialism but also ultra liberal capitalism are in need of profound democratic reform.

(*The Guardian* 31 October 2009: 35)

Kevin Rudd notes as evidence of his damning critique of neo-liberalism that 'even the great neo-liberal ideological standard-bearer', the long-serving chairman of the US Federal Reserve, Alan Greenspan, has conceded that his 'ideology was not right; it was not working', and that 'the "whole intellectual edifice" of modern risk management had collapsed' (2009: 22). Yet, *The Australian*'s notion of 'freedom' and 'democracy' remains committed to that 30-year-old narrative, which grew especially powerful in the decade around the collapse of the Soviet Union. Neo-liberalism is the old economic system within which Murdoch's *Australian* newspaper was – not at all reflexively – attempting to construct the new iconic image of Neda Soltan. Rudd is expressing a political–economic point of view, which we will elaborate theoretically in Chapter 7. *The Australian* has an opposing ideological point of view which many people still share. Our point in mentioning reflexivity here, and throughout the book, is to emphasize both the importance of recognizing the making of icons and the intellectual and ethical need within a democracy to be reflexive about that process of making. This means that we need to be reflexive about our own critical assumptions too.

Reflexivity and becoming an icon

On 7 July 2005, a photo of the first author of this book, John Tulloch, unexpectedly became an iconic image. He was photographed being helped away from the bombed wreckage of a London underground train after the suicide bomber attacks on London that day. Together with two other 7/7 images – of a bombed red London bus and of an injured woman wearing a surgical mask – this image was carried by the media around the world. The international media quickly promoted these three images as 'iconic', representing the resilience and suffering of Londoners that day.

Inevitably this personal encounter with iconic images and prevailing Western discourse on terrorism lends a subjective and reflexive dimension to our discussion. So we, as authors of this book, adopt a different approach to Robert Hariman and John Lucaites (2007) in their important monograph on iconic images in the USA. They define their selection of iconic images quantitatively and empirically (i.e. they select images which have appeared most regularly in collections and compilations of iconic photographs published internationally). Certainly the images which we have chosen are widely regarded as iconic, and we are sure that readers will recognize them as such. But the personal, subjective and reflexive approach we also adopt is not simply experiential, the result of one of us experiencing close-up, and somewhat powerlessly, the construction, circulation and manipulation of his image in the world's media. It is also our way of establishing the wider point that all constructions of the iconic, among media practitioners, public intellectuals, or within academia, are in important ways subjective. The making and unmasking of 'icons' is always relative to the discursive frames adopted by the people who select them for remediation. If, as Judith Butler argues, 'It makes sense to trace the discursive uses of modernity', so too does it make sense to trace the discursive uses of the term 'iconic' within it (2010: 109).

So our process of selection is not empiricist, as is the case of Hariman and Lucaites. Rather we work between two counter-empiricist theories of knowledge – realist and conventionalist (constructivist). These both emphasize, as Terry Lovell describes, the role played by our critical assumptions (and 'theories') in constructing understandings of the world. For Lovell (and for us):

> Modern epistemological realism . . . concedes that knowledge is socially constructed and that language, even the language of experience, is theory impregnated. Yet it retains the empiricist insistence that the real world cannot be reduced to language or to theory, but is independent of both, and yet knowable . . . Theories develop models of real structures and processes which lie at a 'deeper' level of reality than the phenomena they are used to explain. The theory explains the phenomenon because the phenomenon and the 'deep structures' are causally connected.
>
> (1980: 17–18)

Our discussion in this Introduction of the iconic image of Neda Soltan in terms of Kevin Rudd's (and Rupert Murdoch's) 'underlying' context of neoliberalism is realist in this sense.

In contrast, as Lovell argues:

> The limit position which all conventionalisms more or less approach is one in which the world is in effect constructed by and in theory. Given that there is no rational procedure for choosing between theories, relativ-

ism is the inevitable result. Epistemological relativism does not necessarily entail a denial that there is a real material world. But if our only access to it is via a succession of theories which describe it in mutually exclusive terms, then the concept of an independent reality ceases to have any force or function.

(p. 15)

Baudrillard's theory of a 'virtual' world where reality has been wrenched free of empirical grounding and represented only in simulated images (Chapters 4 and 6) is quite commonly taken to be a postmodernist conventionalism; though we, following William Merrin, think differently (Chapter 4).

Working with these two understandings of knowledge production, this book, instead of quantifying the iconic empirically, is interested in examining the iconic theoretically, drawing attention to the qualitative, creative and theoretical making, remaking and remediation of icons of war and terror.

Ways of seeing icons

Following our approach to the theoretical understanding of iconic images, this book is based on four principles. They are critical assumptions underlying our ways of seeing the images we describe here.

The first principle is to explore images of terror and war from the 1970s, when the Vietnam War produced unusually powerful iconic images, to the present. Whereas a recent academic focus in cultural studies has been on celebrities, this book looks the other way, exploring the emphasis on photographic images of war and terror over the last four decades. This particular choice of subject has a personal dimension. Observing the reproduction of his own image on numerous newspaper front pages and on international television in the months and years after he was seriously injured in the 7/7 terrorist attack, the first author became curious about the emotional, professional, political and ideational combination of practices and events that produced iconic images via the media. What made them iconic? This mix of subjective, professional, political, public-intellectual and academic identities, which we also will see operating in Simon Schama's analysis of iconic images (Chapter 1), provides us with a basic interest in writing this book.

Our second principle raises the issue of 'objectivity versus reflexivity'. Not only has it been a commonplace of academic debate in the period since the 1970s, but it has become a concern within photojournalism also, that there are major problems associated with claiming to maintain an objective position in analyzing (or photographing) reality. Of Terry Lovell's three quite different epistemological positions – empiricist, critical realist and conventionalist – only an empiricist position would believe that, provided one's methodology for gathering, photographing and interpreting data is scrupulous and appropriate, the objective analysis of reality is unproblematic. Both the critical realist position, which looks for a 'deep structure' beneath the empirical surface of appearances, and the conventionalist (or social constructivist) position (which in its more radical formulations tends to see 'reality' as an artefact of theory and language) draw attention to the need to incorporate the location of the speaker/writer/researcher reflexively as part of the data to be analysed, as we will do with Schama's *Guernica* in Chapter 1. In sociologist Alan Irwin's definition of 'broad' constructionism, we will point to the discursive formation of icons in Schama's TV programme 'within particular social settings and contexts' (Irwin 2001: 176; and Chapter 11).

Third, in long academic careers in communication and media studies we have noted the emergence and circulation of writers and academics as public intellectuals. Since the early 1970s, when film, media and cultural studies were beginning to flourish, our professional field has also seen a succession of celebrity academics and a bewildering proliferation of theories attached to them. As phases of academic debate shifted, so various versions of realist–modernist and constructivist –postmodernist theories have contended. We want to survey the power of this work about images, forgetting nothing (hence our early focus on John Berger), but not uncritically celebrating anything. In other words, we want to display 'older' intellectual fashions (such as Berger) with the same space and intensity as 'newer' ones (like Baudrillard and Hoskins). Thus, at one level, we will survey the work – from the 1970s to the present – which students in the humanities, social sciences and visual arts have found helpful in exploring images. But at another level, there is a significant empirical dimension to this book. It is a critical scholarly text which makes the theories of the iconic that we explore work in relation to the images of our choosing. This is a way of assessing evidentially in terms of changing theoretical perspectives, sometimes by way of our own empirical research in the field.

Our fourth principle is that the meanings of iconic images matter in the public world. The shocking images of planes slicing into the World Trade Center in New York on 11 September 2001 ('9/11') became part of a local, national and international trauma. But there are some terrorisms – by states, by mercenaries, and by individuals – that went on long before and have continued long after 9/11, as for example at Guernica. Among the 'core values' of Western Culture which Edward Saïd most valued from his own position of cultural hybridity (Chapter 10), was the 'unwavering belief that the rigors of intellectual thought and the courage to speak one's conviction will lead down the . . . road to discovering and demanding equal justice for all' (Bayoumi and Rubin 2001: xxxiv). It is to that positioning within Western intellectual cultures – the position which attempts to use 'core' Western Enlightenment values against the neo-colonial history of Western discourse itself – that many of the critical thinkers, artists and media professionals surveyed in our book aspire as they instruct us, in Schama's words, 'on the obligations of being human'.

The book's themes

Following these principles, this book adopts the strategy of juxtaposing iconic images of a particular decade with the academic and public intellectual writing about iconic images at that time. That gives us the opportunity, where relevant, to compare the often limited, even controlled discussion of these images in the media at that time with critical intelligence available in the same period. Thus the 'napalmed girl' image from the Vietnam War taken in 1972 will be juxtaposed with John Berger's comments about war and iconic images at the same time. And the books by public intellectuals Jean Baudrillard (2002), Paul Virilio (2002) and Slavoj Žižek (2002), which came out to mark the first memorial of the 9/11 attack, will be juxtaposed with iconic images of that day of traumatic terror in the United States.

But we will also choose what we regard as the most insightful work on iconic photographic images, whenever they were written. So Hariman and Lucaites' (2007) significant analysis of iconic images will be used to consider an absence of iconic photos that occurred in the world's media 26 years earlier in Bangladesh. The point is that we want to survey the most intellectually provocative writing about iconic images of war and terror over the last 40 years together with the most powerful photo-images of the same four decades. Where theory and image temporalities coalesce we use them; but we consider earlier theories in the light of more recent ones as well. This is not because we assume the later ones are 'better'; but because we want to draw attention to shifting assumptions in analysing 'the iconic', and to illustrate how those changing assumptions will alter their selection and interpretation.

Chapter 2, about one of the most well-known war icons of the last century, the naked 'napalmed girl' running away – as many also did in Guernica – from airborne terror, begins our comparison of icon and analysis operating conjointly. This draws especially on John Berger's (1972) articulation of the coupling of beauty and horror in art and image making, which Simon Schama also talks about in discussing Guernica (Chapter 1). Chapter 3, in contrast, is about an almost forgotten war: that of the West Pakistan military against its own (East Pakistan) people, soon to be citizens of the new, breakaway state of Bangladesh. Here potentially iconic images were also 'forgotten' and we engage with Hariman and Lucaites' (2007) powerful understanding of the politically civic conditions of the iconic to ask ourselves why. Chapter 4 reminds us of a technologically new type of iconic image that came with the Gulf War, taken from the nose cone of a 'smart bomb'. Here we engage with Baudrillard's (1995) not-to-be forgotten claim that 'the Gulf War didn't happen'. Doing a little of our own empirical media research, and not leaving the 'smart weapon' theme aside, we ask ourselves whether the killing of hundreds of civilians, again from the air, at Amiriyah shelter in Iraq during the Gulf War, 'didn't happen'.

Chapter 4 takes up our theme that different critical accounts of a war will choose different images to pronounce as 'iconic'. Most observers agree that the iconic image of a massacre of villagers at Račak by Serb paramilitary police in January 1999 launched the NATO war in the air over Kosovo. But different critical assumptions within 'old', 'new' and 'postmodern' war theories inflected it in different ways, choosing different images for critical context. Chapter 5 explores the terror from the air that came, as at Guernica, 'out of a clear blue sky': the aeroplane attacks on the United States of 11 September 2001. Here we explore the strong political and air industry claims that 9/11, as though coming from nowhere, 'changed everything'. We discuss political and air security language, as well as academic and public intellectual critiques of this from the different theoretical traditions of Baudrillard, Virilio, Žižek, Young, Hall and Kellner, and also from the pages of a new terrorism journal launched to challenge the 'state-centric' hold on terrorism studies within academic and security industries.

By halfway through the book, we will have begun to explore the 'structure' and 'agency' of theories of iconic photos of war, risk and terror. That is, we discuss theories that embed iconic images in economic systems (Berger, Chapter 2), political systems in tension between liberalism and democracy (Hariman and Lucaites, Chapter 3), state terror (Bangladesh 1971, Chapter 3), but also the active work of photojournalist agencies to make 'forgotten' images iconic (Alam, *Drik*, Chapter 3). We will have observed the self-interest of warring states (and competing intellectuals) in proclaiming that wars and their most powerful images 'didn't happen' (or alternatively 'changed everything'), and the critical engagement of modernist and postmodernist theories in investing the iconic with meaning (Chapter 5). We will have drawn on these competing theories of the 'real', of 'simulacra' and the 'spectral' to consider images of structural walls crashing down to create the '9/11' of historical memory. And we will have considered different modalities through which the iconic has been constructed in intellectual debate: the commoditization of beauty and horror (Chapter 2), the civic life of nation states (Chapter 3), the new technologies of terror (Chapter 4), the different critical discourses of intellectuals (Chapter 5) and the temporalities of political and security discourse (Chapter 6).

But some of the most resonant images of war and terror in living memory will still lie ahead halfway into this book: the 'Shock and Awe' and 'Marlboro Marine' images from the Iraq invasion; the sexual and psychological abuse by US soldiers of prisoners at Abu Ghraib prison, Iraq; the shocking iconic images that emerged from the London terrorist attack of 7 July 2005. The discussion of the 7/7 attack will develop a trend that has been increasing in the second half of the book, which augments structural 'top-down' (economic, political, military, medical, sociological) theories of iconic meaning with agentive 'below-up' ones. So Chapter 7 is still strongly structural and 'top down' (focussing on the political economy of neo-liberalism). Yet it also introduces us to theories of public consent via Gramsci's notions of 'good sense' and 'common sense'. Chapter 8, staying with images of Iraq, begins to look at tensions between 'top-down' and 'below-up' analysis within feminist interpretations of war and terror icons, as more experiential, 'everyday' and subjective approaches are used to understand them. Here the focus is on the images' indexical, iconic and symbolic mobilisation by active professionals in different spheres, from soldiers to political cartoonists to artists. Chapter 9, discussing trauma images of 9/11 and 7/7, extends this 'professional' comparison by considering journalistic, legal, medical-psychological and personal-subjective approaches to the trauma of witnessing terror attacks.

We begin the book discussing the power of one historically iconic painting, and we will end it with contemporary paintings that actively challenge the iconic power of colonial art. Chapter 10 focuses on modernist (critical realist) and post-modernist (constructivist) theories of Orientalism, by way of Edward Saïd (1978) and some of his supporters and critics in academia and the art world. But this academic/art professional debate will parallel an exploration of current images made by Indigenous Australian artists, who both look backwards into a colonial (British) history of power and icon making, and forward towards the hybrid artistic identities of post-modernism. The point of this temporal emphasis – on the deep past as much as the border-shifting present – is both to ground empirically the debate about images, simulation and the real that has taken place in earlier chapters, and to insist that terrorism is not a new occupation. Nor is icon making an activity separate from historical power. State terrorism is as important a subject for the analysis of terror and war as the acts of individual religious extremists: which is why we emphasize *Guernica* from the beginning.

Finally, we conclude by seeking to pin down the many theories and theorists of the iconic that we discuss in our chronological history. Epistemologies are theories of how we know. Thus, we focus here on two of the dominant epistemological positions that constitute the critical assumptions of nearly all of these theorists of the visual. By way of two of their key tropes for analysis – 'walls' and 'borders' – we will bring together a 'hybrid' position for ourselves as theorists of the visual too.

Audiences

This book is not about audience reception of iconic images; except in the very particular sense that it *is* about the naming and interpretation of images as iconic by academic readers and public intellectuals. They are, of course, 'audiences' who remediate powerful images via powerful theories. Yet these theorized effects do equate in systematic ways with recent media audience theory. This is not the place to summarize the recent 'active audience' tradition (see Tulloch 2000). But if we take one of the more interesting surveys of theory covering the last four decades of audience research – and thus the theory span also of our book – Nicholas Abercrombie and Brian Longhurst's *Audiences* (1998), we can find similarities in their broadly focussed analysis, which may help map our own history.

For Abercrombie and Longhurst there have been two main audience research paradigms operating in the period our book covers, replacing the earlier behavioural and uses and gratifications phases. The authors rightly note that these latter were characterized by a neglect of 'concrete social groups and their interactions' and a 'relative neglect of the analysis of texts and their meanings' (1998: 9). It was this missing complexity of both social structure and textual meaning which, they argue, became the focus of the 'Incorporation/Resistance' (IRP) audience theory. They emphasize the role of Stuart Hall within the new IRP tradition, challenging the assumption of societal consensus which had underpinned the earlier behavioural positions, and focussing on the power of media in constructing meanings via the labelling of 'deviants' (never more visible as – at the time of our writing – media coverage of the 2011 London riots).

Abercrombie and Longhurst argue that, in the context of Gramsci's theory of hegemony, Hall and many others within the IRP tradition (e.g. Morley 1980, Radway 1987, Fiske 1989, Livingstone 1990, Philo 1990) stretched the paradigm between the spectrum of all-powerful media 'control' and sub-cultural 'resistance' – between, as Assmann and Conrad conceptualize it, the 'predatory mobility' of globalized capitalism and an alternative globalization 'from below' that 'can back up the counter vision of an international civil society' (2010: 1). Finally the paradigm, reached the extreme pole of 'semiotic democracy' (Fiske's term) and multiple audience 'identities', and began to shatter internally.

It is at this point that Abercrombie and Longhurst celebrate their paradigm of 'Spectacle/Performance' (SPP). Central to this is their notion of the 'diffused audience'. Whereas what they call the 'simple audience' is constituted in local venues with direct face-to-face contact and a high degree of separation between performers and audiences (as in traditional theatres and concert halls), and the 'mass audience' is constituted through a high degree of mediation whereby an 'indefinite number of participants' in 'global spaces' are sent material via a condition of 'one-way traffic' (1998: 64), the 'diffused audience' concept elevates the IRP notion of pluralized audiences to a new level. 'Being a member of an audience is no longer an exceptional event' (as in theatre), 'nor even an everyday event' (as in the interweaving of TV soap opera and the mundane practices of domestic life, as with the 'mass audience'). 'Rather it is constitutive of everyday life . . . It is a claim that the very constitution and regulation of the mundane is in the hands of the media' (p. 69).

This is now, Abercrombie and Longhurst argue, a 'performative society' (Kershaw 1994) in which the everyday performances of our (multiple) identities are so ubiquitous as to be invisible even to ourselves (Abercrombie and Longhurst 1998: 73). 'On the one hand, there is the construction of the world as spectacle and, on the other, the construction of individuals as narcissistic' (p. 75).

This is not the place to take Abercrombie and Longhurst's argument about diffused audiences further into their theory of performance, imagination and enthusiasm within the 'constitution of the narcissistic society of modernity' (1998: 2). We are mentioning it here to indicate our view of the directions that 'audience' research into the reception of iconic images would need to go – across the meeting point of IRP and SSP paradigms. Indeed, that meeting is the ultimate point of our conclusion (Chapter 11) emphasising the need to engage between 'control' concepts like 'walls' and the reflexive 'performance' notion of 'borders' and multiple identities. It is, in an important sense, the path between John Berger's reflexive concern that his TV series to a 'mass audience', *Ways of Seeing*, is 'one-way traffic' (Chapter 2) and the 'images, models of performance . . . which become routine resources for everyday life' (p. 104) that we discuss in relation to the artistic installations of Yinka Shonibare (Chapter 11). But it is also the trajectory and space of interrogation between Berger's ways of seeing and that of Hoskins and O'Loughlin (Chapter 7) who, like Abercrombie and Longhurst, argue for the constitutive relationship between the media and everyday life in what they call the second stage of 'mediatization'.

One of the most important points that Abercrombie and Longhurst make in introducing their notion of the diffused audience is that:

> This is not a claim that simple audiences or mass audiences no longer exist. Quite the contrary. These experiences are as common as ever, but they take place against the background of the diffused audience. Indeed . . . the three audience forms can feed off one another.
>
> (p. 68)

What is true of audience theory is, we argue, also true of the broader theories of iconic representation and remediation that we explore in this book. From John Berger speaking in 1973 to Andrew Hoskins and Ben O'Loughlin writing in 2010, key aspects of what they privilege in their different (IRP and SSP) paradigms of analysis are 'as common as ever', even as they take place now against a background of 'diffused audiences' and 'diffused war' (Hoskins and O'Loughlin, 2010: 3). It is this notion of 'diffusion' which, Assmann and Conrad argue, describes an 'emergent' process 'that evolves beyond agency and control along largely unforeseen trajectories' (p. 4).

1 Guernica

Icon of state terror

Simon Schama in front of Picasso's painting *Guernica* © BBC

In the afternoon of 26 April, 1937, planes of the German Luftwaffe Condor Legion bombed, without warning or declaration of war, the Spanish Basque town of Guernica. It was a Monday, market day in the small town, and many hundreds of civilians were slaughtered from the sky.

In Spain the German attack was seen as support for General Franco's Fascist forces during the Civil War against the elected Republican government. It was terror from the air for the first time in history by a political leader against his own civilian population. In other countries the attack was considered by many as part of a new Luftwaffe Blitzkrieg policy of terror bombing, which was later to reach its climax in the London and Coventry blitzes during the Second World War.

Casualty figures and motives for the terror assault on civilians at Guernica are disputed. But what is not disputed is that the Spanish painter, Pablo Picasso, living in Paris and probably the most famous painter in the world, turned as a result of the bombing from his highly successful painting of nude lovers to something quite different: his painting of state terrorism, *Guernica*.

Also not disputed is that *Guernica* became the first internationally recognized iconic image of terror from the air. It is an image so powerful that 66 years later, in February 2003, when Colin Powell, US Secretary of State, addressed the Security Council of the United Nations to drum up support for the imminent US air attack on Iraq with so-called evidence of 'weapons of mass destruction', his minders covered over a large wall tapestry of Picasso's *Guernica* to hide it from television cameras. As an icon against war and terror, *Guernica* was thought to convey the wrong meaning at a moment when the world's most powerful nation was about to attack another country from the air.

Columbia University history professor and television presenter Simon Schama directly addresses this first iconic image of terrorism against civilians from the air in his 2006 BBC series *The Power of Art*. Of the bombing itself he says:

> When the people of Guernica fled into the streets and fields, the pilots strafed them with machine gun fire. A rain of incendiary bombs finishes the job, turning the town into an ashy cauldron . . . There was nothing in Guernica that could possibly be designated a military target. What was special about Guernica was the brutality and clarity of the objective: to terrorize defenceless civilians from the air, and to send a message to the rest of Spain and to the world. 'This is what we *can* do, and this is what we *will* do.'

Schama says of the hiding of *Guernica* from television cameras for Colin Powell's UN speech:

> It was, I suppose, the ultimate backhand comment to the power of art. 'You're the mightiest country in the world. You can throw your armies around. You can get rid of dictators. But hey, don't tangle with a masterpiece.'

Picasso's iconic image against terror from the air was just too powerful, Schama is saying, to leave uncovered at this moment of high militaristic fervour in Western history. He is, of course, making huge claims for the power of images. But so do all the image theorists we discuss in this book. W.J.T. Mitchell (2011: 137) uses *Guernica* as his benchmark in asking: 'Is there a *Guernica*, a masterpiece of artistic reflection on a historical atrocity, lurking in the artistic responses to Abu Ghraib, the war in Iraq, or the War on Terror? Probably not.' But he still goes on to describe the hooded man image from Abu Ghraib as the master image of our era of war and torture.

We think that in more recent times the power of photography has augmented, maybe replaced, what Schama calls 'the power of art' in relation to war and terror. Iconic photographs – like the one of a little girl running naked and burnt by napalm during the Vietnam War in 1972; of the Twin Towers of the World Trade Center burning and collapsing on 11 September 2001; or of a hooded prisoner standing on a box, arms stretched to his sides and wired to an electric socket at Iraq's Abu Ghraib prison in 2004 – are also extraordinary testaments to the iconic power of the image. There will be other powerful photographic icons of war and terror discussed here.

But before we engage with these, we will spend a little more time with Schama and *Guernica* to indicate both a substantive and a theoretical principle underpinning this book. The substantive point is that, in a book surveying four decades of theories of the visual, our focus will not be only on academic theorists. Quite a number of the analysts of visual icons and images of terror we discuss here are public intellectuals: for example Simon Schama, John Berger (Chapter 2), Susan Sontag (Chapters 4 and 7), Naomi Klein (Chapter 7), political cartoonists (Chapter 8), and art exhibition curators (Chapter 10). Many others (like Baudrillard, Virilio and Žižek, Chapter 6) write both academically and as public intellectuals. This is not surprising because iconic images of this kind have such a profound public resonance internationally. So, public intellectuals' voices are important to us.

Our theoretical principle is that every theory of the visual icon, whether 'public' or 'academic', is based on critical assumptions and it is an important part of our purpose to reveal what those are so that readers can assess critical positioning, theories and grounding evidence together. Thus at the outset we offer no fixed definition of an icon because to do so would detract from the journey ahead. Our emphasis here is on the *production* and *naming* of icons of war and terror.

Schama's discussion of *Guernica* and the power of the image is a good place to start this journey; not least because Schama is so explicit about his critical position. Telling stories about iconic journeys is Schama's professional method and *Guernica* is a foundational image of terror from the air for all that follow. Even as we write, television news coverage speaks of air attacks by Colonel Gadaffi on his own Libyan population in terms of *Guernica*. This is an iconic image stored deep in popular memory and it is, as Schama says, a testament to the future as well as the past.

Schama's television programme on *Guernica* is a remediation – a putting into media forms and meanings – of an earlier iconic history. At the actual time of the Guernica attack (and later) Fascist commentators denied responsibility for the human carnage, blaming the Republicans for it. But that is not Schama's focus, which is a very particular *television* remediation of *Guernica* that we want to explore.

Schama, as he weaves his own narratives around Picasso's *Guernica*, is especially clear about this process of producing and remediating icons.

Schama's *Guernica*

Simon Schama's 'Picasso' episode in *The Power of Art* (2006) begins with a blue/black still image of windowpanes and white clouds that could almost be a surrealist painting. This is the simulated attic window of Picasso's studio in Paris during the Second World War. Lit in the top left windowpane against a darkening sky we see a small bulb, the filaments glowing dull purple. Suggesting the importance of this light motif for the episode, the first camera edit is to a close-up of this bulb. The purple zigzag filaments create an effect, within the glass frame and against a blue-grey ground, that is aesthetically pleasing but strangely ominous.

This dual motif of light and shadow will be a central theme in Schama's narrative about Picasso's iconic painting *Guernica*. It will also underpin his thesis about the power of art played out between beauty and horror.

Over these opening shots we hear Schama's voice, 'It's the depths of winter, 1941'. The image immediately cuts to German jackboots invading the stairwell to Picasso's flat. 'Pablo Picasso is . . . working on the top floor of an old house in Left Bank Paris. The Third Reich owns Europe.'

The viewer is thus set up for dramatic confrontation: of power and risk, of brutal military against the individual artist. Rapid edits segue across continuing blue-grey images. We see Picasso's cowskull sculpture, then the skull of a human being before the image cuts to the skull on the hat of a Gestapo officer. Schama – seen in colour contrast to the dramatized edits of blue-black Gestapo silhouettes – says that Picasso gets periodical visits from the Gestapo who mumble about degenerate art, drop threatening hints that he's hiding Jewish friends and damage his studio. The unwelcome visitor with his death's head insignia is indeed a Gestapo officer, and he notices in the studio a number of postcards of Picasso's most famous work. As Schama said, 'it's an epic depiction of what happened when German bombs fell on a small Basque town in the Spanish Civil War'.

The postcard is *Guernica*: and a drama around the painting is played out between the circling Gestapo officer and Picasso, represented only by cigarette smoke fiercely ebbing upwards in the steely-blue frame. It is a powerful, aestheticized shot. This is 'Picasso'. His resistance is insubstantial, uncontainable smoke and light beams in the face of brutish authority. There follows a subjective point-of-view shot: we see the officer thrusting the postcard of *Guernica* into our/Picasso's face. It is the first time we have seen *Guernica* in this episode, and now we know why the colour choices in the opening sequence have been almost completely blue, black, white and grey. These are the colours of Picasso's painting, *Guernica*.

Over the thrusting presence of the Gestapo officer with his postcard we hear Schama quote him: had Picasso done this? The camera cuts to a reverse shot, not to an actor playing Picasso, but to Schama showing us the postcard before his own face: '"Oh no", said Picasso. "*You* did. Go on. Take one. Souvenir".' It's a powerful conceit: the art presenter in the role of Picasso the art-maker, shaking his head from side to side to punctuate the artist's words reported in Schama's symptomatic presentational style, which leads into his punch line for this opening pre-titles sequence: 'Great comeback . . . But what can art really do in the face of atrocity?'

The word 'atrocity' cues a rapidly edited sequence: brutal black-and-white images of bombs falling from aircraft; the painting *Guernica* in slow zoom filling the screen; a dead bull yanked with a neck rope in a Spanish bullring; a bull's head image from *Guernica*; dozens of Luftwaffe bombers in the sky above us; buildings consumed by night fire; a desperate hand from *Guernica*; a photograph of terrified civilians under attack; *Guernica*'s screaming head; a filmed close-up of a terrified horse's eye; the shrieking horse's head from *Guernica*; the shadow of the cow's horns in Picasso's studio; the lightbulb and eye-like penumbra from *Guernica*; and a slow zoom into the gaping wound at the dead centre of *Guernica*. These edited black, white, blue and grey images systematically inter-mix naturalistic photography of atrocity with Picasso's post-cubist representation of it in *Guernica*. The edited sequence is a repeated drama between light and shadow, terrified survival and power, war brutality and its representation.

This theme of contrasts is immediately taken up visually as we return to Schama sitting in Picasso's studio, shot in chiaroscuro against a window, his black suit in direct contrast to the squared light panes of the glass behind him. He asks 'isn't art best at delivering pleasure? Or is it when the bombs are dropping that we find out what art is really for?'

These words end the prologue, before the programme title *Simon Schama's Power of Art. Picasso.*

Approaching *The Power of Art*

There are different ways methodologically we could have approached Schama's *The Power of Art* series. One would have involved our presence at all stages of the commissioning, pre-production, production, post-production and marketing of the television series; an ethnography of production of the kind we have done before. But we couldn't adopt this approach because Schama's series was broadcast before we knew about it.

Another approach would be textual and comparative, exploring Schama's series within the history of other major British television art series. The BBC's own *The Landmark Arts Series* (2008) took this approach. This focused on the public service 'integrity' versus ratings 'popularity' theme it perceived in television's own art history, from the extremes of what some critics (and cultural studies academics) saw as the 'elitism' of Kenneth Clark's *Civilisation* series (1969), to the 'populism' of Rolf Harris' high-rating *Rolf on Art* (2001–7).

In his DVD commentary about the series, Schama (2006) says that all worthwhile television non-fiction must balance being authoritative and user-friendly. 'You don't want to be so friendly you're nauseatingly blokey' [like Rolf Harris?]. 'On the other hand, you also don't want to talk down to the audience . . . frighten them and make them think they're sitting A-level' [like Kenneth Clark?]. This negotiation between intellectual integrity and popular television does indeed mark Schama's remediation of the icon of *Guernica*.

But our approach here is neither through 'ethnography' nor 'landmarks' discourse. Instead, it explores the series via Schama's own personalized DVD account of how he came to make *The Power of Art*, and then examines these production intentions textually, analysing what went to air in the *Guernica* episode.

Any approach we make to the analysis of an imagistic text – and there will be many different approaches in this book – will have advantages and weaknesses. One disadvantage of relying on Schama's personal account on the DVD *The Power of Art*, given our absence as researchers from the BBC production, is that we have to take his narrative on trust. On the other hand, both of us have been professionally involved for sufficient time in television studios and media to know that what Schama says happened probably did happen. Second, our close textual reading of the episode did reveal that Schama's stated production intentions were very visible in the broadcast programme.

Simon Schama: risk, creativity and conversation

In his DVD commentary, Schama talks about three kinds of risk-taking. First, there is the risk of creating art. Second is the risk of commissioning and making a television series about art. Third there are the risks of modern atrocity in the world 'out there', which Schama believes Picasso's *Guernica* represents in new and iconic ways.

Schama describes the early pitch of his programme idea to the BBC as about the *risk-factor* in creating art. Schama emphasized to BBC executives that great paintings are seldom painted for a museum wall. Thus 'hushed' reverence (as employed in Clark's 1969 *Civilisation* series) 'doesn't always capture the kind of fury and the scary situation of high pressure in which some of the greatest masterpieces were made' (Schama 2006).

As an academic historian, Schama instinctively turns to historical sources to drive home this point. He draws on Cellini's autobiography (1968), begun in 1558, to emphasize the 'creative drama' of risk so often involved in making images. He tells us – and no doubt told the BBC commissioner – of Cellini, about to create his *Perseus and Medusa* sculpture, apparently being close to death and being roused by his apprentices. They were panicking that the smelting of his proposed masterpiece had gone wrong, producing a bulbous puddle of metal alloy rather than the statue planned to rival Michelangelo's *David* in Florence. Schama recounts Cellini's anecdote of rising from his deathbed and hurling all 87 kitchen pots and pans onto the furnace to create more liquid metal. Thus, according to Cellini's narrative, the artist created his masterpiece. Whether this event happened we don't know. What we do know is that it had real effect in Schama's pitch to the BBC. Out of Cellini's death-bed moment of creative risk, Schama found his programme idea, and convinced the BBC that to show the 'actual way in which a painting was created could be as exciting to the viewer as the story of a murder or a love affair or a revolution or a war' (Schama 2006).

For Schama, the initial moment of risk lies in the artist's creation of the image. But he also describes a second order of risk-taking. In television production, after you have made your programme pitch to the BBC and for US co-production, is potentially the time of the 'office hit', which in industry language is something that only sounds great on paper.

Schama and his producer Clare Beavan addressed this production risk in four ways. First, there was Schama's original idea that to avoid yet another television art series which was 'reverent and hushed' in tone it was important to introduce dramatization to make the audience's neck hair stand on end. Second, Schama speaks of how to turn this historian's written craft into television by means of dramatic lighting and camera.

Third was their decision to emphasize the *drama* of creation by focussing on one artwork. Thus, he says, the first line of his 'Rembrandt' episode was 'What is the worst think that can happen to an artist's paining?' It is to 'have to cut up your masterpiece', and we see a figure with a pair of shears doing that. This was a painting rejected by its sponsor, Amsterdam Town Hall, and Schama explains his series style of taking this moment of professional crisis, then looping back to explore how this trouble came about.

We'll see in Chapter 2 that John Berger also opened the first episode of his 'landmark' British art television series *Ways of Seeing* (1972) with a figure cutting up a famous art painting. And he too was using it to demystify the aura of the art museum. But Berger's and Schama's underlying concepts were different. Berger, as a socialist television presenter, cut out the young woman's face from Botticelli's *Mars and Venus* to indicate the commodification and interchangeability of art and advertising images within the capitalist image-trade. Schama, as a mainstream, liberal-minded historian, gives us a savagely edited visual reconstruction of an historical event: of hands clumsily unwrapping a canvas, sharpening a knife on stone and ruthlessly cutting up the canvas.

This shot of Schama on-screen next to a Rembrandt typifies his fourth level of professional risk. He tells us on the DVD of his series of conversations he had with television-art-presenter friends Robert Hughes and Andrew Graham Dixon about the 'prat' aspect of his television role. He illustrates this with an example of his feeling of inadequacy standing, as television presenter, in front of a Rembrandt painting (Schama 2006). This may seem surprising, given that Schama had already published a well-reviewed book, *Rembrandt's Eyes* (1999). But, in this case of television presentation, he felt Rembrandt's eyes were on *him*. 'Well, I've seen people like you before, sonny Jim. You come and go you know, I stick around' [Schama dips his head in self-mocking laughter] (2006).

But in Schama's DVD narrative this feeling of inadequacy is immediately trumped by the *adequacy of historical authenticity*. On the one hand, he talks of how, after 'pratting on' about a Caravaggio painting in Valetta, Malta for a whole day and finding it beyond him, he looked for the pub where an actor-hero of his, Oliver Reed died, only to find it closed. But before he discovered that, while he was still wiping make-up off, tired from a day of 'pratting', suddenly a very small man nudged him with something in the ribs saying 'Please, please, take, take'. Here Schama's identity switches suddenly to what we'll call the professional historian's love of the detail of empirical authenticity. His anecdote about this man with a 'beaky nose and glinting eyes' is itself dramatically mysterious, until the reason for the prodding is revealed. The man, a cathedral verger, thrusts an old, dirty and very large key into Schama's hand and immediately swings him round like a tiny judo wrestler to confront the painting. Schama realizes that the key in his hand is the *same* key on the belt of the prison warder in Caravaggio's painting.

Schama, as scholarly art historian, has already begun to tell us about this painting. He says that around the beheaded John the Baptist, human figures represent everything art is supposed to bring you: beauty, cruelty, atrocity, monstrosity, horror. There is the heroic male nude who looks like a hit man; the beautiful young serving woman holding the decapitated head of the Baptist on an exquisite dish. But now there is the added authenticity of the actual key Caravaggio held.

Schama draws on two different personal identities to pin down this anecdote of the key: first, his professional authority as art historian ('I realized at that moment I was holding the key that Caravaggio had held 400 years before . . . Caravaggio always used live models, so he would have been lent the cathedral key . . . He would have had to do this painting in situ because it was too big for the studio.'); second, as a Cambridge don, when he was given charge of a very old wine cellar which he visited often. Hence he knew all about such ancient keys.

Schama, in conversation with his audience, is working through a range of discourses and identities during his 'key' anecdote to establish what, for him, makes a painting iconic. It wasn't just John the Baptist who was mugged by the hit man; it was Schama the historian who was mugged by the painting too. By holding in his hand an object once held by an artist who was tormented by his *own* sense of inadequacy, Schama achieved a sense of 'spooky proximity' to an artist in the moment of creation 'when it could *all go wrong* . . . And *if* you have that moment of danger . . . you *feel* transported I think by the power of art' (2006).

Schama's multi-layered anecdote about the key is revealing. It is symptomatic of his attempt to be 'friendly' (for example, laughing about his interest in alcohol: the story of the pub and Oliver Reed, and his own frequenting of the college wine cellar) yet not 'too blokey', while also being an erudite art expert. As Schama gesticulates with his arms the width of the Caravaggio painting, or the knife action coming from behind the back of the hit-man, his anecdote lives out the drama that he wants to inject into his television art series. But it also reveals his critical identities as an academic.

The historian's theory and method

As well as weaving together Schama's various performed identities – as friendly but erudite television presenter, as authoritative academic, as a professional individual with a personalized history – we get a clear sense here of Schama's *methodology* as an historian translated to television.

This book's first author was taking his honours degree in history at Cambridge University at about the time (the early 1960s) when Simon Schama was studying history at Christ's College, Cambridge, under the tutelage of Professor J.H. Plumb. The principles of historical methodology were well defined for us. For example, Burston and Green's standard textbook, *Handbook for History Teachers* (1964) described two central ways of studying and transmitting history to students. The first, emphasizing *continuity* between past and present, 'defines history as the study of the origins and evolution or development of the present, and it follows that the most important things in the past are those which are directly contributed to the shape of the present' (p. 2). The authors call this the vertical perspective on history, which views events and institutions like the US presidency, 'as part of a continuous past' (p. 10). This was the perspective of Schama's *The American Future* television series (2008), where key aspects of the USA's political, economic, military and environmental future were examined in the light of the starkly diverging philosophies of its Founding Fathers, Alexander Hamilton and Thomas Jefferson.

The second perspective, history as the study of *contrast* between past and present, Burston and Green said, 'involves seeing the past as it really was, with its own institutions as they were in the past'. This is to see history as a 'series of slices of life', whereby professional historians require 'the careful study of relatively short periods' (1964). Here the historian is concerned not with general laws but with describing the unique social, economic, religious, aesthetic and personal conjuncture of the event being described. This is the 'horizontal', 'patch' or 'special period' approach to history (p. 11). The authors' focus here is on history as 'essentially an imaginative study' (p. 11), using original sources as a means of conveying to students 'the reality of the past' (p. 97). This second methodology, they emphasize, is about 'appeal to historical imagination, to forget the present and immerse ourselves in some past age and its problems' (p. 5); and for them, and for a generation of historians like Schama training at this time, the fact 'that this represents the general practice of historians cannot be denied' (p. 9). This is the methodology of Schama's *Power of Art* television series, where he describes writing history to 'suspend disbelief', immersing the viewer or the student in the density of detail that any particular period of history contains, so that they 'feel they're somewhere else, they're not stuck on the tube on the District line. But they are in Rome, or Amsterdam, or Madrid' (2006).

Schama's methodology places emphasis on empiricism – on how, in sociologist Terry Lovell's (1980) definition, surface empirical detail reveals the truth: hence the way Schama used the very key that Caravaggio held 400 years before (together with the detail from Cellini's autobiography) as the bookends of his 'popular but authoritative' narrative structure in the DVD conversation. The empirical detail as *source* (the key) reveals the truth: not only the truth about historical moments of extreme creativity, but the truth also about television art history that is both authoritative and popular.

This then leads Schama to his third level of risk, and his definition of the iconic:

> [W]hen these artists are working at . . . a level of white hot intensity, they're out to change . . . the way we see the world. . . . And sometimes as a result of understanding in a different way . . . how we experience what it's like to be human, we can affect the larger world, too. But none of these paintings, even *Guernica*, is a kind of party-political broadcast . . . It's just something that adds to the sense of what it's like to be alive. That's what we're trying to do in *The Power of Art*.
>
> (2006)

In two key passages of his DVD conversation with his audience – his discussion of Caravaggio's painting of the beheading of John the Baptist and the concluding summation of his talk – Schama has spoken of *both* beauty *and* 'cruelty, atrocity, monstrosity, horror' as representing 'everything that's supposed to be brought to you by art'. Yet, when it comes to the great *icons* of modern art history, Schama seems to opt for the ones painted in the 'white heat' of frightening creation – of Caravaggio's violent life, Van Gogh's suicidal mentality, Rembrandt's mutilation of his own painting and Picasso forced out of his painterly dallying with the human body into the atrocities of Guernica. Or, more precisely, it is in the blending of artistic identities and forms – of both beauty *and* terror, creative risk *and* reality – that Schama finds his greatest icons, as we will see by returning to his presentation of *Guernica*.

Schama's *Guernica*: textual reading

After the series titles, Schama's narrative does indeed loop back to Picasso's earlier career. Pondering on one of Picasso's semi-nude masterpieces from this period, his 1932 painting *The Dream*, Schama says the artist 'poses Maria Therese in a languid reverie. Gently masturbating, she's literally got sex on her mind' and the camera searches her face to reveal a vaginal forehead outlining the nose. Schama intercuts this with the dreaming, post-coital face of an actor playing the model. It is, he says, a sensuous reverie in an image of great beauty. It is art as playful trance: the work of a cocky, self-indulgent master of his art – and a long way from *Guernica*.

But from here Schama loops his narrative still further back to explain how we may begin to understand this disparity between Picasso's obsession with female 'body parts, artfully re-arranged' and his pathway to the international politics of painting *Guernica*.

First, there's the fact that Picasso had, from his youngest years as an artist, been *iconoclastic*, breaking with conventions of history-as-power, female beauty and naturalistic representation. As illustration Schama compares the Spanish court painter Velasquez with Picasso in his pink period. Velasquez's *Portrait of King Philip IV of Spain*, Schama says, is the ultimate painting of power on horseback, the nonchalant grip of Philip's hand on the reins signifying the strong leaders control of state and war. 'It was the most enduring image of pure power.'

The horse will be a key image of his *Guernica* episode. So Schama edits to Picasso's pink period painting, *Boy Leading a Horse*:

> Instead of a prince in the saddle, a naked boy leading a bare-backed horse through an eerily empty, primordial landscape – there's no hero to identify here, no story, no subject. Just the modern coming straight out of the archaic, as if there had never been anything in between.
>
> (2006)

The sense of the direct relationship between primordial and modern forms in Picasso's artistic iconoclasm is central to Schama's argument as we look back to the future of *Guernica*. In Schama's narrative, spoken to film newsreel shots of the rumbling threat of Nazism and Fascism in Europe, we hear that Picasso was not losing any sleep over current world events. Unlike other contemporary artists like

George Grosz who 'knows there's a war to be fought' and whose 'brushes are armed for the offensive', Picasso – locked into his ever more tangled love-life and its associated paintings of beautiful female 'body parts' – is still, in the words of a close friend, the least political person he had even encountered.

So Schama looks for a second stage in Picasso's transition towards *Guernica*, and finds it in his growing obsession with Goya. Schama's camera pans slowly across images of execution, torture and decapitation in Goya's *Disasters of War* (circa 1810), as he describes the two artists' developing relationship. Goya had been the first, Schama notes, to have made art look directly in the face of the barbarous cruelty of modern warfare; his *Disasters of War* the first to turn art's beautified human body into a sick joke. Picasso was infected with Goya's obsession; and the earlier Spaniard's bullfights with their ritualized slaughter pulled Picasso inexorably back to Spain.

It was, in Schama's account, that earlier iconoclastic interest of Picasso in the direct link between primordial and modern forces that was the conduit to this new artistic (but also national and international) perception. To edited visuals of inter-cut images combining Goya's bullfights with colour film of contemporary savagery in the bullring, Schama begins to build his history forward from sensuous beauty to the atrocity of Guernica:

> In the mid-1930s the spectacle was threatening to spill from the bullring. Spain was to be torn apart. It was already hopelessly divided. There was a modern Spain – urban, secular, industrial; a Spain of thriving socialist movements and agitating anarchists. But there was another more ancient Spain. A country of immense landed estates, poverty-stricken peasantry, a Spain suffocated by the heavy presence of the Catholic Church. Picasso called this the black Spain . . . Neither was prepared to accept the verdict of elections . . . Each side, Left and Right, old and new, believed the other not just to be the opposition, but the enemy of re-born Spain itself. Each side demanded the other's annihilation.
>
> (2006)

Schama's history of 1930s Spain is spoken over the prolonged colour sequence of a contemporary bullfight in Madrid, where Picasso was visiting in the mid-1930s. A bull paws, charges and wheels, as does the matador. To the words 'each side demanded the other's annihilation', Schama's camera goes into powerfully dramatic slow motion, the bull pawing the ground one final time, a primordial object of natural violence, while the matador has the greater technology, a finely and aggressively pointed sword as he, too, charges and plunges. The bull slowing, staggers, collapses and dies, blood spilling in the dust. The analogy with Spain on the edge of civil war soon becomes evident. Franco's Fascists are backed by the latest technology of the German Luftwaffe and 40,000 Italian troops on loan from Mussolini. The Republicans, supported by idealistic, poorly-armed volunteers will soon be swept aside; and Picasso continues to ponder the link of primordial and modern in his art. Schama shows us Picasso's mid-1930s bullfight drawings inter-edited with live colour footage of violent action between animal and animal, animal and human in the bullring. He has prepared for the final section of his programme, the shift of Picasso to 'politics' when the Fascist forces start shelling Madrid and the Prado Gallery, home to Picasso's beloved Goya.

Schama now quickly completes Picasso's journey to *Guernica*, as the artist accepts the role of honorary director of the Prado, selects the paintings to be evacuated to Valencia and waits in great anxiety to hear news of their safety. 'It's a signal to the world that he's chosen to stand with the Republic. Picasso has got politics. Picasso's thoughts and passions are now locked into the Spanish struggle'.

And then, Schama says, life caught up with art. We see a plane in the sky above Guernica. He talks of its 7000 strongly anti-fascist population going about its market-day business in the Basque's ancestral homeland, with their own language, culture and proud identity. A black speck appears, says Schama, in the blue sky at about four in the afternoon. We hear the drone and see a plane as it seems to drift in the blue afternoon sky above the small Basque town, and just as casually drop four bombs. Then, suddenly, the air was full of waves of German and Italian planes with more than 5000 bombs hitting the defenceless town.

Thus, Schama says, '*Guernica* has become the shared heritage of an appalled humanity and the mirror of suffering civilians in *every* conflict'. *Guernica* was, he adds, 'not just a painting, it was a prophecy'. *Guernica* represented the first 'Shock and Awe'. To emphasize this, he inter-cuts images photographed by Picasso's new lover Dora Marr of him painting *Guernica* with the martial-machismo footage of German, Italian and Spanish Fascists on the march, and with much more passive faces and scenes of contemporary terror and state violence: in Palestine and in 9/11 New York at ground zero. Last, in this sequence, we see the face of a traumatized, abandoned child in a contemporary refugee camp, the camera slowly zooming into her weeping eye and then cutting quickly into the eye of the screaming woman in *Guernica*.

The images of 'primeval' death and light-as-life have haunted Schama's text almost subliminally and they now come together to introduce the different parts of the painting that changed Picasso from iconoclast to maker of the greatest iconic image of modern warfare.

Schama speaks authoritatively about the size of Picasso's ambition, as we observe images from *Guernica* that we have seen before in this episode: the hand-held light, the screaming horse, a primeval bull's head:

> What Picasso was setting out to make was something foreign to the very nature of modern art, art *he* had defined. He was about to make a truly modern *history* painting. It was the tallest order of his life, to turn from icon-breaker to icon-maker. So everything he's ever touched in his art and his life had to come together for this one moment: the excitement of modernism, the obsession with the art of the past, and his own intimate experiences of love and grief.
>
> (2006)

Each of the levels of risk, and Schama's ways of managing them that he spoke about in his DVD conversation, is woven through this *Guernica* episode. First, the historical moment of *creative risk*, in the Spanish Civil War and then in Nazi-controlled Paris, has been contextualized and resolved in a painting 'as exciting to the viewer as the story of a murder or a love affair or a revolution or a war'. Indeed, Schama suggests that *Guernica* includes each of these things. Drawing on Marr's photography of Picasso painting, he describes the developing changes in *Guernica* as Picasso mixed, juxtaposed and blended his different domestic and political identities. As a jealous Marie Therese and Dora Marr fight in the studio, and Marie Therese's child by Picasso covers her hands with the still wet paint of *Guernica*, domestic tragedy and distraught mothers transmute into Picasso's iconic war painting.

Second, each of the ways in which Schama and Beavan addressed their *production risks* is evident throughout. The use of dramatization – of the Nazi officer or the Prado's Mercedes trucks ploughing with headlights blazing through the country night towards Valencia as the anxious Picasso waits on their safe arrival – is blended with the conceit of the joke at the expense of the German officer. Schama avoids 'pratting' in front of the painting by being drawn into the joke. This is Schama as Picasso, holding the postcard of *Guernica* in front of him.

Dramatic lighting lies in wait throughout the episode at moments of 'crisis', not just in the scene with the Nazi officer, but in the Prado evacuation scene and each moment of savage political emphasis. Thus Schama's words 'a Spain suffocated by the heavy presence of the Catholic Church – Picasso called this the black Spain' are accompanied by the device of an unusually long camera pan through a black, blank screen, from the faces of nuns lit strongly in the blackness to Schama, himself a black figure presenting his history in the daylight street. This visual trope of the contrast of light and dark is carried through the programme by different television devices: via a light in its Andalucian shade swinging repetitively in the dark; in Schama's on-screen storytelling mode itself, as he is usually represented in semi-chiaroscuro, sitting half-silhouetted in windows at the various Picasso studios; and in his discussion of *Guernica* itself to the inter-cut images of the glaring light-bulb in the painting and the small bulbs swinging in dingy torture cells.

Schama takes us authoritatively from Picasso's earlier, slightly more optimistic sketches for the painting to the finished work, as the camera follows his words in detail with close-ups. He shows us an early sketch for *Guernica*, drawing attention to the clenched socialist fist of a dead Republican soldier thrust upwards in resistance, which transmutes in the final painting into a defeated, helpless, slack-jawed and defeated corpse.

This isn't, Schama says, Picasso as Republican partisan. Instead, the painter has turned back to Goya's own icon of death and execution, *The Third of May* (1814), where Napoleon's machine-like soldiers gun down the Spanish rebels. Again, this is 'the response of an artist seizing at cruelty and massacre' which, in the crucifixion pose of the man about to be shot, is 'coloured by an ancient Christian hope, especially deeply rooted in Spain, that of salvation'. Comparing Goya's and Picasso's great paintings, Schama observes a continuity that turns art on its head, overthrowing the long convention that light signifies beauty and sublime dignity. In the Goya, light signifies torture, since there is a light box at the feet of the soldiers and these 'machine-men go about their dirty business, just following orders'.

Similarly in the Picasso, Schama notes the pyramid of bodies thrusting up through the painting, straining towards the evil eye containing at his core a single electric light bulb. This, says Schama, is 'the incandescence of the death squad and the targeting bombers; the bare light bulb of the torturer's cell'. And yet, against it the strong, beautiful arm of the young woman in *Guernica* holds her candle-light, in an epic battle between art and evil.

Finally in his *Guernica* sequence, we see an acted Dora helping Picasso to cover the body of the dying horse 'with a field of sharp, little downward strokes' which make the body 'dissolve into a sea of newsprint, or the light of a projector . . . unreadable marks . . . Towering above there is the force of art, breaking through the drone of news'.

Schama is making his definition of 'great art' and 'mundane media' clear enough, except of course that he himself is using the television medium to construct his art icon. Now Schama stands in front of the *Guernica* painting at last, 'pratting on' after all, but now with a mix of intellectual and artistic devices behind him in his narrative. He says of Picasso that in this painting the artist crashes into the lazy routines of his public's everyday life, getting deeper than all the everyday images of violence and disaster we are bombarded with, and wipes away our yawn over perennial massacre. So, 'what *can* art do when the bombs start dropping? It can instruct us on the obligations of being human'.

Accompanying these words are images from the Vietnam War, 9/11, Second World War bombers and 'smart weapons' over Iraq. This, Schama claims, was Picasso's pinnacle of achievement when the creative fires burned.

Conclusion

Earlier in the episode, standing in front of *Guernica* at the Reina Sofia Museum in Madrid, Schama observed that the painting is, after all, back on a museum wall. So is it now just a safe relic of history? No, it is not:

> Guernica's always been bigger than art, untameable by mere museum walls. It's one of the very rare creations that gets into the bloodstream of the common culture. It's become the shared heritage of an appalled humanity, and the mirror of the suffering of civilians in *every* conflict.

(2006)

This is Schama's definition of the iconic power of art; and this is how he named it 'iconic'.

It is a definition embedded intellectually and practically in his understanding, as a Cambridge-trained historian, reflecting his mentor J.H. Plumb's profound belief in public intellectuals conveying history accessibly to a wide public. But in his *Guernica* episode Schama displays an icon in its making via images of beauty and atrocity, as each struggles for the power of light.

We have been talking in this chapter about the naming and *remediation* of an icon of atrocity by a presenter with many identities whose methodology is two-fold: an empiricist history and a television production concerned with multi-levels of risk. The remediation of icons is a complex media matter.

2 Ways of seeing the napalmed girl

Icons of agony and beauty

South Vietnamese forces follow terrified children fleeing down Route I near Trang Bang, South Vietnam: the 'napalmed girl'. Photograph taken by Huỳnh Công (Nick) Ut © Press Association

No photograph of the Vietnam War was more iconic than the 'napalmed girl'. It was taken by Associated Press photojournalist Huỳnh Công (Nick) Út in 1972. The subject is Kim Phuc, the nine-year-old napalm-burned girl running towards camera crying. Many observers have felt it played a major part in bringing the war to an end by reinforcing the loss of US public goodwill. As Hariman and Lucaites describe it:

The little girl is naked, running right toward you, looking right at you, crying out. The burns themselves are not visible, and it is her pain – more precisely, her communicating the pain she feels – that is the central feature of the picture. Pain is the primary fact of her experience, just as she is the central figure in the composition. As she runs away from the cause of her burns she also projects the pain towards the viewer. The direct address defines her relationship with the viewer: she faces the lens, which activates the demanding reciprocity of direct, face-to-face interaction, and she is aligned with the frontal angle of the viewer's perspective . . .The photograph projects her pain into our world.

(2007: 175–6)

We return to Hariman and Lucaites' analysis of photographic icons in Chapter 3. In this chapter we want to explore a different theoretical line about the public context of icons, extending Simon Schama's contrast of 'body parts' of beauty and horror – especially because the Vietnamese girl's pain and exposed nakedness mark the urgency of this image. Our focus is the socialist writer and public intellectual John Berger, who, like Hariman and Lucaites, is deeply concerned with the relationship between image and viewer. What Hariman and Lucaites call 'face-to-face interaction', Berger describes as dialogue.

Body parts: the agony of war photography

Berger did not, as far as we know, write about the image of the napalmed girl. But we know the kind of things he would have said had he done so, because in the same year that Nick Ut took Kim Phuc's photograph, Berger presented *Ways of Seeing* on television and wrote a short piece, 'Photographs of Agony', about the Vietnam War images by British photojournalist Donald McCullin. McCullin had taken photographs just after the US air force launched extremely heavy bombing raids on North Vietnam, with little media comment. In addition to the huge bombs, which could flatten an area of up to 8000 square metres, the planes dropped small 'antipersonnel' bombs, some full of plastic barbs and others with antennae designed to explode and maim on human touch anyone helping the wounded.

Berger describes a photograph by McCullin which represents this systemically cruel, anti-civilian war from the air. 'It shows an old man squatting with a child in his arms, both of them are bleeding profusely' (1980: 41):

McCullin's most typical photographs record sudden moments of agony – a terror, a wounding, a death, a cry of grief. These moments are in reality utterly discontinuous with normal time . . . The camera which isolates a moment of agony isolates no more violently than the experience of that moment isolates itself . . . The image seized by the camera is doubly violent and both violences reinforce the same contrast: the contrast between the photographed moment and all others.

(p. 43)

Anyone who has watched friends die in warfare, or who has experienced instant savage violence in a terrorist suicide attack, will know what Berger means by that contrast between two kinds of time: the continuous time of everyday life and the sense of a sudden but ever-present time of instant violence when the enemy's gun trigger or the suicide bomber's switch finger explodes quotidian time, in an instant. But *viewers* of the image, Berger says, tend to feel this temporal discontinuity as their own personal moral inadequacy. Such inadequacy may shock them as much as the crimes being committed in the war. Either this inadequacy is seen as only too familiar or else it prompts a kind of penance – such as making a donation to OXFAM or UNICEF. 'In both cases, the issue of war, which has caused that moment, is effectively depoliticized' (Berger 1980: 43–44). Berger is similar in this view to Jean Baudrillard, who sees our viewing of imagistic reconstructions of wartime horror as making us complicit 'in the extermination process, with our role as tortured witnesses functioning to absolve ourselves and dissipate the horror' (Baudrillard 1993: 92; Merrin 2005: 66). Berger would also share Judith Butler's view that graphic images of war 'sometimes do no more than sensationalize events. When that happens, we respond with outrage periodically, but the outrage is not transformed into a sustained political resistance' (Butler 2010: xiv).

Body parts: images of beauty 'naked or nude'?

If you conduct a web search you will find a number of versions of the 'napalmed girl' image. There is one of Kim Phuc taken from the side, close up. Another is taken from the front, with her running, showing photographers taking pictures of the burnt children from behind. But only one version dominates web pages quantitatively; and the same image appeared on front and double page spreads in international newspapers: of Kim Phuc with her arms outstretched, naked body exposed, soldiers behind the children, and beyond them the napalm clouds. Horst Faas and Marianne Fulton (2000) in their article 'How the Picture Reached the World' noted that nude photography, especially of children, was frowned on professionally. But Fass, Associated Press' (AP) Saigon photo department head, predicted this photograph would win a Pulitzer Prize, and, based on the marketing power of this forecast, reached a compromise with the New York head office that no close-up of Kim Phuc's nudity would be used.

Coincidentally, in the same year that Kim Phuc's photograph was taken, John Berger was presenting powerful accounts of nudity and the 'body parts' of beauty and violence. In Episode 2 of his television series *Ways of Seeing* (1972), Berger talks about the well-received art series of 1969, *Civilisation*, in which Kenneth Clark had famously made the distinction between 'naked' and 'nude', as between a body without clothes and a work of art. In his 1972 series, Berger offers a different interpretation. 'To be naked is to be oneself'. In contrast, to be nude in European painting and the modern publicity advertising that feeds off it is 'to be seen naked by others and yet not recognized for oneself'. To be nude is to be seen as an object, just as an animal, or a house, or a silver goblet in a painting is an object. Nudity, in European oil painting, says Berger, is a sight (and a predominantly female site) for those (men) who are dressed. This is why, he argues, Manet's nineteenth-century painting, *Déje-uner Sur L'Herbe*, caused such a scandal, because it placed a fully nude woman with a group of fully clothed men. Reflexively it put within the picture frame the convention of nudity which usually was hidden: that is, of clothed men (and patrons of art) outside the frame looking at 'naked' women. So, Berger says, Manet's painting was a profound comment on all the art nudes that went before it.

There are, Berger believes, perhaps only a few painted European nudes where the artist has revealed the woman as herself. He shows us paintings by Rubens, Rembrandt and George de la Tour as examples. These, he argues, are women painted naked 'as personally as love poems', not women lined up for the male spectator–owner who will assess and judge them as sites of nudity.

He discusses Rubens' painting of his much younger second wife, *Helene Four-ment in a Fur Coat*. Two subjectivities are *in dialogue* here, says Berger: of the naked women and of the painter who loves and desires her. They are in a dialogic not a voyeuristic relationship. Berger's argument is that Rubens, possibly unconsciously, has made Helen's body 'impossibly dynamic' by displacing the upper and lower parts of her naked body by about nine inches, hidden beneath her fur wrap.

> Her body confronts us, not as an immediate sight, but as . . . the painter's experience . . . More precisely, it permits the upper and lower halves of the body to rotate separately, and in opposite directions, round the sexual centre which is hidden. . . . Her appearance has been literally re-cast by the painter's subjectivity.
>
> (Berger 1972: 61)

Berger's discussion of a few paintings, which portray the naked (not nude) woman as both dynamically sexual in herself and in partnership with a man who is much more than a voyeur, relates to two other aspects of this episode. The first is Berger's own account of the vast majority of paintings in the European nude tradition, 1400–1900. In these conventional paintings, Berger argues, women are condemned to never being naked. As nudes they are as formal as if they had their clothes on. The beautiful nude is given the prize (as in *The Judgment of Paris* paintings). But, for Berger, the visual prize is that of being owned by men, of being 'available' – and he shows us Sir Peter Lely's secretly commissioned painting for King Charles II of Nell Gwynn. She is fully nude, other than the small cloth across her pubic area with which a young boy plays. She looks passively at the spectator, a sign for Berger of submission to male demand which the King would show off to envious friends. Berger contrasts this with the portrayal of nakedness as a celebration of active, mutual sexual love between male and female in Rubens' painting. But in most European oil painting of nudes the other person, the one who matters, is the stranger outside the frame looking at the woman. In this context, Berger compares a series of paintings with advertising photographs. These are all images of women responding with passive charm to the male observer.

Secondly, to conclude his 'Naked or Nude' episode, Berger showed his first edit to five women and filmed the conversation. His intention was to access current

public feminist debate engaged in *dialogue* with his own understanding of the convention of the European nude genre, where women are normally silent. Women
speak on camera about the questions raised by the programme: above all, how
men see women in publicity photographs or have seen them in the past in paintings, and how this influences the way women see themselves today. These women
talk about their self-representation as indeed being a matter of visual images, in
which women are generally passive. For example, one woman is interested in
Berger's comment on nudity as a disguise that you can't take off. She adds:

> we are always dressing up for a party, putting on a uniform of one kind or
> another – as mother, worker, pretty young chick; and nudity is the 'I'm ready
> now for sex' uniform. So nudity is not being free.
>
> (1972)

Another woman speaks of her mirror-obsessed narcissism as she looks at herself
not as naked but nude, as she thinks others would see her, and feels that this has a
lot to do with being trailed around art galleries by her parents as a child. The issue,
for her, is the feeling of inadequacy. Her habit of constantly looking at herself in
a mirror has the effect that if she actually sees herself by chance in a shop window
it is a tremendous shock because 'you see yourself as you are, windswept, badly
dressed, untidy, tired, etc'.

An alternative photography

'Inadequacy', then, in Berger's account, is a response to media images of both female
nudity and the bodily ravages to wartime civilians like Kim Phuc. It is likely that
he would also have considered the camera shot of Kim Phuc's 'sudden moment of
agony' as depoliticized, although he would have certainly taken note of its role in the
anti-war movements internationally. For Berger, the next step after feeling personal
horror and inadequacy over war imagery should be 'to confront our own lack of political freedom' – the only effective way of responding to the photograph. But, Berger
argues, the double violence of the photographed moment actually works against this
realization, which is why these images can be 'published with impunity' (1980: 45).

Berger promotes an alternative use of photography where photographers position themselves not so much as reporters of an event for the rest of the world but
as a recorder of the event for those involved (p. 62). This distinction is crucial because the
latter kind of photograph is 'not taken to please generals, to boost the morale of
a civilian public, to glorify heroic soldiers or to shock the world press: they were
images addressed to those suffering what they depict' (p. 64). Both the communicative nature of Nick Ut's photograph, linking the victim with the viewer, and Ut's
care in taking Kim Phuc to hospital and becoming her lifelong friend, indicate a
strong personal identity between photographer and a photograph 'addressed to
those suffering what they depict'.

Berger's aim in discussing an alternative photography is to construct a context
for the image using 'words, comparisons and signs'. These devices, Berger says,

'mark and leave open diverse approaches. A radial system has to be constructed around the photograph so that it may be seen in terms which are simultaneously personal, political, economic, dramatic, everyday and historic' (pp. 64, 67).

This radial system, which reinserts the personal (whether the beautiful naked body or the war-ravaged body of Kim Phuc) into the political and reinserts everyday into historical time, is hard to achieve. Berger argues that there are only a few great photographs that achieve this alternative aim; and he discusses the period between the World Wars when photography 'had been liberated from the limitations of fine art, and it had become a public medium which could be used democratically' by masters of the medium like Paul Strand (1978) (Berger 1980: 52).

He observes that equally there are only a few great painters of the naked body that achieve this alternative aim of recording events for those involved. There is an important continuity in Berger's valuation of images of the human body – whether fragmented in violence or represented as sexualized 'body parts'. This continuity is in the importance of recording human experience in *dialogue* between subject and artist/photographer. But both in war and in commoditized sexuality Berger found this dialogue lacking amidst a plethora of 'body parts'. His challenge to the 'body parts' of war and commoditized sexuality is via personal and political reflexivity.

Reflexivity and John Berger's *Ways of Seeing*

The first episode of his 1972 television series *Ways of Seeing* opens, even before the titles, with the unexpected image of Berger in an art gallery cutting a 'body part' of a young woman, the head of Venus, out of Botticelli's painting *Venus and Mars*. Beginning a series that aims to be polemical but reflexive at the same time, this image sets the pattern of simultaneous personal, political and ideational reflexivity, which is evident everywhere in Berger's work. He argues that since paintings in their original settings of chapels, stately homes and galleries are static, the most obvious way of manipulating them on television is by using movement and sound. The television camera can zoom in to extract a detail from the whole (as Berger does in the opening image when he physically cuts out part of the body of Venus, drawing attention at the very start to the action of the camera, and to his role in 'calling the shots'). In this way, Berger says, the television image changes the art-work's meaning for audiences. An allegorical figure of poetic metamorphosis in Botticelli's painting becomes 'a pretty girl anywhere', as in a publicity advertisement.

Another reflexive example is in Episode 3 when Berger discusses landscapes. He considers Kenneth Clark's interpretation of Gainsborough's *Mr and Mrs Andrews* in his 1969 *Civilisation* television series. Berger quotes Clark's text which speaks of Gainsborough as so inspired at the very beginning of his career by the 'pleasure in what he saw' that he positioned Mr and Mrs Andrews in a 'sensitively observed' cornfield. To this quotation from Clark, Berger's camera cuts from the full painting with its foreground seated figures to a detail of the cornfield 'sensitively observed', and then to the vista behind the seated couple of their extensive lands and their sheep, spreading into the perceivable distance.

Berger comments 'Now look at it another way, the way I would use it for my argument'. We see a close-up of Mrs Andrews and then the camera pulls back to reveal the pair, with, tacked on the tree, a hand-written 'Trespassers Keep Out' notice. This is not in the original painting, of course. It is Berger's own tag, his signature on the painting and on the series. A close-up focuses on the fact that the man is holding a gun, an image of violence. Berger says, 'Theirs is private land. Look at their attitude towards it. The attitude is visible'. We see a close-up of the woman's rather cold, distancing face, and the man's legs, gun and dog, as the camera tilts up the weapon to his face. He, his dog and his gun, Berger's camera tells us, are here for hunting. In contrast, Berger's voice-over continues, 'If a man stole a potato at that time, he risked a public whipping. The sentence for poaching was deportation. Without a doubt, one of the principal pleasures this painting gave to Mr and Mrs Andrews was the pleasure of seeing themselves as the owners of their own land' (the camera pans across the landscape). 'And this pleasure was enhanced by the ability of oil paint to render this land in all its substantiality' (the camera shows the whole, very detailed painting). The technical capability of oil painting to convey, with meticulous brush stroke and colour, every detail of the object possessed – whether land, food, farm animals, women or precious objects – is a theme of Berger's analysis throughout the series.

Berger's discussion of *Mr and Mrs Andrews* is in a socialist context that was widely influential in the 1970s when he made the series. Berger's political position in this discussion is both clear – he sides with the 'unrecorded poor' – and reflexive. In case we don't pick up the point of his opening images of scene one, or his 'Trespassers Keep Out' label on Gainsborough's painting, Berger ends Episode 1 of *Ways of Seeing* by highlighting his own power over the programme. He says that in his other three episodes he will try to relate the experience of art directly to other experiences and to use the television means of reproduction 'as though pictures were like words rather than like icons', or holy relics – or like advertisements that embody how we see the women and possessions surrounding us in our everyday lives.

But, Berger adds, unfortunately he has no direct dialogue with audiences in his television presentations.

> Remember that I am controlling and using for my own purposes the means of reproduction needed for these programmes . . . You cannot reply to me. . . . As with all programmes, you receive images and meanings which are arranged. I hope you will consider what I arrange, but be sceptical of it.
>
> (1972)

Berger's emphasis in this reflexive conclusion to the first episode is on dialogue as a foundation of equality; and he puts this in opposition to the 'iconic' which he understands as received imagistic wisdom, given from on high, from authority, whether via the image of Christ or of English aristocratic landowners or advertising images.

A public intellectual context

In the first two chapters of this book we are examining how public intellectuals – the liberal historian Simon Schama and the socialist novelist John Berger – name icons in their public work on television. While Berger's *Ways of Seeing* book (1972) had an enormous influence on art college courses, his television series presented him as a public intellectual to a mass audience.

Theatre director Simon McBurney has emphasized how he had studied Berger as an undergraduate:

> It was that heady time when everyone was in thrall to Barthes and the French structuralists, this whole new way of looking at art and literature, and Berger, in retrospect, stood out because his voice was absolutely direct, and practical and clear. It was his clarity and, of course, his compassion, that entered my consciousness and has stayed with me ever since.
>
> (McBurney, cited in O'Hagan 2005)

McBurney is right about Berger's clarity and compassion. But in saying Berger's voice stood out from that of Roland Barthes and other influential thinkers of the time, McBurney is describing Berger's pedagogy not his intellectual position. Unlike Simon Schama, whose grounding as a public intellectual draws together conventions of traditional historical scholarship and television practice, John Berger has been the kind of public intellectual who blends theories, fusing and debating the strongest critical ideas of his age, and enlarging them in his own art practice of painting, novel writing, poetry and criticism.

Like Schama, but in different ways, Berger has multiple identities as a public intellectual. Two of his intellectual identities, his commitment to Walter Benjamin and to 1970s feminism, are overt. The others we identify here, to Roland Barthes and to the emerging 'cultural turn' in academic debate, are less well known but are important to understanding his emphasis on images and the 'dialogic'.

Walter Benjamin

Berger acknowledged the influence of the German social philosopher Walter Benjamin in *Ways of Seeing*. He drew strongly on Benjamin's rejection of the sense of 'aura' experienced by people in the presence of unique works of art. For Benjamin traditional art's aura was associated not so much with its innate value, but with feudal, religious and bourgeois institutions of power. These were external valuations placed on the art work: as religious icon, as class icon or as commodity icon.

In *The Work of Art in the Age of Mechanical Reproduction* (originally published in 1936; see Arendt 1968), Benjamin was optimistic that the age of art aura might be over, despite its centrality in the Nazi era. For Benjamin, the 'contemporary crisis' was more than the imperialistic Nazi regime that drove him as a Jewish socialist first from Germany, then from France and finally to his tragic suicide on the France–Spain border in September 1940. But for Benjamin the larger scope of the crisis was the relationship between capitalism, technology and war.

Modern industrialization, he argued, included its own dark side because of the power of capital. Speaking of the 'war is beautiful' aesthetics of Futurism, which justified 'the big tanks, the geometrical formation flights, the smoke spirals from burning villages' (Benjamin 1973: 244), Benjamin argued that the combination of capitalistic rivalry and imperialistic warfare in the 1930s represented a discrepancy between production and the use of that production: 'Instead . . . of dropping seeds from airplanes, (industrialization) drops incendiary bombs over cities; and through gas warfare the aura is abolished in a new way' (p. 244).

But, he believed, new technology properly used would allow humankind to penetrate new spaces. Benjamin was infused with optimism over the photographic and filmic innovations of the 1920s, especially in Russia. He believed in photography and film as 'the first truly revolutionary means of reproduction' (p. 226) separating art from its aura and its ritual function. Instead art 'begins to be based on another practice – politics' (p. 226). Painted art, too, had its revolutionary movement. A favourite reference for Benjamin (pp. 239–40) was the anti-art literary works of the Dadaists, who in response to World War I thrust into the public eye a 'shock' art of obscenities, humour, visual puns and everyday objects.

Berger's *Ways of Seeing* is clearly influenced by all of these ideas. For example, near the beginning of Episode 1 Berger says the invention of the camera changed everything. He speaks of the reflexive-modernist film *Man with a Movie Camera* by the revolutionary Russian film-maker Dziga Vertov; its vertiginous style opening up city streets and buildings by using all the new camera techniques Benjamin described. Images, Berger argues, are transportable away from their original iconic and ideological sites of ritual and privilege, and can be seen by masses of people world-wide, in their own homes, even while art galleries desperately cling to the notion of the aura and authenticity of art images. Like Benjamin, Berger believed also in detaching art from a cultural hierarchy of specialists and making it available to a mass of people who could apply it to their own lives. Like the Dadaists who are Benjamin's model for a new 'shock' art, Berger tags Gainsborough's *Mr and Mrs Andrews* with a label to challenge the painting's aura as 'original', thus re-contextualizing the 'alluring appearance' of its rich people and opulent landscape. Using his television camera reflexively, Berger brands 'his' Gainsborough 'with the very means of production' (Benjamin 1973: 240).

Roland Barthes

Barthes' book *Mythologies* was translated into English and published in the UK for the first time with an extended essay on myth as a semiological system in 1972, the same year that Berger presented *Ways of Seeing*. Barthes talks of myth as a 'type of speech chosen by history' (1973: 110) with no substantive limits, since a whole range of subject areas make themselves available as signifiers for myth-making. For Berger, 'publicity images' are one of these substantive areas of myth.

But whereas myth has no substantive limits, Barthes argues, it does have *formal* limits; it operates a two-tier semiotic system.

Barthes' best-known example of this two-level myth-system is his analysis of a cover photograph from the magazine *Paris Match* of a young black soldier, eyes uplifted, saluting the French tricolore. Barthes says that when he sees this image, instantly

> I see very well what it signifies to me: that France is a great Empire, that all her sons, without any colour discrimination, faithfully serve under her flag, and that there is no better way for the detractors of an alleged colonialism than the zeal shown by this Negro in serving his so-called oppressors.

> (Barthes 1973: 116)

For Barthes, at this first level of description – or denotation – 'here is the image of a black soldier saluting the French flag'. The meaning is simple enough for any reader with basic competences in recognition of skin colour, military uniform, national flags, etc. But it is at the second level, of myth itself – or connotation – that the concept offered becomes more complicated.

At this second level of mythical form, Barthes argues, the image of the saluting black soldier 'empties itself, it becomes impoverished, history evaporates' (p. 117). The everyday history of the black soldier turns 'suddenly into an empty, parasitical form' (p. 117). What was the black soldier's background? By what family and personal struggles did he get here? We never hear; and the form is parasitic because now the soldier stands for French imperiality.

For Barthes, myth plays between these two semiotic layers providing its power: of language meaning (where we see in visual detail an actual black soldier) and of mythical concept (of a benign, inclusive French imperialism). This is a kind of *arrest*, in both the physical and legal sense of the term: French imperiality condemns the saluting Negro to be nothing more than an instrumental signifier, 'the Negro suddenly hails me in the name of French imperiality' (p. 125).

Barthes' use of the word 'arrest' in emphasizing the power of the photographic image is the same verb used negatively by Berger to describe both generic war images and advertising images. This is not coincidental, since a similar understanding of the depoliticization of the image is evident in both Berger and Barthes. Myth, says Barthes, is depoliticized speech. Myth 'is constituted by the loss of the historical quality of things: in it things lose the memory that they once were made.' This relationship between dominant myth, photographic images, history and memory is the context of both Berger's words and his visual style in *Ways of Seeing*.

Reading him via Barthes explains Berger's long, silent sequences of ordinary people in bleak landscapes dominated by advertising hoardings. In the television series and in Berger's discussion of war photographs we see this same relationship between publicity images which 'arrested' and 'impoverished' everyday histories, and the same emphasis on the depoliticized, duplicitous erasure of human memory and action. For Berger, the fragmentation of human bodies both in advertisements of the 'beautiful' and in war photojournalism is a world of myth and dreams, always potentially arresting viewers from action, trapped in a world that 'goes without saying'. His Barthesian view here is similar to Baudrillard's view that history is exterminated by its 'spectacular promotion' into the 'space of advertising', allowing us 'to take leave of the actual historical event' (1992: 233–4, cited in Merrin, 2005: 69).

Barthes thus advocates a third-level language system, of 'robbing myth'. 'Since myth robs language of something, why not rob myth?'(1973: 135). By 'robbing' myth, Barthes means adopting a language which points to itself, is reflexive, and refuses to drain the black soldier of his history on behalf of a naturalized new concept. But robbing myth is also distinguished by something else: a determination to bring history back to the first-level signifier – the black soldier, the nude woman in an advertisement or a naked child in Vietnam.

Feminist theory

John Berger invited feminists to join his *Ways of Seeing* discussion of the episode 'Naked or Nude?' All the women involved engaged supportively with Berger's analysis of conventional paintings and publicity images of the female body. This is not surprising because Berger was drawing on ideas and critiques current in the women's movement in the late 1960s and 1970s. To represent these, we can look at Rozsika Parker and Griselda Pollock's *Old Mistresses: Woman, Art and Ideology* (1981), which was enormously influential throughout the 1980s and beyond. We choose *Old Mistresses* here because, although published in 1981, it represents collective work in the women's movement throughout the 1970s, challenging, as the book cover says, 'the existing impoverished history of art with its narrow and exclusive conception of art and artist', with the intention 'to intervene in art history itself' – both intentions shared by Berger.

Berger and the 1970s women's movement shared the view of art as 'one of the cultural, ideological practices which constitute the discourse of a social system and its mechanism of power' reproduced in languages and images (Parker and Pollock 1981: 115). Both focused on structures of power in the art/media institutional world to include conditions of production and reception. Both examined the history of painting – and the genre of history painting itself – from the early Renaissance to the mid-nineteenth century, exploring the power of myth and history-construction based on human figures. In this sense, the work of Parker and Pollock overlaps with that of Barthes, his photographed black soldier saluting the flag replaced in their work by the painted nude woman as the focus of discussion of signification and meaning.

Like Barthes and Berger, feminists were centrally interested in 'what images signified and what could or could not be represented' (Parker and Pollock 1981: 115). Both Berger and 1970s feminists interpreted the conventional portrait of nude women as 'passive, available, possessible, powerless. Man is absent from the image but it is his speech, his view, his position of dominance which the images signify' (p. 116). Both saw their work as challenging the mass media's representation of women as spectacle, 'objects of display, to be looked at and gazed at and stared at by men' (Mulvey, cited in Parker and Pollock 1981: 132). And, like Berger (and Barthes), Parker and Pollock focus on the draining of the painted object's history, transforming it via a hegemonic ideology of representation (French colonialism, patriarchy, advertising publicity).

Both Berger and feminists examined the power and role of the critic; and Berger would have agreed with Parker and Pollock that the 'critic of modern art is a central element in twentieth century art practice, one who conditions the reception of the work of art' (Parker and Pollock 1981: 136). Both explored alternative representations of women to challenge that of the passively available women of men's construction and desire. Both explored new meanings for women by deconstructing 'the ideological *work* of art, the effects of artistic practices and representations' (p. 133). In particular, both wanted to 'shift meanings and to break open common sense' (p. 143), to refuse 'to celebrate American consumer society' and instead subject 'contemporary political and artistic circles to searing commentary' (p. 151).

It is important to acknowledge that 1970s feminism extended Berger's analysis in various ways, especially psychoanalytically in terms of male fetishistic-narcisstic fantasy (Mulvey cited in Parker and Pollock 1981: 131–2), with a particular focus on sexual 'body parts'. Berger, however, does not take this feminist/psychoanalytical path in his work, and it is notable that it is the feminist women in his *Ways of Seeing* episode 'Naked or Nude?' who frequently talk about male/female narcissism. For Berger, this going inward to the personal psyche had always to be connected to the socio-political, and with the politics of our everyday lives.

The politics of everyday life

John Berger has lived in rural France for more than 30 years. He says he first went there to be closer to the lives of the village poor that he was writing about in his novel, *A Seventh Man*. Journalist Sean O'Hagan (2005: 1–2) saw this as part of Berger's deep democratic conviction and cited author Geoff Dyer's experience of dining with him in his French village, enjoying their conversation with people as socially separated as the local plumber and the renowned photojournalist Henri Cartier-Bresson.

'Conversation' or dialogue is central to Berger's method as revealed in *Ways of Seeing*. It is why, frustrated at not being able to have a dialogue with his television audience, he included conversations between women and between schoolchildren in half of his episodes. 'Conversation' is also key to his intellectual and literary style, and in this respect Berger was in the forefront of an enduring intellectual and social movement that began in the 1970s. Elsewhere – in academic social sciences – it came to be known as the 'cultural' or 'ethnographic turn'. In his book *Cultural Politics of Everyday Life* (1993: xiii), John Shotter describes this intellectual tradition as 'the attempt to understand what it is to act within a "position" in a culture'.

Suspicious of the power of professional and academic disciplines, which Foucault described as a surveillance moment in the history of modernity, many intellectuals had begun to question their own position. Shotter argued that academics needed to move to the margins of social life – as Berger did physically in moving to rural France – rather than to the centre, because it is at the margins that people lack power. Shotter writes:

> The kind of power of interest to us is not power at the centre, but that at work *between* the centre and margins. It is those without power who find at every turn resistances to the realization of their desires.
>
> (Shotter 1993: 40)

Shotter, unlike many postmodernists, upholds Kant's question:

> the question of whether (and in what sense) people themselves can be self-determining; must they always (in some sense) be under the yoke of others? It is this latter, emancipatory concern of the Enlightenment that I do not want to give up.
>
> (pp. 12–13)

But Shotter's 'conversation' emphasis changes some aspects of the Enlightenment's emancipatory focus. His approach moves beyond

> the study of the inner dynamics of the individual psyche (romanticism and subjectivism) or the already determined characteristics of the external world (modernism and objectivism), the two polarities in terms of which we have thought about ourselves in recent times.
>
> (p. 12)

The central focus is now on the contingent flow of continuous communicative interaction – the *dialogic* relationship – between human beings. At the same time such a focus on interaction needs to emphasize *practical* knowledge:

> by studying the different ways in which different people, at different times in different contexts, resolve the dilemmas they face *in practice*, we can both characterize the resources available to them in those contexts at those times, and 'plot', so to speak, their political economy, that is, the fact that they are very much more scarce in some regions and moments of our social ecology than in others.
>
> (p. 15)

It is the *monological*, distanced analytical mode of the Enlightenment that Shotter, like Berger, rejects. Those at the centre, encased in their theories and disciplines, Shotter argues, exclude and silence the voices of those at the margins. The methods we use – no matter what position we take (benevolent, sympathetic, etc.) towards the people we study – cannot 'make sense of "their" lives in "their" terms . . . What they say is treated as "data", they themselves are not treated seriously as being able to speak the truth about their own lives' (p. 48).

We have here not only the particular kind of Enlightenment rationale that took Berger to live in rural France but also his rejection of the 'relation of domination' of professional art critics like Kenneth Clark in his analysis of Gainsborough's *Mr and Mrs Andrews*. Using his camera to focus on the gun in the painting, Berger considers the fate of the marginal people on those lands who were caught for poaching. This attempt to enter the everyday lives of the 'marginal' runs through Berger's work, whether presenting *Ways of Seeing* from London or writing novels in the Haute Savoie.

This distinction between monological *talk* and dialogical *conversation* is central to the ethnographic 'local' turn across the humanities and social sciences over the last four decades. For example, Canadian historian Paul Rutherford, writing about the US 'propaganda state' during the Iraq war, says 'what died was debate, what prevailed was monologue' (2004: 186). He concludes from his qualitative study of audiences of Iraq war media coverage that the problem was that there

> was no channel to communicate with any of the governors who counted . . . In short, the hollowness of present-day democracy resulted from an institutional failure, the fact that citizens, no matter how well informed, how thoughtful, were unable to affect the course of global policy, even when they flooded into the streets.
>
> (Rutherford 2004: 142–143)

John Shotter emphasizes that new knowledge grows out of the voices of ordinary people in conversation and that citizenship cannot be instituted in a top-down power play by elites (1993: 202).

In his essay 'Flesh and Speeches', written in July 2005 just after the terrorist attack on London, Berger wrote that the politicians who rushed in from Gleneagles where the G8 leaders were meeting had instantly subsumed victims' words 'to speak in their name, whilst serving their own interests' (2007: 101–2):

> The so-called war against terrorism is in fact a war between two fanaticisms . . . One is theocratic, the other positivist and secular. One is the fervent belief of a defensive minority, the other the unquestioned assumption of an amorphous, confident elite . . . One claims the right to spill innocent blood, the other the right to sell the entire earth's water. Outrageous to compare them! Yet the *outrage* of what happened in London on the Piccadilly line, the Circle line and the No. 30 bus was the misadventure of thousands of vulnerable people, struggling to survive and make some sense of their lives, being inadvertently caught in the global crossfire of those two fanaticisms.
>
> (Berger 2007: 104–5)

From the iconic images of the Vietnam War in 1972 to those of the terrorist attacks in London on 7 July 2005 there is a coherence in Berger's narrative: about the vulnerable and 'marginal', about the monological discursive power of religious, political and economic icon-making, and about the continuing potential to speak 'in conversation', 'above ground, together' (2007). This is what Berger means when he says in *Ways of Seeing* he wants to see 'pictures . . . like words rather than like icons'.

Skin dreams and far-away places

Following Walter Benjamin, Berger argues that the invention of the camera has changed not only what we see, but how we see it. At the beginning of the historical period covered in *Ways of Seeing*, Berger notes that worshippers converged on the religious icon. Behind the icon they saw God; and they might even close their eyes and not look at the image because they *knew* God was there in that unique place. But today in the mass media, he argues, for most people the icon and the image belong to no particular place. The image comes to you and is surrounded by your furnishings, family, friends and the life outside your window. The days of pilgrimage to see icons are over. It is the images and icons that travel now. Thus, Berger argues, the meaning of a painting no longer resides in its unique painted surface which you can only see in one place at one time. The painting's meaning has become *transmittable*, like the news of an event. Iconic images have become 'information of a sort'.

But what kind of 'information of a sort' is it? And what is its contemporary cultural context, in comparison with those of the religious chapel or the stately home? To answer this, in his final episode 'The Language of Advertising', Berger brings the series back to where it has really always been: the present time, the world of mass mediated images, of advertising and publicity. Here he argues that advertising's publicity shots manufacture glamour. The things which it sells are made glamorous 'by being inserted into contexts which are exotic enough to be arresting'. Such imagery may be public but it is the dreams that are intimate. He describes two such dreams – the 'skin dream' and 'scene of a far-away place' – which are directly relevant to our discussion of the naked image of Kim Phuc.

In the 'skin dream', says Berger, you can touch the body surface, the skin without a biography. Berger illustrates this point with contemporary advertisements: images of many colourful painted hands touching a woman's naked back; of a male hand near a woman's thigh; of a woman's hand on her own thigh, sensuously fingering under the top of her sheer nylons; of the bare breast of a woman almost available under a gauzy veil. The skin you can see, to dream to touch, is sensual, smooth, always unblemished.

To illustrate dreaming of a 'scene of a far-away place' Berger uses a travel advertisement image of a woman lying semi-nude on a bed alone, thinking about travel 'somewhere else'. The camera reveals her dreams as we see an image of a nude woman stepping from sand dunes towards an endless blue sea; and an advertisement showing white women in white underwear in the desert, with Bedouin men on horses. We see other white women in the desert with Arab men. White sand is evident in all these 'orientalist' advertisements (see Chapter 10). White sand is exotic, but it also is softly material, supportive of the female body that, in all these images, tilts itself to be frontal to expose skin and flesh to the viewer, not to the men who observe from inside the image. These images are, says Berger, of distances without horizons, and the promise is to be in two worlds at the same time, 'just where Europe ends'. This dream world at Europe's edge, he says, is represented as potentially violent, infidel, full of unknown passions; but 'not close enough to us to offer a threat'.

Making Berger's analysis work for us, we can observe that the image of the napalmed Kim Phuc in Vietnam was about burnt skin terror as she tears off her clothes covered in napalm jelly. It is not advertising's 'skin dream'. In that sense it was 'naked' not 'nude'. It was a 'scene of a far-away place', but not one about sexuality. And, if it is violently 'full of unknown passions', these passions surely emanate from the people who did the bombing, '*our side*', by implication the soldiers (or journalists with their cameras) in the photograph behind the screaming children.

Conclusion

For Berger, the body-part photograph of violent pain, or of nudity as pleasurable consumerism, involves the representation of strangers that shout 'Look!' but have no history of their own. In contrast, in his *Ways of Seeing* images Berger tries to offer alternative narratives and contexts: of ordinary people in ordinary city life and of the silent camera which 'listens' to these 'stories' as it films them.

A child walks in front of a large 'Captain Morgan Rum Yo-Ho-Ho' advertisement dumped in the middle of a dreary space that could otherwise be a public park. A small mini-skirted figure trudges past a blank brick wall and white door, her almost static image dominated by the yellow rising sun of a paint advertisement, its cheerful salesman thrusting his finger out at us, three-dimensionally in contrast to the drab two dimensions of the wall, the door and the woman's line of movement. A solitary, poorly dressed middle-aged woman walks hesitantly, stopping uncertainly at a traffic light on an empty and featureless corner – empty except for a big hoarding advertisement for cigarettes. A street person is surrounded by rubble, bottles, litter, and is leaning against a huge poster hoarding, 'Think Cool', 'The Common Market. Get the Facts'. Silence on the soundtrack of television is unusual. Ten seconds of silence seems a long time. So this is an unusually long, one minute sequence of city shots without sound, each segment itself protracted and doing nothing much, except for the advertisements. Berger, who has been letting us watch silently, then asks: 'What surrounds these posters?' In the past, he says, oil paintings were surrounded by gold frames symbolizing the wealth of the owner within the picture and around it. Now advertising posters surround ordinary, uncertain people going about their everyday lives even while hailed by publicity's mythical dreams. Although he doesn't say so, Berger implies that these glowing, jewel-like colours of advertisements in the dull surrounds of everyday British city life are the new icons, as ritualized and mythical as religious icons in chapels and churches once were.

At the same time, though, Berger offers an alternative narrative of our everyday lives. In the absence of any two-way dialogue, he has used different techniques to create that dialogue within *Ways of Seeing*. This is his attempt, as he says of the 'radial' photographic image, to position his television camera images in the context of 'other words, comparisons, signs'. We think that an image of Kim Phuc that *never* became an icon, her everyday, clothed reality (which Nick Ut later went to see) – sacrificed to the actions of the soldiers and photographers seen behind her – might have been one such 'radial' image of 'comparisons, signs'. In Berger's terms it would have been 'alternative' to the iconic image of the 'napalmed girl' we know so well.

In the next chapter, we further examine the iconic image of Kim Phuc by drawing on work by Hariman and Lucaites (2007) on iconic images and US public culture. Our focus is on the rhetorical relationship between image and viewer. In doing so, we also question why another image, arguably as powerful as the 'napalmed girl' photograph, did not become iconic internationally.

3 Two Bangladeshi boys and public culture

Iconic or absent?

Two boys are surrounded by spent rocket bombs in Jessore, Bangladesh in 1971.
Photograph taken by Abdul Hamid Raihan © Drik Picture Library

Two small boys, one naked, the other wearing only a tee-shirt, stand amidst the
detritus of war; rocket bomb casings are strewn around their feet. Together they
stare at ravaged fields, homes, crops and a solitary bomb-scarred tree. This is
in Jessore, Bangladesh in the final month of the war of independence, when state
terror was unleashed by the Pakistani government to the point of genocide.

Hundreds of thousands of citizens left their homes and fled to neighbouring states between March and December 1971. Reportedly, about two million Hindu, Christian, Muslim and Buddhist civilians were killed and an estimated three hundred thousand women were raped by the military.

Nick Ut's photograph of Kim Phuc taken in June 1972 was front-page news internationally and became iconic of the Vietnam War itself. In May 2003 political cartoonists were still using it to comment on the US-sanctioned tortures at the Abu Ghraib prison in Iraq. Yet only six months before the 'napalmed girl' image first appeared, Abdul Hamid Raihan took the photograph of the two Bangladeshi boys and this did not become iconic internationally. Photojournalist Shahidul Alam, who co-ordinated the Rivington Place London exhibition, 'Bangladesh 1971' where we first saw this image, has written about the exhibition photographs, some amateur, some by professional journalists, who had risked their lives to preserve the images. 'These faded images, war weary, bloodied in battle provide the only record of what was witnessed. Nearly four decades later, they speak' (Alam 2008). These images were, in Berger's words, 'records of the event for those involved'. Most surviving negatives are scarred and some were buried to hide them from the military. *The Times* did print in December 1971 the photograph of a desperately wounded child in Bangladesh, his arm a bandaged stump. But the caption told us the child was 'caught in the crossfire' between two invading armies, the Indian and the Pakistani. In this newspaper report the boy was positioned as an innocent victim of military conflict. There were also by-lined articles in the world's press talking about reported civilian killings and rapes by the Pakistani military. These were not the main narrative, however, and the newspapers printed no images of the kind that Alam showed at Rivington Place.

Why was only one image of a naked child terrified in war, of the 'napalmed girl' in Vietnam, distributed globally and became iconic? How do we account for extraordinary and lasting media coverage in one case, complete absence in another? In this chapter we draw on Hariman and Lucaites' (2007) powerful book on iconic images and public culture, *No Caption Needed*, to discuss this.

Vietnam war icons and communicating public culture

In Hariman and Lucaites' discussion of the 'napalmed girl' image (quoted at the beginning of Chapter 2) there is notable repetition of terms of interaction between Kim Phuc and the viewer: 'communicating the pain she feels', 'projects the pain towards the viewer', 'direct address', 'demanding reciprocity', 'face-to-face interaction'. Extending the 'cultural turn' approach of Berger, their focus is on a 'pictorial turn', emphasising the rhetorical relationship between image and viewer in public culture. Their analysis focuses on modes of emotional address. 'The photograph projects her pain into our world'. In examining this relationship, Hariman and Lucaites propose that the confrontation for the viewer is both about convention (what we expect) and transgression (which outrages us):

> Just as she is stripped bare of her clothes to escape the burning napalm, she tears the conventions of social life, a disruption signified by the photo's

> violation of the news media's norms of propriety . . . Yet war by its nature is
> a violation of civility, normalcy, civic order. Thus, a visual record of war will
> have to negotiate an internal tension between propriety and transgression.
>
> (Harimand and Lucaites 2007: 176)

Hariman and Lucaites argue that this non-prurient image of a naked young girl
circulated internationally according to a deep set of norms where journalistic and
societal proprieties were cast aside for a moral purpose (p. 176). The transgression
of showing her naked body revealed a deeper form of concealment – 'the damaged
bodies behind the US military's daily "body counts," "free-fire zones," and other
euphemisms' (p. 176). This dramatic photojournalism, they argue, broke away
from the official narrative that justified the Vietnam War.

Significantly, this is a different theoretical claim to the one presented in Chapter
2, in so far as Berger fears that icons generally collude with religious and secular
celebrity-elite conventions, whereas Hariman and Lucaites believe that visual icons
work at a continuing point of tension between convention and subversion. Berger's
socialist 'Ways of Seeing' is what Hariman and Lucaites call 'ideology critique' and
they rightly see this as one of the dominant theoretical frameworks for understanding modern media. But they also believe such a position is dependent upon 'a deep-
seated suspicion of the relationship between imagery and power' (p. 20). Its suspicion
is that some 'sophisticated persuaders' can manipulate mass audiences of naïve or
ignorant viewers, and 'iconic photographs would seem to confirm the long-standing
suspicion of visual display in Western philosophy' (p. 3). Berger's ideology critique of
the advertising image is part of this suspicion of 'sophisticated persuaders'. In contrast, Hariman and Lucaites, recognizing that more aspects of Western culture are
being shaped by photography and other visual media, argue that social theory itself
is mediated by various forms of observation (p. 5). Thus, for Hariman and Lucaites,
two conceptual positions are crucial to the new study of visual rhetoric. First, it must
re-engage with visual modernity via a renewal of the classical study of rhetoric, but
with 'the emphasis . . . shifted from the individual's pursuit of advantage to the collective construction of identity, community and power' (p. 4). Second, it must challenge
ideology critique (discussed in our Introduction as IRP) in both its hegemonic and
resistance modes to dominant readings.

They recognize that media studies has spent nearly half a century in tension
between theories of ideological control on one hand and an 'ethnographic' emphasis on the other, in its varying 'active audience' or 'sub-cultural' understandings of
popular resistance. But for Hariman and Lucaites there is much more occurring
than either the 'ideological relay' of media meanings from elites to publics or the
local 'subversion' of textual meanings according to gender, class, ethnicity, age
or sexual preference. Instead, photojournalism creates a public culture in tension
between hegemony and resistance:

> In that middle realm other forms of rhetorical effectivity come into their own:
> social knowledge becomes more than dominant-subordinate relationships,
> collective memory serves more than elite interests, citizenship becomes a

distinctive form of social identity, and the resources for communicative action can be more than just the master's tools.

(p. 10)

Hariman and Lucaites are clear in their focus on understanding icons primarily in public news media and in icons' wide circulation as markers of public subjectivity (p. 27). Underpinning their analysis of the rhetorical power of iconic images are five assumptions about the images' public appeal: 'the iconic photograph is an aesthetically familiar form of civic performance coordinating an array of semiotic transcriptions that project an emotional scenario to manage a basic contradiction or recurrent crisis' (p. 29).

Aesthetic familiarity

Photojournalism, Hariman and Lucaites argue, is a public art that cannot rise above or repudiate ordinary expectations (p. 29). It is grounded in conventional materials and devices. The iconic image is 'a moment of visual eloquence' but not experimentation. Icons work with stock devices. Their representation is naturalistic, with 'nothing uncanny' allowed. Their iconography uses familiar images, such as a mother with child or soldiers saluting a flag. Journalistic conventions are applied in terms of balanced composition and appropriate decorum. Their visual grammar is routine. Advertising publicity lore ('image before text') and professional media mythology ('photographs get us close to today's action') are strongly evident. Hariman and Lucaites see the napalmed girl image, too, as drawing on the conventionality of news images of the Vietnam War. 'Day after day the public saw a jumble of scenes – bombings, firefights, helicopter evacuations, patrols moving out, villages being searched, troops wading across rivers – that could seemingly be rearranged in any order' (p. 177). The 'napalmed girl' incident was yet another of these scenes. The image is starkly naturalistic, and is balanced in frame as the four children running in front are matched by a similar arc of four soldiers walking behind. This photograph gets us as close to the brutal action of war as seems possible. But there is one breach of photojournalistic convention and decorum: the girl is naked.

Civic performance

To be iconic, Hariman and Lucaites emphasize, the image must also add value to conventional forms. The iconic photograph must go beyond photojournalism's ritual repetition of special people, events and emotions (p. 32). It must have for literate cultures the mythical power and intensity that sacred ritual has in non-literate societies, thus acquiring 'the capability to reveal . . . what is . . . not being said or seen in print' (p. 33). There is a shift here from Berger's position. He argues that dialogical language must confront the icon. Hariman and Lucaites argue for the power *of* the icon – 'the unsayable' – over language. Of the napalmed girl photojournalistic image they observe that young girls conventionally are not shown in public stripped naked, while US soldiers were conventionally pictured fighting just wars for noble causes and 'handing out candy to children in occupied lands' (p. 176). So the image simultaneously violates public propriety about child nudity and 'ruptures established narratives' about military action (p. 176). The authors say that by the time Kim Phuc's image was circulating globally, the US public was increasingly recognizing that the government was waging an illegitimate, unending war, seemingly without purpose. By now in this war there was no certainty that this horrific event was not a typical, repeated action. It was in this prepared ground that the napalmed girl visual rhetoric became iconic. Hariman and Lucaites also argue that the civic performance of the iconic photograph is rhetorical in its political intention – it is composed to persuade publics (p. 33).

> The girl's nakedness provides a performative embodiment of the modern conception of universal humanity. She could be a poster child for the Universal Declaration of Human Rights . . .The dramatic charge of the photo comes from its evocation of pity and terror.
>
> (p. 179)

Thus, whereas Berger stresses the collusion of beauty and terror within advertising lore, Hariman and Lucaites emphasize the public rhetorical power ('evocation') of visualized pity and terror.

Semiotic transcriptions

Iconic images, they argue, must attain to both coherence and difference. An icon's popular appeal must be open to plural and often inconsistent perspectives. Thus Hariman and Lucaites say an iconic photograph's performance must include multiple representations coded in terms of 'romance, tragedy, gender, class, nationalism, technocracy, and many other forms of collective organization' (p. 34). Individual readers can then mobilize for different identifications with the image. For example, Hariman and Lucaites make a strong case for the 'therapeutic' consensus established by parts of the media industry via Kim Phuc's images. Noting that the history of an icon is never static, they discuss the social knowledge communicated by a later photograph of Kim as an adult peace activist in the West. In this image it is her back, not her front, which is naked, showing healed napalm scars. And now she holds her new baby, thus instilling a different way of seeing the original image and its embedded history. Questions of collective responsibility are displaced in this later photograph by questions of individual healing:

> A record of immoral state action [in the 'napalmed girl' photo] has become a history of private lives . . . Questions of collective responsibility – and of justice – have been displaced by questions of individual healing . . . [and] a narrative of . . . a new, unblemished, innocent generation . . . [T]he reinscription of the iconic image by the second image . . . reinvokes a therapeutic discourse that has become a symptomatic and powerful form of social control in liberal-democratic, capitalist societies.
>
> (pp. 184–7)

But the authors also point to countervailing later images of Kim Phuc, especially in other areas of the media such as political cartoons. For example, one cartoon by Dennis Draughon (2004, cited in Hariman and Lucaites 2007: 202) in The *Scranton Times* startlingly drops in the tortured hooded figure from Iraq's Abu Ghraib prison behind Kim Phuc as she runs from the napalm. So she is now set during the Iraq occupation thirty years after her own war. Clearly the image of Kim Phuc is open to plural meanings. Yet photojournalism must also coordinate identifications, fusing differing codes together in what Hariman and Lucaites call strong economies of transcription. Iconic images coordinate different patterns of identification 'which together provide a public audience with sufficient means for contending with potentially unmanageable events . . . In place of identification with a heroic version of the dominant subject, the napalm photograph encourages identification with alien victimage' (2007: 34–5). Thus, they argue, the original iconic photograph is used to heighten the emotional and moral content of Draughon's new cartoon image:

> Her nakedness reveals the vulnerability of his shrouded body, her scream voices the agony within his hooded silence, her violated innocence represents his torture . . . Once again, war crimes are occurring because of US policy; once again, the public is trapped in a space between pain and indifference; once again, the war will not go away.
>
> (p. 202)

Despite the remediation of the 'therapeutic' Kim Phuc and her message of forgiveness, her past life as the 'napalmed girl' will just not go away. That iconic image of trauma continues to appear, 'ghostlike' (p. 204) in a succession of cartoons challenging economic and imperial expansion. Citing Barthes, Hariman and Lucaites ask: when can photography be mad or tame? They argue that the 'napalmed girl' image is repeatedly tamed by the banality of its circulation, by personalizing the girl in the picture, by drawing out a liberal narrative of healing, by the transition into the celebrity photograph of Kim's regeneration as 'peace activist'. But, on the other hand, it remains an indelible image of terror that 'obsessively repeats itself, that keeps the public audience interned in the real time of fatality rather than the fantasies of renewal, staring at screams that cannot be heard and haunted by ghosts that will not speak' (pp. 188–9).

Emotional scenarios

Media performance is always, say Hariman and Lucaites, 'traffic in bodies' (p. 35) and through this vehicle iconic photojournalism provides audiences with powerful emotional experiences. The focus on bodily expression *displays* emotions, thus placing the viewer in an affective relationship with people in the photograph. Within this emotional dimension, iconic images operate rhetorically, becoming 'circuits of emotional exchange' (p. 36); and this is especially so politically because they evoke civic pride or public outrage. 'Democratic publics need emotional resources that have to be communicated through the public media . . . Iconic images are emotional because they are born in conflict or confusion.' (p. 36) Thus, Hariman and Lucaites note the conditions of modern US warfare become visible in the napalmed girl image. This is imperial action in a distant country far from the public's direct control. Massive, technologically intensive firepower is being used to spare soldiers' lives at enormous cost in 'collateral damage'. The image of the napalmed girl image captures this world tonally – the sky is blocked by smoke and the young girl is bathed in light that in reality is a searing 'liquid fire':

> [T]he elements of the sublime are present but out of order, gone demonic . . . The photo depicts a 'troglodyte world' where moral norms have been either inverted as children are being targeted or abandoned as soldiers walk through the scene not caring. The image calls a public to moral awareness, but its rhetorical power is traumatic.
>
> (p. 183)

Contradictions and crises

A political state is a complex system which, Hariman and Lucaites say, contains at least three sources of 'foundational contradiction' (pp. 36–7). First, political power comes from combining diverse groups or interests, and this coalition can fracture when demands are not met or when class conflict rises to the surface. Second, in the normal condition of politics, some social goods are mutually contradictory: one cannot always optimize liberty and security at the same time. Third, representation is incapable of reproducing the social totality and, as a consequence, no political discourse or image can avoid signifying biases, exclusions and denials. In this situation of embedded contradictions, visual icons are powerful aesthetic resources for mediation of conflicts that can have no definitive resolution. 'Because all societies, and particularly democratic societies, are grounded in conflict, there is continual need for performances that can manage conflict. The stage is set for iconic circulation' (p. 37). The Vietnam War saw the display of some of the most profound social contradictions in the US since the Great Depression of the 1930s. Public criticism of US foreign policy represented volatile arguments of gender, class, age and ethnicity challenging the contradictions between US 'liberty' and the 'security' of another people across the world whom US aeroplanes seemed to want to 'bomb into the stone age'. This image of Kim Phuc, Hariman and Lucaites argue, brought to the surface all of the denials and exclusions of visual rhetoric in Vietnam.

Between hegemony and resistance

Hariman and Lucaites look for a 'middle realm' between hegemonic ideology critique and sub-cultural resistance theory. Here they analyze five 'vectors of influence that seem important for photojournalism and particularly for iconic photographs': (i) reproducing ideology, (ii) communicating social knowledge, (iii) shaping collective memory, (iv) modelling citizenship, and (v) providing figural resources for communicative action (p. 9). In terms of ideology, Hariman and Lucaites' under-standing, like Berger's, is premised on Barthes' account of myth as a 'set of beliefs that presents a social order as if it were a natural order' (p. 9). They contend that Kim Phuc's image is impoverished as personal history, a 'combination of naked expressiveness and personal anonymity' (p. 199). But, they argue, at the same time that the photograph empties her personal–social history in war-torn Vietnam, it is also 'expressive' of the fragmentation already occurring *within* the imperial power and in US public culture, as citizens become emotionally aware of the hypocrisy behind daily 'body counts' and media rhetoric about 'free-fire zones'. Similarly, in their analysis of another iconic photograph – the shootings of anti- Vietnam War protestors at Kent State University in 1970 (when four students died and nine were wounded) – Hariman and Lucaites note the personal anonymity of the woman crying out at the centre of the image. What was important to the viewer was not the actual detail of the crying woman but the expressive power of the image and the social knowledge it conveyed.

We see, Hariman and Lucaites (2007) say, a young woman kneeling, screaming over the dead body of a young man; and as an iconic image it is especially powerful in its representation of raw feeling:

> The girl's anguish registers not only personal affect but also the profound social rupture that has occurred. The US government was not supposed to shoot its own citizens for gathering in public or protesting against government actions. Political conflict at home was not supposed to be a war. By shooting thirteen students the Ohio National Guard had seriously wounded American society's basic sense of legitimacy. By crying out across the dead body as if to say 'How could you?' the girl fuses an overwhelming feeling with a funda-mental belief.
>
> (pp. 140–1)

The Kent State image, Hariman and Lucaites observe, draws on a fund of social knowledge; and in understanding the connection of social knowledge to shaping collective memory, they draw on Marxist philosopher Louis Althusser's theory of interpellation – that is, the power of the image to 'call up' a particular response from a viewer: 'The girl's cry is a direct demand for accountability and compensa-tory action – a terrible wrong must be acknowledged and made right – but it is not stated directly to the viewer' (pp. 142–3). Figural resources of the image convey this moral sense of the need for action. The girl in the image is addressing the state, understood as off-stage, to the right of the actual viewer of the image: 'How could you do this?' But the image also addresses the viewer in a particular way:

> The girl is screaming at those beside us while being offered directly to us for our judgment or action. Thus the photo's combination of emotional display and visual interpellation creates a strong sense of moral crisis, a point at which the audience must decide where it stands.
>
> (p. 143)

In establishing a powerful feeling of moral choice, the iconic image is, they argue, modelling citizenship. The democratic process is being countered by an act of violence that originated outside the photo-frame to silence this man in the crowd and to disperse others. Thus the photograph 'becomes a simulacrum of the public sphere, where free discussion among citizens and public accountability are the only legitimate means for countering state coercion' (p. 144). Hariman and Lucaites make big claims for their iconic images. They argue that the entire usage of cultural forms within the Kent State image is presented 'through a visual image that is centred in an inarticulate cry' (p. 144). But here the power of the image and the lack of an accompanying verbal text becomes a rhetorical advantage because it makes citizenship the key feature of interpellation. 'For the dominant elements of the visual presentation also give that structure a profoundly emotional inflection. In short, the photo reconstitutes citizenship as a constitutional act' (p. 144).

From a democratic to a liberal polity

Hariman and Lucaites' analysis is central to their thesis about contemporary tensions within the liberal-democratic world-view. Their use of the word 'liberal' is centred on the view that society should allow optimal realization of individual liberty. In contrast, the authors insist, it is collective preferences – social goods like health, education, equality before the law – which underpin democracy. In their view, the period covered by their book, from the image of the 1936 'Migrant Mother' during the Great Depression to the Challenger explosion and the images of 'ground zero' after 9/11, marks a shift in the tension within liberal democracy. For them the napalmed girl photograph of 1972 represents in the US 'the point at which the balance in the public culture shifts from appeals for democratic solidarity to a discourse of liberal individualism' (p. 22). Similarly, the Kent State image acts as an invocation of the solidarity and public good that is deemed lost. 'Her scream is more than the expression of individual grief . . . for it carries the social energies swirling around her while venting the deep betrayal that occurs when a citizen is killed by their own government' (p. 145).

Two Boys in Bangladesh

In contrast, the graphic image of two naked boys in Bangladesh in 1971 did *not* become iconic. Does their complete absence from public view for nearly forty years support or indicate omissions in Hariman and Lucaites' framework of analysis?

If we take two images of pain and personal damage that we found most powerful at the 'Bangladesh 1971' exhibition, that of the two boys and of photographer Naib Uddin Ahmed's 'Shamed Woman' who had been raped by the military, neither engages directly with the viewer: the two boys have turned away from us, and the young woman covers her face completely with her hair and clenched hands. Arguably though, both images have 'the capability to reveal or suggest what is unsayable' (Hariman and Lucaites 2007: 33), and both are, photographically, rhetorical performances 'composed to persuade' (p. 33). Moreover, both images are clearly emotional scenarios encouraging 'an affective relationship with the people in the picture' (p. 35). Although the images are no doubt open to 'multiple and often inconsistent perspectives' (p. 34) – especially the image of a raped woman, who is generally an object of shame in Muslim communities – they clearly represent 'foundational contradictions' (p. 36) in the Pakistani political system. So on almost all counts – aesthetic familiarity and transgression, civic performance, semiotic transcription, emotional scenario, and political contradictions – these images fulfil Hariman and Lucaites' definition of the iconic.

So, is the combination of just those two absences – of face-to-face reciprocity, and of semiotic collective coherence – sufficient to explain why these images have not become internationally iconic? We do not think so, and have argued elsewhere (Tulloch and Blood 2010) that the images' invisibility since 1971, as well as their quest for iconic status only in the last few years, reveals a significant absence of agency in Hariman and Lucaites' account – both top down agency

One of the estimated 400,000 birangona, meaning 'brave women', who were raped during the 1971 war. Photograph taken by Naib Uddin Ahmed © Drik Picture Library

from governments and military and below up agency in terms of new social movements. We pursue our argument using Hariman and Lucaites' five vectors of photojournalistic influence.

Reproducing ideology

Hariman and Lucaites argue that the 'ideological code produces a way of talking about the world . . . that is necessarily "impoverished" in order to sustain its own contradictions' (p. 9). This Barthes-type combination of personal anonymity and expressiveness operates in Raihan's photograph of the two small boys. They are standing alone but in human communion. But what is absent here from the frame – the millions of dead and dispossessed, the thousands of raped women – is as powerful as what is included. The photographer, Raihan, whose shadowed head just creeps into the harshly sunlit scene at bottom of frame, was recording what he was politically commissioned to do as a war volunteer: portraying symbolically, as well as naturalistically, the human rights devastation by continuous acts of state terrorism. This was a 'resistance' *agency*. But there was another agency which was more powerful at the time. This photograph was not absent from the world's media because of poor news values, but because of harsh war conditions, the difficulties put in the way of Western journalists by the military, the absence of a professional media infrastructure to transmit them to the world – and the fact that after Bangladesh's independence was achieved, there was a continuing silence (over moral shame) and contradiction (between changing politics) surrounding many of these images. For example, in the new Bangladesh, children's schoolbooks represented the shifting politics of different governmental and military factions, yet were consistently dominated by the images of military heroes.

Communicating social knowledge

What is needed in the case of Bangladesh, as an extension to Hariman and Lucaites' somewhat functionalist notion of 'structure' and 'agency', is an understanding of agency within the media industries themselves. In 1990, a small group of media professionals, including photojournalist Dr Shahidul Alam, set up the Dhaka picture agency, Drik, to represent 'the majority world'. This term is itself more agentive than the 'third' or 'developing' world descriptions they rejected. These majority world images were not to be 'fodder for disaster reporting, but a vibrant source of energy' (Alam 2011). Drik set up the South Asian Institute of Photography, with Alam as director, where photographers are trained to take up social issues absent from mainstream media. As Alam puts it:

> In the past, the majority of images produced and seen in mainstream media, certainly in the West, had been . . . by either white Western photographers or staff working in NGOs; and because it has been that way, it has catered to a particular agenda . . . to raise funds.
>
> (Alam 2007: 3)

He questions the Western concept of 'development' where raising funds 'requires putting people in positions where their only identity is as icons of poverty'. This 'donor' genre of photojournalism, as Hoskins and O'Loughlin describe it, is mediated by 'compassion', since 'NGO's and humanitarian organizations wish to avoid denunciation and the "blame game" and concentrate on presenting suffering in ways that simply allow for an empathy between victims and potential donors' (2010: 51). Similarly, John Berger argues, this framing of moral response 'accuses nobody and everybody' (Berger 1980: 43–4).

It was against this conventionalized 'donor' context that Alam, in collaboration with Mark Sealy, director of the photographic agency Autograph ABP, mounted the exhibition in April–May 2008 at Rivington Place in London (and later at the Side Gallery, Newcastle). In contrast to Drik's own 'vernacular' everyday-life sites for its photography in Dhaka – like rickshaws and buses – this gallery exhibition represented Alam's 'minority world' remediation in the West of the images of genocide. This made them, in the view of reviewers like Tahmina Shafique (2008) and Bangladeshi novelist and *Guardian* reviewer Tahmima Anam (2008), active and iconic internationally. As Hoskins has commented, 'A photograph . . . on display in . . . galleries of exhibitions inhabits a very different physical space to the moving image. Its physicality affords the photograph a historical status that the television image has for many years been deprived of' (2005: 20, 135).

But complementing the exhibition at Rivington Place was a Bangladeshi Film Festival at Rich Mix cultural centre in April–May 2008, which showed narrative and factual compilation films which, for the first time in an area of London containing many Bangladeshi migrants and diasporas, represented the genocide by West Pakistan's military in Bangladesh and the systematic and prolonged rape of women in the army camps, which led to shame and sometimes suicide. As the Rich Mix film programme put it, these films, complementing the photographs at Rivington Place Gallery, spoke

> for the many who have given their lives for their freedom, for those who have been left behind, who live with the pain, for the perpetrators of the crime who must be confronted with their deeds, and for the youth to know the birth pangs of their nation.
>
> (Rich Mix programme 2008)

Thus the gallery and the cultural centre were part of the multiple media modalities which Hoskins and O'Loughlin have described in their discussion of whether 'images of war show or hide' (2010: 26). Together Rivington Place and Rich Mix allowed the emergence of hitherto unseen images which connected and diffused 'the image into intrinsically unpredictable and ongoing interpretive realms, communities and individuals' (Hoskins and O'Loughlin, 2010: 26; and see Chapter 7).

Shaping collective memory

In Bangladesh, what Hariman and Lucaites call 'repeated memory' has been constructed and maintained by the state sponsored National Museum in Dhaka and by school textbooks which repetitively – but with a changing focus provided by changing military and civilian governments – emphasize the relative claims to 'truth' of this or that male-hero initiator of independence rhetoric. In contrast, criminologist Wayne Morrison argues, The Liberation War Museum in Dhakha has constructed its central thematic trope around the issue in Bangladesh of surviving genocide in 'living contrast to our states of denial' (Morrison 2006: 299). With NGO backing, this museum has implicitly challenged state-sponsored displays at the National Museum. Arguably the Rivington Place exhibition was repeating internationally the Liberation War Museum's policy, just as the rickshaw, boat and school playing field exhibitions of photographic images by Drik are a local, everyday life forum for 'majority world' images. As a visit to their photographic website will reveal, Drik's aim has been to indigenize photographic production, while also trying to be aware of different identities and politics among journalists. Its policy has also been to feminize its photographic texts, both through its 'Bangladesh 1971' images and through photographers like Alam's substantial portfolio of productive women workers and leaders in 'development' countries from Thailand to Kashmir.

Hariman and Lucaites worry about the re-gendering of the public sphere via images like the grieving woman at Kent State University and the 'napalmed girl'. They argue that, set against a masculine monopoly of violence and state action that is increasingly irrational, such gendering may harden alignments of power, violence, and masculinity:

> Worse yet, as women only cry out and scream while remaining helpless, public speech becomes hysterical and without agency, and as their meaning is transferred to the visual medium that is featuring a woman's body, the public becomes subject to the male gaze while being reduced to the politics of spectacle.
>
> (Hariman and Lucaites 2007: 197)

This concern parallels that of Berger and 1970s feminism about the male gaze and the female nude. Yet, the 'Bangladesh 1971' images in fact challenged these gendered polarities. The Rivington Place window display featured a photograph by Rashid Talukder, 'Students on the Street', taken during the non-cooperation movement of 1970, showing lines of women dressed in light saris striding in three columns along a road with rifles over their left shoulders. As *The Guardian* reviewer Anam wrote, this and a further image were successful in challenging our gendered expectations:

> Another photograph is a seemingly idyllic image of two women wading through a pond with a basket of flowers. But the caption reads: 'During the liberation war, female freedom fighters would smuggle grenades in baskets covered with water hyacinth'.
>
> (Anam 2008)

Among these women we see no screaming but plenty of deliberation and a complete merging of public and private spheres. Where there were images of raped, brutalized women in the exhibition, as in Ahmed's *Shamed Woman* who is seen covering her face with her hair and fists, there was no screaming either. Rather the emotional affect was conveyed by the silence, the determined screening of her face and the classically triangular monumentality of the framed body. She was not a woman for the male gaze either.

Modelling citizenship

Hariman and Lucaites make the point that the 'iconic photo . . . may be the leading edge of globalization on US terms' (2007: 19), but they don't explore the implications of this comment. In contrast, Shahidul Alam, in an interview on US alternative radio has spoken about foreign 'presence' in the political economy of Bangladesh:

> [T]he famine that we had in '74 is believed largely backed by the US preventing PL-48 wheat coming into Bangladesh . . . But even today, where we have what is officially a neutral caretaker government, it is generally perceived that the military has a strong role behind the scenes and certainly the United States, while it espouses democracy, has singularly supported autocratic regimes, which it has found more convenient to handle.
>
> (Kolhatkar 2007: 4)

For Alam, globalization on US terms also means globalization of their 'minority world' images, particularly of 'development' (Kolhatkar 2007: 4). In contrast, Drik's aim is to model citizenship around local communities and ethnic differences: 'awareness and understanding of people and their cultures . . . what we've tried to do is take pictures of everyday life, which, in itself shows that people are active and have great differences' (p. 4).

Providing figural resources for communicative action

Hariman and Lucaites note that the iconic Kim Phuc image creates a searing eventfulness that breaks away from any official narrative justifying the war (2007: 176). In her naked vulnerability, she 'is a call to obligation' (p. 178). This sense of heightened emotional intensity, conveyed by the vulnerable, screaming children of Vietnam, is crucial to Hariman and Lucaites' argument about the power of emotions conveyed visually at moments of extreme terror. This allows, they argue, a new sense of communion and advocacy in public culture.

The two Bangladeshi boys staring at the devastated land in the absence of their parents draw on some of the figural resources that Hariman and Lucaites find in the Kent State photograph. In the rocket bombs image of the two naked boys, as in the Kent State photo, there are two vectors of sight. The boys stare diagonally across the frame, looking silently out of frame, perhaps at the soldiers who have caused this carnage. This diagonal is reinforced by the direction of most of the rocket bombs that lie at their feet. But a secondary vector follows the line of those rocket shells nearest to us, via the line of the photographer's shadow at bottom of frame, to the viewer of the image. From this perspective, looking successively deeper into the picture – from rocket bombs to boys to field with bomb-scarred tree to wrecked dwellings – the enormity of what is absent unfolds as though in parallel waves. Peace is absent (the foreground shells). Parents are absent (the isolated, naked boys). Productive livelihood is absent (the destroyed crops in the fields). Home is absent (the wrecked dwellings).

Shahidul Alam began his photojournalism career photographing children and has continued doing this because he found early that even when without food, without homes washed away by floods or destroyed by armies, and without family members who have died, still 'the children surrounded me. They wanted a picture' (Alam 2008). But Alam notes that because the owners and editors of Bangladeshi newspapers are the urban elite, village people 'exist only as numbers, generally when plagued by some disaster'. They are just as susceptible to 'donor genre' photography as newspapers in the West (ibid.).

But Alam has continued to take photographs of children in disaster areas, such as Kashmir in 2005. While photographing these children,

> My thoughts are far away . . . I remember the children screaming . . . during the Indo-Pakistan War of 1971, when I watched in helpless anger as Pakistani soldiers shot the children trying to escape their flamethrowers. The United States had sent their seventh fleet to the Bay of Bengal in support of the genocide that was Operation Searchlight which led to the deaths of 3 million Bengalis in what was then East Pakistan.
>
> (ibid.)

Alam adds poignantly that as he photographs children today he also remembers the Palestinians and the Lebanese 'that the world is knowingly ignoring', and he can hear the bombs raining down – and the children screaming. 'Piercing, wailing, angry, helpless, frightened screams. . . . I wonder if those screams can be heard . . . I wonder if through all those screams the warmongers will still be asking, "Why do they hate us?"' (ibid.).

Like the photographers discussed in the 'Bangladesh '71' exhibition, Alam is attempting with his shots of traumatized children what both John Berger (Chapter 2) and Judith Butler (Chapter 8) call 'alternative' photographic framing. This is his agency.

Conclusion

Unlike Hariman and Lucaites, we have been working here through a collection of *travelling* images. The main reason for this lies in our difference of theoretical emphasis. For Hariman and Lucaites iconic images separate themselves out from other photojournalistic images via the sedimentation of time. But in our analysis icon-*making* is more instant and active. The 'Bangladesh 1971' UK exhibitions in London and Newcastle were part of an active agency in foregrounding traumatic images of state terror to human beings. The attempt was to make them iconic among local communities by reconstructing histories and memories. This 'travelling' operated in Barthes' sense of 'robbing myth' – by robbing 'minority world' images of their same-as-it-was 'compassion fatigue' (Hoskins and O'Loughlin 2010: 37). The specific location of the exhibition and film festival was designed to capture the attention and understanding of new Bangladeshi generations as a basis for inter-personal communicative action. They were also aimed at British people who might see the neighbouring communities of Tower Hamlets and Brick Lane, as Tahmima Anam wrote , in a new light. Hoskins and O'Loughlin argue that the 'presence of diasporic or migrant audiences is central to the new media ecology; in any country there will be people who bring different geographical, ethnic and religious perspectives to local or national news' (2010: 44). In the case of the 'Bangladesh '71' exhibition, the images themselves travelled, through time as well as across space, to empower Bangladeshi migrant audiences with those different perspectives.

4 'The Gulf War did not take place'

Smart-weapon icon

A CNN website, 'The Unfinished War', shows an undistinguished image in its section on smart weapons used during the 1991 Gulf War. The grainy grey of the photograph is typical of the 'missile-eye' television images released by the Pentagon at the time. It is, as the website says, a smart bomb image that provided 'one of the most memorable television clips of the war, pinpointing an elevator shaft at the Iraqi Air Force headquarters in Baghdad' (CNN 2001).

We didn't, of course, see the image this way at the time it became iconic internationally. It was then a regularly repeated moving image on television news, always accompanied by a spoken voice-over as the precision 'pinpointing technique' (signified by its cross-hair marker) was explained and the camera in the nose of the missile rushed us down towards its target. This iconic image signified the enormous computer-driven superiority of 'our side'. As Hoskins and O'Loughlin put it, this kind of image amounted to a 'fundamental disowning of injury' which was achieved via 'a crystallization of memory around a belief in precision strikes and "limited" warfare', which marked what they call the 'first phase of mediatization' (2010: 115; see also Chapter 7).

The CNN website says that these precision-guided munitions (PGMs) were not widely used in 1991. More than a quarter of a million conventional bombs were dropped on Iraq and less than 10 per cent were PGMs. Yet they accounted for 75 per cent of the damage. The website added that the use of smart weapons led to a new military theory: 'surgical strikes.' Nearly two decades later the popular internet site YouTube continued to display these 'surgical strike' videos from the war (leander37 2010). But, as we will see, this precision medical metaphor is highly problematic.

Enemy combatants, let alone civilians, were rarely seen in these fast-moving images – only the target cross-hair marker and the inevitable puffs of smoke. One notable exception occurred at a news conference when Commander in Chief of the US Central Command, General Norman Schwarzkopf ('Stormin Norman'), showed one such smart weapon video and pointed to a car driving over an Iraqi bridge moments before a Patriot missile struck. In his ebullient style Schwarzkopf called the driver 'the luckiest man in Iraq' (Cody 1991).

Arguably, the smart-bomb attack images are the ones French social theorist Jean Baudrillard intuited as emblematic of the 1991 Gulf War. They are certainly a key example of what he calls the 'hyperreality' of a world of increasingly fast global communication networks where the real object of war seemed to have been superseded by its simulation. Baudrillard argued that 'the Gulf War did not take place', because its 'meaning' could only be found via images, 'simulacra' such as the indistinct smart-bomb image of the elevator shaft.

In this chapter, we explore images from the 1991 Gulf War and examine Baudrillard's controversial claim. As a celebrity intellectual famous for his Gulf War 'will not happen/isn't happening/did not happen' media articles, Baudrillard *himself* was circulated, both by internet and within academia. We will examine some of the more interesting of Baudrillard's academic critics in relation to Gulf War images; and drawing on one of the most critical of these, Douglas Kellner, we explore the apparently horrific consequences conveyed by another of the iconic images from the 1991 Gulf War, the PGM destruction of the Amiriyah shelter in Iraq. These photographs seem in absolute contrast to that of the smart-weapon with which we begin the chapter. Yet, as we shall see exploring internet images of Amiriyah, this awful 'reality' was itself conveyed by quite varying images as further simulations.

'The Gulf War did not take place'

Baudrillard's *The Gulf War Did Not Take Place*, published in French in 1991 and translated into English in 1995, was originally three essays published in the French daily leftist newspaper *Libération* and London's *The Guardian*. Baudrillard argued that the style of warfare in the 1991 Gulf War differed dramatically from previous wars; the 'war' existed only as 'live' images on radar and television screens:

> It all began with the leitmotif of surgical, mathematical and punctual efficacy, which is another way of not recognising the enemy as such, just as lobotomy is a way of not recognising madness as such.
>
> (Baudrillard 1995: 43)

Because the coalition forces, led by the US, chose not to engage with Iraqi forces or take risks normally associated with warfare, Baudrillard argued the coalition fought a virtual war (pp. 68–9). While enormous violence occurred, the Gulf War as such, he argued, did not take place. Baudrillard reasoned that Saddam Hussein did not use his full military capacity in the war, that his power was not reduced significantly by it, and that he was not removed from power as Western leaders had wanted. So the victors did not win, the enemy went undefeated: 'The Gulf War did not take place.'

> What is tested here in this foreclosure of the enemy, this experimental reclusion of war, is the future validity for the entire planet of this type of suffocating and machine performance, virtual and relentless in its unfolding. In this perspective war could not take place.
>
> (p. 64)

Baudrillard's writings on the Gulf War achieved notoriety and were criticized by many observers. First, he was challenged on factual grounds, since many thousands of people died, and Saddam Hussein's regime was limited by post-war aerial surveillance. Secondly, he was criticized on theoretical grounds for his nihilism, relativism, even valorization of the system of simulacra he was describing. Susan Sontag, in her final book on theories of the photographic image, *Regarding the Pain of Others* (2003), critically re-examined her own enormously influential early work, *On Photography* (1977). But near the end of her 2003 book, written around the ideas and emotions surrounding the Iraq War, Sontag engaged with the 'French theorists' of the image, Guy Debord and Jean Baudrillard. The death of reality, she argues, as presented in Baudrillard's work, has been accepted without much reflection (Sontag 2003: 110–11). This is especially so in the West, where, she writes, news has been converted into entertainment.

> To speak of reality becoming a spectacle is a breath-taking provincialism . . .
> It assumes that everyone is a spectator. It suggests, perversely, unseriously,
> that there is no real suffering in the world. But it is absurd to identify the world
> with those zones in the well-off countries where people have the dubious privi-
> lege of being spectators . . . of other people's pain [through] war and massive
> injustice and terror. There are hundreds of millions of television watchers
> who are far from inured to what they see on television. They do not have the
> luxury of patronizing reality.
>
> (Sontag 2003: pp. 98–9)

However, perhaps Sontag misunderstands Baudrillard. Even some of Baudrillard's harshest critics have found value in his theories of the image; while other academics have argued for the profound importance of his media theory as a *challenge* to the world of simulation he describes.

Hammond's Baudrillard: political agency and the loss of meaning

One productive academic inflection of Baudrillard's ideas is Philip Hammond's *Media, War and Postmodernity*. Hammond's core argument is:

> that war and intervention since the Cold War have been driven by attempts
> on the part of Western leaders to recapture a sense of purpose and meaning,
> both for themselves and their societies. This in turn has led to a heightened
> emphasis on image, spectacle and media presentation.
>
> (Hammond 2007: 11)

He argues that the fundamental shift in Western politics with the collapse of the Soviet Union was the 'end of Left and Right' and 'the death of politics' (p. 11).

Hammond views Western interventions from the 1991 Gulf War to President George W. Bush's 'war on terror' as opportunistic and reactive to perceived emergencies rather than acting to achieve some strategic project (p. 16). One such opportunistic threat was Saddam Hussein's attack on Kuwait, to which the West reacted with 'Desert Storm', its 'emergency' name for legitimizing the 1991 Gulf War.

Thus, Hammond argues, the disillusionment of former Left (but now postmodernist) theorists, and the defeat of the 'revolutionary potential' (Baudrillard 1995: 85, cited in Hammond 2007: 18) culminating in the collapse of the Soviet Union, led to 'the "ironic" postmodernist attitude, refusing to get excited by the propaganda, dismissing it all as only images', and to Baudrillard's 'hyperbolic and seemingly nonsensical insistence that the war "did not take place"' (Hammond 2007: 18–19). This was meant, Hammond says, as a denial of the assumption that the Gulf War was a significant historical event that either supporters or opponents could see as part of some grand narrative of liberation. 'The Gulf War was less a battle with Saddam than a struggle to make sense of the West's role in the post-Cold War world' (pp. 19–20).

This loss of political purpose gives rise, Hammond argues, to factors seen as symbolizing the post-modern war: high-technology smart weapons, and the importance of media spectacle. In this context, war, as Baudrillard contended, becomes bloodless: 'an asexual surgical war . . . in which the enemy only appears as a computerized target' (1995: 62, cited in Hammond 2007: 21).

Television coverage of the Gulf War was highly aestheticized – that is, portrayed in an artistic, idealistic manner – *as well as* made to seem 'surgical'. On the first night of the War, as explosions lit up the sky around Baghdad, US television commentators seemed to be in raptures at the beauty of the shapes, colours and forms of the military attack. In a world without politics, Hammond argues, the *media spectacle* becomes a substitute 'for an inspiring cause to rally public support' (2007: 21). This is why Baudrillard could write, 'The war . . . watches itself in a mirror: am I pretty enough, am I operational enough, am I spectacular enough . . . to make an entry onto the historical stage?' (1995: 31–2, cited in Hammond 2007: 21). But in Hammond's view, this degree of attention to self-presentation in the war was self-defeating. 'The emphasis on creating the right image heightened the sense that the war was somehow unreal: the feeling that it was, as many commentators remarked at the time, "like a video game" (Knightley 2000)' (2007: 21).

Kellner's Baudrillard: Critical theory and French theory borderlines

In a series of books and articles, Douglas Kellner has adopted a critical realist position in discussing Baudrillard and 'New French Theory'. In particular, pre-empting Sontag's critique of 'French theorists', Kellner positions himself on the side of Critical Theory to survey the strengths and weaknesses of Baudrillard's 'postmodernism' (an attribution which we will see later is challenged by William Merrin).

Kellner notes that both New French Theory and Critical Theory 'explode the boundaries' between traditional disciplines (1989: 1). But Critical Theory in its critiques of ideology also challenged the divisions that contemporary capitalism was imposing within the empirical world of power and control:

In these ideological operations we see *abstraction* at work: ideologies which legitimate the superiority of men over women, or of capitalism over other social systems, so as to attempt to justify the privileges of the ruling classes or strata . . . Thus I believe that abstraction is fundamentally related to the key features of ideology such as legitimation, domination, and mystification, and that the drawing of *boundaries* (between allegedly inferior and superior systems, groups, policies, values, etc.) also plays a fundamental role in this process.

(Kellner 1989: 2)

For Kellner there is a causal relationship between abstractions and the drawing of boundaries, observable in both the operation of capitalist logics and philosophy (p. 2). He values both German Critical Theory and New French Theory (that is, Barthes, Derrida, Foucault, Baudrillard, Lyotard and others) for resisting this. Kellner acknowledges that *any* intellectual procedure must involve a degree of abstraction from daily reality and he summarizes his position by

noting that 'abstraction' per se is . . . neither 'good' nor 'bad'. Rather, it is a question as to whether one contextualizes one's concepts and abstractions . . . to illuminate social processes and phenomena rather than to decontextualize one's abstractions or concepts so as to distort and mystify social reality.

(p. 4)

Yet, while positioning himself within Critical Theory (p. 4), Kellner believes that it fails 'to account for changes in the social conditions and techno-political infrastructure of capitalist societies from the 1960s to the present' (p. 5). It is here that Kellner sees the importance of Baudrillard who 'provides a theory of the new conditions of postindustrial, postmodern societies, which themselves allegedly obliterate the boundaries between established categories, classes, political parties, etc.' (p. 5).

Kellner notes how Baudrillard, starting from a Marxist position in his early work, focussed on capitalism's increasing concern for managing consumption. Baudrillard believed that commodities were now characterized by more than use-value and exchange value (as in Marx's theory of the commodity), but also by sign-value, such as the mark of style, prestige, luxury, power, etc. Similar to Berger, Kellner agues: '[T]he phenomenon of sign-value became an essential constituent of the commodity and consumption in the consumer society' (pp. 5–6).

Kellner explored how Baudrillard followed through the logic of this earlier position, leaving Marxism behind to produce 'a rather extreme and in some ways paradigmatic postmodern social theory' (p. 5). In his writings since 1975:

Baudrillard projects a vision of a media and a high-tech society where people are caught up in the play of images, spectacles, simulacra, communications networks, etc. that have less and less relationship to an outside, to an external 'reality' to such an extent that the very concepts of the social, political, or even 'reality' no longer seem to have any meaning.

(p. 6)

As Kellner puts it, Baudrillard claims that we are in a new era of simulation in which social reproduction (information processing, knowledge industries, media, cybernetic control models and so on) has replaced production as the organizing principle of society. Thus, labour, the central focus of Marxist theory, is no longer a force of production but is itself a 'sign among signs' (Baudrillard 1973: 23, cited in Kellner 1989: 6). Crucially for Baudrillard, therefore, political economy is no longer the foundation, the social determinant, or even a structural 'reality' through which phenomena can be interpreted and explained (Baudrillard 1973: 53ff, cited in Kellner 1989: 6):

> Instead we live in a 'hyperreality' of simulations in which images, spectacles, and the play of signs replace the logic of production and class conflict as key constituents of contemporary capitalist societies.
>
> (p. 6)

In Baudrillard's postmodern universe, for Kellner, the society of simulations takes on the appearance of 'hyperreality'. This comes to constitute the real as people imitate hyperreal simulation models. The distinction between model and reality, real and hyperreal disappears (pp. 6–8).

On one hand, Kellner criticizes the negative responses to Baudrillard of critical theorists like Habermas, in placing his postmodern theory 'under the sign of irrationalism' (p. 9). On the contrary, Kellner argues, New French Theory has produced a powerful description of new phenomena like cybernetics, computerization and the information society 'which Critical Theory today must deal with if it is not to become irrelevant to the current problems of the present age' (p. 9). On the other hand, Kellner insists that Marxist categories retain central importance:

> For it is capitalism that is determining what sort of media, information, computers, etc. are being produced and distributed precisely according to their logic and interests. That is, in techno-capitalist societies, information . . . is being more and more commodified, accessible only to those who pay for it and who have access to it.
>
> (p.10)

Thus, Kellner proposes exploring a new configuration of capitalism, with postmodernism as the cultural logic of capital, never forgetting that the hegemony of capital is still the fundamental principle of organization (p. 10). He calls for 'situating abstractions back into a specific and complex set of differential relations, contextualizing one's concepts . . . 'within a set of historically specific and complex social relations (p. 11). In particular, Kellner wants more evidence that there *is* the clear borderline between modernity and postmodernity which Baudrillard claims to have crossed.

Kellner, Baudrillard, the Gulf War, 9/11 and the Iraq invasion

In 2003, on the verge of the Iraq invasion, Douglas Kellner wrote an article (2003a) summarizing some of the work in books he had written on the Gulf War (1992) and media spectacle (2003b). This was part of his quest to explore the 'new totali-zations' being undertaken by capitalism in the areas of consumption, the media and information.

Like us, Kellner speaks of the Gulf War as producing 'spectacles of precision-bombs and missiles' (2003a: 10–11). But for him these spectacles were embedded in the real, everyday minutiae of political and economic strategy:

> The Gulf War of 1990–1991 was the major media spectacle of its era, capti-vating global audiences, and seemed to save the first Bush Presidency before its ambiguous outcome and a declining economy defeated the Bush presiden-tial campaign of 1992.
>
> (pp. 9–10)

Kellner argues that the Bush administration's change in attitude to Saddam Hus-sein was partly pragmatic, in terms of local US politics; partly geopolitical, to establish the US as a dominant international police force; and partly to gain more control over Iraqi oil supplies. The Gulf War peace agreement, however, allowing Saddam Hussein to stay in power, and the failure of the US to aid the Kurds in the north and Shi'ites in the south after encouraging them to rise against Hussein, cast a pessimistic pall over the war:

> Images of the slaughter of Kurds and Shi'ites throughout the global media provided negative images that helped code the Gulf War as a failure and that negative spectacle of failure combined with a poor economy helped defeat Bush in 1992.
>
> (p. 10)

Symptomatic of Kellner's 'totalizing' intention is his comparative method, draw-ing attention to structural continuities in the US which bound together the war policies of presidents Bush, father and son. By early 2002, he argues, Bush Jr. faced a situation similar to his father after the Gulf War:

> Despite victory against the Taliban, the limitations of the war and a fail-ing economy provided a situation that threatened Bush's re-election. Thus George W. Bush needed a media dramatic spectacle that would guarantee his election, and once more Saddam Hussein provided a viable candidate.
>
> (p. 11)

Kellner offered 'many hidden agendas' in the Bush offensive against Iraq in 2003. Seeking re-election in 2002, Bush was looking for a major symbolic triumph against terrorism to deflect public attention from the domestic economy, and from the limited foreign policy success in Afghanistan (given that Osama bin Laden had not been found). Further, the main images of Afghanistan 'that circulated through the global media were of civilian casualties caused by US bombing and daily pictures of thousands of refugees [which] raised questions concerning US strategy and intervention' (p. 11). Secondly, neo-conservative ideologues within the Bush administration aiming at a hegemonic international policing role for the US wanted a policy of pre-emptive strike, and a successful attack on Iraq would normalize this policy. Third, postulating a father/son psychological power relationship going back to George W. Bush's succession of personal failures in adult life, Kellner notes that 'the "Oedipus Tex" drama, where George W. Bush desires to conclude his father's unfinished business and simultaneously defeat Evil to constitute himself as Good, is driving him to war with the fervour of a religious Crusade' (p. 11).

Even in his short, 11-page article summarizing the extensive continuities in US economic-strategic policy from the Gulf War, through 9/11 and the Afghanistan War to the Iraq invasion, Kellner is keen to emphasize the point made in his 1989 article of the need for 'contextualizing one's concepts . . . within a set of historically specific and complex social relations' (Kellner 1989: 11), while at the same time establishing a meta-narrative about systemic similarity (as between the two Bush administrations) within US capitalism. He commented that the Iraq invasion in March 2003 resulted from many factors and it would be simplistic to say any one (like control of oil or domestic US politics) was the key. A critical cultural studies approach, he argued, should investigate all dominant discourses, images, and spectacles to reveal manipulation, propaganda and questionable policies:

> [I]n a highly saturated media environment, successful political projects require carefully planned and executed media spectacles. What I have been arguing here is that both the September 11 terror attacks and George Bush's Gulf War were prime examples of such spectacles, and that George W. Bush's . . . war against Iraq could be read in this light.
>
> (Kellner 2003a: 12)

Media spectacles in Kellner's analysis were not, as in his view of Baudrillard's theory, the world itself. Rather, they were 'carefully planned and executed' performances in a realist world of 'underlying' structure and agency.

Merrin's Baudrillard: Symbol and semiotic

For us, the most convincing analysis and critique of Baudrillard is William Merrin's *Baudrillard and the Media* (2005). Merrin rejects the conventional view (as in Hammond and Kellner) of Baudrillard as a postmodernist. Instead, he traces Baudrillard's theory back to a radical interpretation of Emile Durkheim as developed by his collaborator Marcel Mauss and other key Durkheimian thinkers like Roger Callois and Georges Bataille. As Merrin argues, Baudrillard's fundamental 'concept of "symbolic exchange" is directly derived from this tradition's identification and privileging of an immediately actualized, collective mode of relations and its transformative experience and communication' (Merrin 2005: 12).

For Durkheim, there was a radical separation in primitive society between everyday life and the 'symbolic' communication of religion and ritual; and this generated a 'state of effervescence' and 'real communion' (Durkheim 1915: 220, 230, cited in Merrin 2005: 12–13).

> Religion operates, therefore, 'to raise man above himself and make him lead a life superior to that which he would lead if he followed his own individual whims' Thus our highest experience is attained collectively and socially through a communion with others.
>
> (Durkheim 1915: 414, cited in Merrin 2005: 13)

After Durkheim's death, Mauss developed his work in *The Gift*, an anthropological study of a system of exchange and reciprocal gift giving – or 'potlach' – in Polynesian, Melanesian and Native American societies. This ritual, for Mauss and Durkheim as for Baudrillard, was the human space of the *symbolic* – 'an image of an intense, competitive and dramatic scene of exchange, contrasting with the later individualized, utilitarian, formal, impersonal and contractual relations of economic exchange' (p. 13). Yet Mauss' concept of the gift as symbol

> retains its dual character as both positive communication and agonistic confrontation. It is based on a challenge to the other that necessitates a personal response, staking one's own humanity in a cyclical struggle for recognition, supremacy and face. Like the Durkheimian sacred, therefore, the scene of the gift is a social, collective one, raising the participants in a moment of meaning and communication, producing a higher life in its contagious transformation and risking it in the rivalry of the challenge.
>
> (Merrin 2005: 14)

Two important aspects of Merrin's Durkheimian analysis of Baudrillard are relevant here. The first is the association of the gift symbol with *both* a higher form of human sociality *and* with human risk – an association we will see is central to Baudrillard's analysis of the 9/11 terrorist attacks in the USA. The second, is Merrin's convincing demonstration that Baudrillard, far from being the postmodernist apologist for a world of simulation, is, among academics, one of its most systematic foes, seeking throughout his career (like other Durkheimians) the 'lost' symbolic human communication of the 'sacred' in the face of ever-present, late capitalist simulacra. In the symbolic exchange of the gift, 'the object "is inseparable from the concrete relation in which it is exchanged" . . . Once given it is an "absolutely singular" phenomenon, actualizing the "unique moment" of the relationship and becoming "the concrete manifestation of a total relationship"' (Baudrillard 1972: 64, 65, cited in Merrin 2005: 17). In contrast, the 'sign originates with the breaking of this bond, no longer gathering meaning from it' but 'taking on a relationship to all other signs in the semiotic system in its precoded difference, being unilaterally, individually appropriated for that meaning' (Baudrillard 1972, 65, cited in Merrin 2005: 17).

These two features of Baudrillard's Durkheimian position – risk and symbolic exchange – are emphasized centrally by Merrin:

If its experience is one of fullness, it is also dangerous, hostile and even lethal, risking not only the face but also the life of the participant. It is not simply an ideal community; it is also a struggle for power, rank, recognition and humanity.

(2005: 18)

Merrin correctly notes that, in contrast to 'active audience' theories strong within media studies for some three decades, 'Baudrillard explicitly presents a theory and an analysis of media power and its operation' (p. 24). And he adds that Baudrillard's emphasis on this operation of media power also asserts that the contemporary West is vulnerable 'not at the level of the economic "but at the level of the production of social relations"' via the media, 'surviving only by creating the illusion of those symbolic relations it abolishes' (p. 26). There is, Merrin argues, a persisting tension within this mediated illusion of symbolic relations. 'Baudrillard suggests that this tension is never resolved, with every society facing the potential "perdition" of its abolition of the symbolic and the potential counter-gift of those who refuse its simulation' (p. 26).

In Merrin's interpretation it was Baudrillard himself as theorist in the case of the Gulf War (and Osama bin Laden's terrorists in the case of 9/11) who provided this counter-gift of the symbolic.

Baudrillard, the non-event and the Gulf War

As Merrin argues, 'Originating in his early critique of semiotic media, and continuing through his contemporary pronouncements on world events, Baudrillard's theory of the event can be seen to run throughout his work' (2005: 64). He notes that the first real 'events' Baudrillard analyzed in a media context were the student riots of May 1968.

Already his emphasis here is on the media's role in disarming the challenge of this 'symbolic' explosion . . . It was this mediation that administered the movement 'a mortal dose of publicity', he argues, depriving it of 'its own rhythm and meaning'.

(Baudrillard 1969: 174, cited by Merrin 2005: 64)

By the time of the Gulf War, Baudrillard had developed his theory of the 'event', and Merrin describes his discussion of Western television and its audiences' 'profound indifference to the symbolic reality on the ground' (p. 91). Far from being a nihilistic denial, as his critics argued, Baudrillard's essays before, during and after the Gulf War, aimed

at shocking their audience out of their complacency by extending the absurd swindle . . . of this war, and a genuine, impassioned, sustained polemic infused with an anger, wit, scepticism and power. They were premised on an opposition to the war and to the western powers and to the western project of destroying the symbolic alterity and singularity of other cultures, from a critical position grounded in, not this western system, but the realm of the symbolic emerging from it and staking all on the gamble of its own method to strike against the military and media operation.

(p. 95)

Two aspects are key to understanding Merrin's comment: the 'western system' of 'military and media operation'; and the gamble, or 'counter gift' of Baudrillard's own theoretical method.

As regards the 'western system', its operations consisted of both military and media non-events. Baudrillard deliberately misused von Clauswitz's famous phrase that war is politics by other means, describing the Gulf War as 'the absence of politics pursued by other means' (Baudrillard 1995: 30). He argued that this was a 'non-war' because, far from being a military contest, it was 'a preventative, deterrent, punitive war' to prove the west's power (p. 56) and to domesticate and eliminate the symbolic 'alterity' of the Arabic "other"' (Baudrillard 1995: 36–7, cited in Merrin 2005: 83). But it was also not a war, Baudrillard claimed,

> in the absence of the symbolic relationship the concept [of 'war'] contains. Echoing the simulation model of 'communication' where sender and receiver do not meet, the military similarly exclude all contact, refusing to recognize or engage the enemy in 'annihilating him at a distance'.
>
> (p. 83)

Similarly,

> If the military simulation of war provides one reason for its non-eventness, the media's processing and production of the conflict is another. For Baudrillard the audience experiences only a 'virtual war' in 'the absence of images', the 'profusion of commentary', the 'speculative' coverage, and the 'uncertainty that invades our screen like a real oil slick'.
>
> (Baudrillard 1995: 29, 30, 32, cited in Merrin 1995: 84)

For Baudrillard, this was a 'symptomatic' war, full of professional pundits who filled the media screen with 'the ultra-succession of phony events and phony discourses' where we felt 'the emptiness of television' as never before (Baudrillard 1995: 51, cited in Merrin 2005: 84).

Unlike the risky face-to-face of the symbolic potlatch, 'no "war" was "happening" for a western audience, whose electronic extension entailed no risk, no relationship and no involvement. *They* would not be shot, wounded or bombed' (p. 91). The western television audience experienced only an 'affective and moral distanciation in the scopic thrills of watching the Baghdad skyline being bombed and the grainy, smart-bomb video footage'. This was war as 'viewing pleasure' (p. 91).

Only a single Iraqi casualty was seen in Britain when *The Observer* published the picture of a charred face at the windscreen of a vehicle (3 March, 1991).

The real disaster in the Gulf, we were told, was ecological. We saw more dead birds than we did dead bodies. And yet we also saw *more* of this war. The coverage was marked by a technological hyper-reality, epitomized by real-time broadcasts accelerating us across continents to the Saudi border, to the launch of missiles from Gulf ships and then to the centre of Baghdad to follow their progress. Here the real dissolved into the hyperreal – an excessive mode of perception and experience instantly realizing and heightening the moment to hold us hostage, as Baudrillard says, before empty actuality and the visual psychodrama of the news. The defining images of this hyper-reality come, however, from the inhuman perception of 'the bomb's-eye view' (Broughton, 1996), offered by the nose-cams of smart or guided munitions.

(p. 91)

But there was something else countering this military/media world of simulation for publics and audiences: there was the notoriety created, first in public newspapers, then academic books, by Baudrillard's 'The Gulf War did not take place' (1995). For Merrin:

Baudrillard's admitted invention of the Gulf War (Baudrillard 1993: 94) was a strategic, critical reading of the conflict. It was intended as a challenge to the occurrence, meaning, credibility and historical place of the war; albeit one based on its occurrence, responding, like a counter-gift, to the overwhelming evidence of its reality to invert its processes, aiming to 'contest the very self-evidence of war, when the confusion of the real is at its height' (Baudrillard 1994: 64).

(p. 94)

This was Baudrillard's 'escalation' method, challenging the simulacra events of military and media with one of Baudrillard's own.

   As Merrin describes it, this is

Baudrillard's potlatch with the real: that escalating theoretical project in which both theory and the world are at stake. For Baudrillard, therefore, theory is also a symbolic challenge. His aim is not simply a descriptive statement of the real but its critique and transformation; hence he offers original, speculative, engaged, strategic readings, hoping to hasten its processes and push towards the point of implosive collapse and reversal. . . . For Baudrillard, *theory must be an event in the world.*

(p. 158)

Spectacles and propaganda: 'Amiriyah did not take place'

Baudrillard does not believe in the traditional (quantitative and qualitative) empirical methods of social analysis. Rather, as Merrin explains, his has been a process of theoretical 'speculation to the death'; theoretical simulations which are 'invented, perverse, intentionally provocative and counter-intuitive claims and analyses' (2005: 52). Moreover, as Merrin himself acknowledges, Baudrillard's 'event-strike' methodology has little or nothing to say about developments in contemporary electronic technologies, variations within and between media industries, internal processes of media production within specific institutions and cultures, readings of specific media texts and images, and different audiences with their gendered, aged, classed and other culturally-based interpretations of media spectacle.

It is in these areas that critical realists like Kellner focus. In concluding his 2003 article, Kellner noted the potential of the internet to challenge mainstream media messages and provide the real context that was missing. Although concerned by misinformation and 'reactionary discourse' on the web, he noted the role the internet had played globally in developing the anti-war movement, nurturing its anti-globalization and global justice focus.

So, following Kellner's cue, we set ourselves an assignment where, borrowing from Baudrillard (while ignoring his rejection of empirical analysis), we explored whether the 'Amiriyah massacre' of hundreds of people by US smart-bombs 'didn't take place'. If the smart-bomb image of 'precision pinpointing' an elevator shaft at the Iraqi Air Force headquarters was the most positive propaganda icon of high technology militarism during the 1991 Gulf War, then the PGM attack on Amiriyah shelter was certainly one of the most negative. According to the accounts from many western NGOs, the Iraqi government and some Western journalists, more than 400 civilians were killed at the Amiriyah air-raid shelter when on 13 February 1991 it was bombed by US PGMs.

We conducted an internet image search for about ninety minutes to test Kellner's optimism. We began by exploring typical student search sites like Wikipedia and university home pages. We also explored mainstream media, government and alternative media sites. In order to focus our comparison of mainstream and alternative information, we used as a common filter variations on just one image from Amiriyah that appeared widely in the media: a photograph taken from inside the upper room of the shelter, looking up at the roof destroyed by a smart-bomb.

Alternative media and Amiriyah

First, we should make some cautionary comments on whether mainstream media is as closed as Kellner suggests. Our own research into the British media's coverage of the Kosovo (Chapter 5) and Iraq Wars suggests otherwise; and our brief web search for Amiriyah seemed to confirm this. For example, two mainstream sites, the *Washington Post* and the *Seattle Post-Intelligencer* (the latter serving a community that became 'a hotbed of peace sentiment', Rutherford 2004: 39) while using similar images of the wrecked shelter, differed widely in their interpretation. They varied according to their different source-identifications (US military or Iraqi witnesses), different classification of who died (Iraqi elite families in a military command post, or poor women and children in a bomb shelter), different material focus ('expertly dropped' bombs by two Stealth fighters, or incinerated toys, books and personal belongings of the dead) and even differently directed titles (for

An Iraqi man holds a peace offering at the Al-Amiriya bomb shelter in Baghdad, where, by Iraqi count, 408 civilians died after a US bomb and missile destroyed it in 1991. Photograph taken by Paul Kitagaki © Hearst Communications

example, the *Washington Post*'s title 'The Fog of War' is itself an expression used by military personnel to account for 'collateral damage').

Government internet

Second, to establish the degree of similarity or difference between mainstream media and government 'control' sources, we looked at government websites. The White House website had as its main colour image the bombed room in the upper floor of the Amiriyah shelter, with its steel entrails gesturing down to the heads of a crowd of people: 'Visitors tour the Amiriyah bunker: The Iraqi government has preserved the bunker as a public memorial' (George W. Bush White House Archives n.d.).

From the moment of its title, 'Crafting Tragedy', the White House article sets out to say, 'This didn't happen – not this way'. To gain immediate legitimacy, the article quotes Article 51 of the Protocol to the 1949 Geneva Convention. This states that civilians should not be used to make areas immune from military operations, especially if the attempt is to shield military targets from attack. The White House then lays out its claim:

> Based on what he has done in the past, if conflict with Iraq should occur, Saddam is almost certain to lay a trap for the world's media. He apparently

believes that dead Iraqi civilians are his most powerful weapon in trying to create revulsion against any military action that might occur against Iraq.

(ibid.)

The website stated that during Operation Desert Storm, coalition forces chose military targets carefully with strict rules of engagement 'intended to avoid bombing innocent civilians'. The website admits that even with 'strict rules' and 'precision munitions' in the campaign, some civilian casualties occurred. Yet, the clear message is that Saddam Hussein used Iraqi civilian deaths to try to undermine international and domestic support for the American-led coalition forces.

Both images and words are used to support this case and reference is made to the 21 January 1991 US bombing of what the Iraqi government claimed was a baby milk factory in Baghdad. The US insisted that Iraq was using it as a biological weapons factory. The images – for example, of a Mosque co-located with an ammunition depot and of Iraqi aircraft moved to a historic site – support the White House's description of Hussein's propaganda strategy of situating civilians and cultural assets near military targets.

The White House website describes what happened at the Amiriyah shelter, detailing the use of guided missiles and international television coverage of charred bodies at the 'Amiriyah bunker' in Baghdad. The website says the shelter was originally built for air raids during the Iran–Iraq war but was then converted into a 'military command-and-control center':

> Unknown to the coalition was that selected civilians had been admitted to the top floor at night, while the Iraqi military continued to use the lower level as a command-and-control center.

(ibid.)

The report cites Khidir Hamza, former director general of Iraq's nuclear weapons programme, who stated in his book *Saddam's Bombmaker* that during the Gulf War he had noticed 'some long black limousines slithering in and out of an underground gate in the back. I asked around and was told that it was a command center . . . I decided it was probably Saddam's own operational base' (Hamza 2000, cited in George W. Bush White House Archives n.d.).

This website report's evidence is meticulous. It includes the 'seeing is believing' evidence of the surveillance photographs, where, it says 'Some of the regime's co-locations were clearly detectable through overhead imagery'. It also emphasizes the verbal evidence about the two levels in the shelter by the professionals who installed them; the earlier history of Saddam's deceit and propaganda; and evidence from Iraqi defectors. All of this material must weigh heavily on our interpretation of the photograph of visitors in the still damaged 'public memorial' that is positioned at the bottom of the website article. By now, we 'know' that beneath these people's feet was the real object of the attack: an Iraqi intelligence centre.

But, of course, the fact that the engineers confirmed there were two levels was not new evidence at all. Journalists knew that from the wreckage they discovered, and some argued that there was evidence of sheltering civilians in both. Further, the reliance of US intelligence on 'anti-Saddam', 'defecting' or 'captured' Iraqis turned out to be catastrophic for US reconstruction policy in the later Iraq War, so we may wonder whether it was not equally so at Amiriyah.

Alternative information: globalization justice movements

Alternative web sources of information provide, Kellner argues, 'a variety of sites that might make possible political discussion and organization' (Kellner 2003a). Here lies Kellner's hopes for the internet; and certainly within the time we permitted ourselves we found plenty of variety.

The Visual Statistics Studio's site (n.d.) showed a detailed close-up photograph of the inside of the Amiriyah shelter below the hole made by the first smart-bomb in the upper chamber. In the image the melted concrete has solidified in hanging folds, like lava. The steel reinforcement hangs useless, like a cage, beneath the hole up to the Iraq sky. Next to this image, there is an artist's impression of a laser-guided bomb. The images match in colours of grey (the bomb's body, the concrete of the shelter), red-orange (the Iraqi desert below the bomb, the colour of the wrecked steel) and blue (the sky above Iraq, the trailing cables in the ruined shelter). In this account Amiriyah was no elite shelter.

> The Amiriyah shelter is located in a poor, working-class neighbourhood made up mostly of apartments. There are no nearby military facilities. There is a school across the street . . . In the shelter there were no adult males – only four-hundred and eight human beings – women with their children. At 4:30 in the morning, most of the victims were sleeping in bunk-beds stacked along the walls.
>
> (Visual Statistics Studio n.d.)

Above the images of the PGM and the hole in the roof of the upper chamber, the website page is headed with two other photographs: an image in blue and grey of 'a child's hand burned into the wall', and the black-and-white close-up face of an Iraqi girl: 'This picture is not a picture of an Iraqi girl who was in the shelter at the time of the bombings, but could have been. It is a surrogate face of children who no longer have one' (ibid.). At the bottom of the article are the most shocking images in colours of red-orange and grey, which show the faces of children burned into the wall. The first of these images shows how 'As the second, incendiary, bomb exploded, it carbonized people and the walls, creating imprints of bodies, faces, hands, small hands of children'. The second image is the 'Wall imprint of a mother holding her child.' The third shows the clear, skull-like image of a 'Face burned into a wall.' The page is completed by an emotive 'witness' text.

> Neighborhood residents heard screams as people tried to get out of the shelter. Shortly afterwards, the second bomb passed through the hole made by the first bomb. . . . The screaming abruptly stopped. The flash of the explosion

was hot enough to sear foot- and handprints to the walls. Combustible articles – hair, clothes, blankets – caught on fire. When the rescuers opened the doors to the shelter, they saw scenes of incredible carnage.

(Visual Statistics Studio n.d.)

This website article is extracted from a Visual Statistics book *Ethical Canons and Scientific Inquiry* that attempts to open international ethical concerns to quantitative analysis and empirical scrutiny. But the book has a polemic at the head of its first chapter, 'About Ethical Canons and War'. It is an account of the US production of lethal neutron bombs that kill people without destroying buildings or other infrastructure. The site says that in 1981 President Ronald Reagan ordered full production of Lance missiles equipped with neutron bomb warheads. The text adds that the President often mentioned in his speeches that there are few problems that cannot be solved by consulting the Bible. 'One wonders if he was guided in his decision to produce the neutron bomb by Joshua 6:24: "They burned the city with fire, and all that was therein"' (ibid.).

Bringing religion, science and ethics together is one kind of global justice movement for alternative opinions. We found a very different kind under the 'peacebutton' webtitle, 'The Week in History: February is Black History Month' . This site detailed the following 'black' history for one particular day in recent history, February 13. France conducted its first plutonium bomb test in the Sahara Desert. The group Women Strike for Peace stormed the Pentagon, carrying photographs of Vietnamese children who had been victims of napalm. Two precision-guided missiles destroyed the Amiriyah subterranean bunker in Baghdad used by 408 Iraqi civilians as an air raid shelter during the Gulf War. 'The deaths of all made it the single most lethal incident for non-combatants in modern air warfare.' Each of these 'February 13' histories is accompanied by an appropriate photograph. Its Amiriyah history features, on the scorched walls, individual colour photographs of children who died at the site. It is clear that this website is both anti-war and pro-civil rights for Black Americans and is another example of Kellner's internet sites 'playing an important role in facilitating development of a global anti-war movement' (Kellner 2003a).

But what is the 'truth about Amiriyah' offered by the differing websites we explored (Wikipedia, university course sites, White House, Visual Statistics, peacebutton)? Did they offer 'alternative information'? (Kellner 2003a) Was there consensus that this 'massacre' really happened?

First, there is consensus that many Iraqi civilians, mostly women and children (separated from the men for reasons of privacy) were killed horribly in Amiriyah shelter, and most sources numbered these at more than 400 people (some believed that the numbers were far higher, but noted that the shelter records were incinerated). Nearly all websites acknowledged that the Amiriyah killings of civilians did happen; but the interpretation of why they were there depended on whose propaganda you believed. However, the gruesome images burned into the walls and the charred bodies had been seen by many observers, including BBC journalists. Only a Michigan State University course webpage offered the important alternative observation that some civilians in Baghdad, but not at Amiriyah, may have been killed by Iraqi 'friendly fire' .

Second, those web image sources we accessed were wide-ranging, offering, as Kellner suggests, a 'wealth of opinion and debate'. These included the White House; mainstream journalists concerned to be 'neutral' and 'balanced' but offering very different pictures of the event; Left ideology-critique exponents with a similar understanding of the war as Kellner; and 'ethical-scientific' anti-war groups.

Third, the images of Amiriyah nearly always gained some of their meanings through associated images and text. These were not so much in Baudrillard's sense of a 'hyper-real' universe of signs and simulacra, but rather in Kellner's sense of embedded historical context. A comparison of the 'surveillance' epistemology and imagery of the White House site with imagery in two of the anti-war sites makes clear the importance of analysing this discursive and simulated context. In simple terms, there was not a vertiginous 'hyper-real' relation between image and image, image and text in any one site. Rather, images were inter-related, and image and text were anchored in terms of quite precise discursive positions on the 'reality' and 'propaganda' of Amiriyah.

Fourth, wherever the truth lay, the images of incinerated women and children at Amiriyah shelter undoubtedly marked the beginning of a new propaganda media war fought over the use of smart weaponry in what Ignatieff (see Chapter 5) calls the new 'virtual wars'. The CNN website, where we began this chapter, concluded its account of Gulf War smart bombs with this comment on the Kosovo War:

> [I]f smart weapons create the illusion of bloodless war, they do not create the reality . . . The newest precision-guided bombs, which get their position from Global Positioning System (GPS) satellites, went exactly where they were told. They hit the Chinese embassy in Belgrade, Yugoslavia, demonstrating that the smartest weapons are only as good as the intelligence that aims them.
>
> (CNN 2001)

Fifth, we note the enormous shift that the US attack on the Amiriyah shelter had on perceptions. It marks a dramatic move away from the 'hi-tech' weaponry propaganda of the PGM image to the horrific indexicality of incinerated faces on the shelter walls. It is also important to note that these images were more often than not kept from the public by the mainstream media. Yet such terrible images were easily available, as the second author of this book can verify. At that time he sat shocked in a small darkened room at Leeds University monitoring satellite 'raw' feeds from the ground in Iraq beamed to television news organizations globally. As Andrew Hoskins notes, still images of the memorialized, ruined artefact of Amiriyah sustained a 'memory of place . . . out-of-synch with the temporalities and the "emptying" of place that remain synonymous with much of the mediated Gulf War' (2004: 95).

Conclusion

This chapter has juxtaposed two broad theories of icons and war: conventionalist theory via Baudrillard (and Hammond) and realist ideology-critique via Kellner.

The chapter has explored the notion that the high-tech PGM image became iconic because it was constructed (and circulated to the media) by elites at the Pentagon and White House. The alternative 'human rights' construction of Amiriyah hinges on another high-tech resource, the internet. The chapter continues in this way the theme of our book emphasizing the conditions of production and remediation of icons of war and terror.

It does not, however, disagree with Baudrillard (as interpreted by Merrin) in terms of either his 'event-strike' methodology or his symbolic/semiotic theory – though Merrin is right to criticize Baudrillard for his own unreflexive reliance on the symbol as a 'lost' reality. As Merrin says, 'That symbolic which he attempts to define and defend as – in effect – an experiential reality outside and opposed to the simulacrum is itself exposed as a simulation and simulacral ground' (2005: 152). Our own, very limited empirical exploration of the internet is not aimed at 'disproving' Baudrilllard's 'non-event' theory. Rather, it points to some of the areas that Baudrillard's assertion of the symbolic-real ignores, as both Kellner and Merrin, in their different ways, attest.

5   Picturing Kosovo

Virtual, new or old war?

The Račak incident, the killing of 45 Kosovar Albanians in the village of Račak, 15 January 1999 © Press Association

In January 1999 a photograph from Račak, Kosovo appeared in the world's press. Senior media colleagues on the ground in Pristina said it marked a turning point in launching NATO into the war with Milošević's Serbia. They were supported in this view by UN Secretary General Kofi Annan, US Secretary of State Madeleine Albright and numerous other observers. The power of a specific image to generate what military historian Corelli Barnett (*Daily Telegraph* 1999: 6) called the 'first aggressive war in a Europe at peace since Nazi Germany invaded Poland in Sept 1939' must surely rank as one definition of the iconic. It is the same politicized kind of icon as the Bosnian Trnopolje images which, Hoskins and O'Loughlin (2010: 95) argue, demonized 'the whole Serbian people via the media, thus legitimating the necessity and inevitability of US military intervention'.

In this chapter, we examine this powerful 1999 Račak image of Milošević's ethnic cleansing but we contrast it with a counter-framed image – the deaths of three Albanian Kosovar children that sparked the 2004 Kosovo riots. In this context, what does 'Račak' tell us about photojournalism and the iconic? What theories can we draw on to inform this discussion? Theoretically, we examine what has become known as military humanism and discuss challenges to this doctrine.

The Račak image

The Račak image came in more than one version. In one we see a gully on an icy hill in the countryside near the village of Račak. It runs diagonally from bottom right to top left of the picture frame. Along this diagonal several dead ethnic Albanians are scattered, anchored at bottom right by the closest body. He is a young man in a white shirt, arms stretched out above his head. His head is bleeding, thrusting out towards the very edge of the frame, almost into the space of the viewer. This image appeared in *The Sun* on 18 January 1999, and was re-used by this British tabloid during the Kosovo War in March 1999.

In *The Observer* on page one and the *Sunday Times* on page two on 17 January 1999 there was a Račak massacre photograph of another young dead man by Radu Sigheti, taken from slightly higher up the bank to the right of the first body. The image employs the same bottom right foregrounding of a dead man. But he lies face down with right arm beneath his head, not on his back like the other. He wears a red jacket and blue jeans, and there is blood on the hand thrust out towards the viewer.

Near the back of both photographs there is one man alive. This older man, who wears a close-fitting white Albanian peasant hat, stops the eye because he himself is standing stock-still in image centre. He seems dazed into uncertainty, shocked at what the Serbian special police have done. This older man looks forward at the dead young men at bottom of frame. But he looks out also at us as though communicating his life and his memories as frozen too. Lying before him are young and older men from his village; his future and his past struck down in one dawn raid by the Serbs. Possibly one or more of the bodies in the gully are his sons, or his brother, or even daughter: there were three dead women reported in the estimates of between 45 and 49 people massacred.

The *Sunday Times* headed its photograph with the words 'Village massacre: victims with heads smashed, eyes gouged, scattered at Rajak.' An accompanying article by Juliette Terzieff (1999: 21) talks about eyes torn out, decapitation, an ear cut off, bullet wounds in the neck, faces blown away at close range. It says the ages of the dead varied between 12 and 74. On the same day *The Observer* published the photograph, and next to it a report headlined 'The village that died, when the butchers came at dawn'. *Observer* journalist Chris Bird (1999: 1) began, 'You heard it first. Men and women moaning quietly behind the walls of the stone houses, hushed by the sound of snow melt running down the dirt track'. He enters a typical ethnic Albanian family compound and finds 58-year-old Riza Beqiri – a man perhaps the same age as the one we see in the photograph. Bird says Riza 'lay next to the wall, a stiff white hand still clutching his walking stick', reminding us again of the living man in the photograph, who also held such a stick. Riza Beqiri was, Bird tells us, 'Number 38' in the NATO observers' patient body count.

The journalist describes how he then went up the 'hill slippery with ice' to the gully.

At the top, above the village, the body of a middle-aged man lay sprawled, his trousers stiff with frost. He had been shot in the head. A few yards further up lay the body of an elderly man. Part of his head had been blown away.

He quotes a British Army medical officer saying that all of them were shot in the head. This was, in the words of William Walker, Head of the Organization for Security and Cooperation in Europe (OSCE) monitoring mission in Kosovo, 'a massacre'.

In March 1999 when the NATO bombing war over Kosovo and Serbia began, haunting photographs of Kosovar refugees multiplied in the world's press, drawing from the iconic power of the dead bodies at Račak. One Račak photograph by Louisa Gouliamaki in January 1999 had been of a boy looking into camera as he carried a younger child on his back, with adults in the background, all walking one way. *The Guardian*'s (18 January 1999: 8) caption for it was 'Ethnic Albanians flee Račak village yesterday as Serb police shell site of the massacre of 45 civilians on Friday'. Now, in late March 1999, readers of the world's press saw similar villagers being forced to flee much further. Many newspapers carried a photograph of a small tractor-driven cart packed with refugees, an older ethnic Albanian man sitting at the controls driving straight to camera, leading his family to safety in Macedonia or Albania or Montenegro. Behind these people, we were told, lay the Serb Army and special police force torching villages and making the refugees flee.

In the first week of the war, when many of these photographs were published at the height of Milošević's 'ethnic cleansing' campaign, *The Sun* newspaper published a story, 'Kosovan boy tells people of horrors' (Patrick and Busfield 1999). The summarizing photograph *The Sun* used as an icon for this and all the ethnic cleansing massacres, seen and unseen by reporters, is the image of the dead man in a white shirt from Račak. He is a dead version of the patriot about to be shot in Goya's *Third of May*, white shirted arms stretched out. Kosovo was pictured by the media in this period of January–March 1999 as a site of brutal 'ethnic cleansing' by Serb militia and police.

Drowning at Mitrovica: A reverse image

But then, five years after the war, in March 2004, we unexpectedly saw images of 'reverse ethnic cleansing.' On 17–18 March 2004 violence broke out after three young Albanian Kosovar children drowned trying to swim across the river Ibar near the divided city of Mitrovica. There was a Kosovar Serb enclave north of the river, Kosovar Albanians inhabited the southern part of the city and NATO's Kosovo Force (KFOR) guarded the bridge between. The only surviving boy told television reporters that they had been chased into the water by a dog and hostile Serb men. This event, closely following tensions surrounding the earlier shooting of two Serb youths, triggered growing unrest. Riots in many parts of Kosovo broke out and mobs of up to 50,000 people were reported looting Serb homes, burning Serb churches and attacking United Nations Mission in Kosovo (UNMIK) vehicles.

A typical photograph representing the riots published in *The Times* on 20 March 2004 on page 15 shows an ethnic Albanian girl standing in an archway before the ruins of a Serbian Orthodox monastery in Prizren, Kosovo. The graffiti on the arch above the young girl's head says 'Morto I Serbi!' ('Death to Serbs!' (2004: 14)). This contrast between the 1999 'ethnic cleansing' and 2004 'reverse ethnic cleansing' images represented the international media's difficulty in picturing Kosovo. As Hoskins argues of media templates like 'ethnic cleansing', the 'media often skews present events in a narrative locked in a past that may constrain interpretation (and memory) rather than enable fresh understanding' (Hoskins 2004: 11).

But there was also a new image of Kosovo on newspaper front pages; of burning United Nations vehicles in European capital cities Belgrade and Pristina. In *The Guardian* photograph on 19 March 2004 (page 15), enormous yellow and orange flames burst from a vehicle and cover most of the image. At the centre, visible on the roof of the upturned car, is the painted insignia UN. The United Nations had become the object, not the active subject, at the centre of trouble and conflagration (p. 15).

Something had clearly gone very wrong with the 'liberal West helps innocent ethnic Albanian refugees' scenario conveyed by the photographic images five years earlier. But for a time the Račak photographs had become iconic, employed as simple testimony to the ethnic cleansing of innocent victims by brutal killers, embodied in the Serb leader Slobodan Milošević. These images, which were circulated assiduously by Kosovar Albanian communities both within Kosovo and in diaspora communities such as New York, had done much to project NATO into the war.

The war of 'humanitarian intervention'

In April 1999, one month into the air war over Kosovo, British Prime Minister Tony Blair made a speech in Chicago highly significant for international principles of war and statehood. Blair argued that the recent NATO military intervention in Kosovo had set an example of the altered balance between state sovereignty and human rights. He suggested that the UN Charter presuming that states should not commit acts of war except in self-defence needed changing in the light of genocidal acts during the 1990s in Rwanda and in the Balkans (including Kosovo). Genocide could no longer remain a purely internal matter, either on humanitarian grounds or in the light of the huge refugee flows generated which impacted economically on surrounding nations. Academics Bideleux and Jeffries (2007) argue that even though these were strong arguments for the NATO-led Kosovo War, it was a major step toward a new 'human rights imperialism', since it could 'be seen as an ominous step down a slippery slope towards . . . more obviously questionable forms of Western imperialism, such as the US-led occupation of Iraq' (p. 551).

If that is so, the iconic images from Račak, and their related sequence of 'ethnic cleansing' photographs, have greater significance than the motives of the killers on that day. So how were 'ethnic cleansing' images debated in the media, and in academic theories current at the time? What does 'Račak' tell us about photojournalism and the iconic?

British newspaper discourse January–March 1999

We examined ten British newspapers over the two months leading up to week two of the Kosovo War in March 1999: *The Sun, Daily Mirror, Daily Mail, Daily Express, The Times, Daily Telegraph, The Guardian (Observer), The Independent (Independent on Sunday)*. We chose to analyze these two months (from the Račak massacre to the end of March 1999) because we wanted to examine the media context immediately preceding Blair's Chicago speech. What were the images and discourses circulating in the media, of which Blair would have been aware, as he selected and edited the debate to channel it into the rhetoric of his new 'military humanism'?

With one exception, the British press supported Western military action against Serbia. They agreed that it was a last but inevitable resort, as years of diplomatic efforts had not achieved results. All agreed that air strikes alone would not be enough. Only the additional deployment of ground forces would achieve a satisfactory outcome; and most newspapers struggled with the unwillingness of the US and UK governments to commit ground troops. The *Daily Mirror, Independent, Daily Telegraph, Times* and *Daily Express* all argued that Račak was a turning point in the road to war.

The Sun and *Daily Mirror* concentrated on the 'ethnic cleansing' humanitarian argument and demonized Milošević as the 'butcher of Kosovo', a 'twisted mind', a 'blood-soaked tyrant.' Typical was the cartoon by Tom Johnson in the *Daily Mirror* (31 March: 6) that showed Milošević, Hitler, Saddam Hussein, Pol Pot and Nero baking in a bath in Hell. *The Sun* attacked anyone who raised criticisms or questions about the Kosovo War as the 'whinge and whine brigade', 'apologists for Milošević'. Both newspapers gave unconditional support to the Western alliance and emphasized the courage of 'Our Boys', as *The Sun* likes to call them. Typical here was the cartoon by Griffin in *The Sun* on 25 March on page 8 that showed a map of Europe centrally featuring Serbia and Kosovo, with broad looping arrows coming in to Kosovo carrying US, UK and German bombers, to the caption 'Who do you think you are kidding Mr Slobba?' – a play on the theme song, 'Who do you think you're kidding Mr Hitler', from the popular BBC television comedy *Dad's Army*. Here, the focus was on the prolonged diplomatic prevarications of Slobodan Milošević, now deemed to have come to their proper, military, ending. Gaskill's cartoon in *The Sun* on 26 March on page 8 celebrated the alliance of two European powers who were once enemies. The cartoon has two boxes: in the first (marked '1939') German Luftwaffe and British RAF fighter planes blast each other head to head; in the second box ('1999') German and British planes fly side by side towards Serbia, signalling each other in comradeship as both pilots fire a missile towards Milošević.

These cartoons drew on the genre of 'attack maps' which in newspapers like *The Sun* were confident representations of the newspaper's ideology. *The Sun*'s (1999) editorial on the day the war started made things seem simple: 'Countries like Britain and America are the guardians of liberty and democracy. We fight for the oppressed. The Serbs are slaughtering innocent men, women and children. This cannot be allowed to go unchallenged'. The editorial was supported by page one headlines: 'Clobba Slobba' (25 March), 'Nowhere to Hide – We'll Bomb Until Slobba Surrenders' (26 March), 'Might is Right – Blair Rallies Britain' (27 March) and by a series of Gaskill cartoons – for example, one showing Milošević in Serb Army gear putting his gun to the head of a refugee tractor driver, saying 'Move it!' while a NATO missile aimed at him says 'Hold it!' (24 March: 8).

Only the *Independent on Sunday* opposed the action completely, on the grounds that it was illegal and would be militarily ineffective. Other British newspapers were more ambivalent, acknowledging the humanitarian argument but concentrating on political, military and legal problems as well. Key reservations in these areas included the following:

a)   Political: The crisis was the West's own fault for past indecision and delay; there was danger of the conflict spreading to Macedonia, Albania, Greece and former Soviet states because of ethnic minorities in these nearby countries; the desirability of an independent Kosovo was problematic; the Kosovo Liberation Army (KLA) was 'unreliable'; there was little unity between the allies; the credibility of NATO and the UN was at stake as floods of refugees suffered even more from Milošević than before the war; and the public 'back home' was unconvinced. A summarizing photograph in *The Times* in Britain showed anti-war protestors outside the Ministry of Defence in Whitehall with placards. 'Clinton screw Monica not Serbia', referring to President Clinton's affair with Monica Lewinsky and possible impeachment (*The Times*, 26 March: 6).

b)   Military: The objectives of the war were unclear (an independent Kosovo, or a Kosovo semi-autonomous within Yugoslavia?); the Serbs were tough, well-equipped and allied troops might be bogged down for years, creating 'another Vietnam'; the bombing was hardening Serbian support for Milošević.

c)   Legal: The legitimacy of NATO action without UN support was questioned; NATO as a defence alliance was acting outside its remit and was beginning to anger the 'sleeping bear', Russia.

d)   Moral: There were many other areas of humanitarian crisis and this was a military attack on an ally that had not harmed British interests.

There were ambiguities in words or images in each of these areas in the British press. For example, in the political domain, Simon Jenkins wrote that the KLA had been encouraged by the bombing war to believe that NATO troops would help them to win their freedom from the Serbs. Yet they themselves 'have committed atrocities and provoked counter-atrocities' (*The Times*, 24 March: 20). Supporting this doubt about the 'innocent/evil' dichotomy of Kosovo/Serbia, a cartoon by Steve Bell in *The Guardian* (24 March: 20) showed two identical vulture-like birds in separate frames, their wings raised, gun on hip like Western sheriffs, with the NATO star on their chests. One vulture says, 'Behave, Serb Bastards, or I bomb now!!', the other says, 'Behave, Albanian Bastards, or I don't bomb now!!'

In terms of military legitimacy, *The Observer* (17 March: 28) in its Račak editorial had written:

We must recognise that we now live in an era of what Mary Kaldor calls 'new wars' . . . Kosovo is a classic example. The conflict is not like conventional war, nor is it wholly anachronistic . . . There must be a new cosmopolitan framework for action that permits disinterested and legitimate intervention. Put bluntly, there have to be soldiers on the ground in sufficient numbers to keep the two sides apart.

In the first week of the Kosovo War, 'new wars' academic, Mary Kaldor wrote in *The Guardian* that bombing was unlikely to succeed against Milošević. She argued that such 'new wars' are directed against civilians and civil society, and she cited as an example Milošević's closure of the Serbian independent radio station B92.

Moreover, the new wars have a tendency to spread through the pressure of refugees, through networks of gun-running and other forms of illegal trading and through knock-down effects on ethnic nationalism.

(Kaldor 1999a)

Kaldor questioned NATO's estimate that 100,000 ground troops were needed in Kosovo. Emphasizing that in new wars violence is directed at civilians and that warring parties avoid conflict, she believed that far fewer troops would be sufficient. She challenged the view that unless NATO bombed it would lose credibility. On the contrary Kaldor, arguing for ground troops, wrote that NATO would lose credibility if it privileged the lives of its own monitors (who had been withdrawn) over those of the Kosovar citizens left behind.

There were other contemporary issues circulating in the world's press that impacted on media perceptions. During the first week of the Kosovo war, the Law Lords in Britain brought in a judgment about General Pinochet, said to be directly responsible for the torture and murder of many thousands of civilians after his coup against the democratically elected Allende government in Chile on 11 September 1973. The Lords decreed that Pinochet could be extradited from Britain to Spain to face prosecution. The case would go later to Appeal, but meanwhile that week Margaret Thatcher, former British Prime Minister, chose to take tea with her friend Pinochet.

This was a week in which images and words about monstrous dictators and their innocent victims were flowing freely. A series of cartoons featuring Pinochet in the context of the Kosovo War were produced. A *Times* cartoon by Peter Brookes (25 March: 24) showed a British warplane dropping Pinochet over Spain en route to Serbia. Two days later, another Brookes cartoon (27 March: 22) showed Pinochet again, this time with Milošević and Irish Republican politician Gerry Adams, who was blamed that week for the IRA refusal to decommission its weapons, thus threatening the year-old Good Friday peace accord. Brookes pictured all three as 'Toxic Mushrooms'. On 29 March, *The Times* cartoon on page 20 returned to this theme, indicating considerable doubt in the UK about the legal conduct of its own leaders. This cartoon has Blair and Clinton in the dock together with Milošević and Pinochet, while a lawyer's hand thrusting into the frame from below holds an

'International LAW' indictment. A *Daily Mirror* cartoon on 30 March on page six, at the height of reporting Serb atrocities against ethnic Albanian Kosovars, crossed the innocent victim/evil despot categories still further by showing Thatcher taking tea, not with Pinochet but Milošević.

Clearly these cartoon images were at least ambiguous, not only about the legal but also the humanitarian legitimacy of the bombing war; as was the *Daily Mirror*'s page-10 cartoon of 29 March. At a time when the *Mirror*'s front-page headlines were describing the 'ethnic cleansing' of the Kosovar Albanians as 'The Exodus', and describing Milošević as 'Pol Pot II', its political cartoon questioned the 'humanitarian' nature of 'smart bombs'. The image shows two bombs talking as they are about to strike the ground of Kosovo: 'You're a smart bomb! So what are we achieving and when will we achieve it?' This cartoon is inset in an article by Tony Parsons, ' Kosovo just isn't worth lives of British troops', in which he says 'A fat lot of good all our smart bombs did against the butcher of Baghdad'.

Even newspapers as thoroughly committed to the War as the *Daily Mirror*, which regularly overlapped its categories of 'Butcher of Belgrade' and 'Butcher of Baghdad', could be uncertain about the legitimacy of this 'humanitarian war' as it skated between the political, military and legal categories of the issue. *The Times* blurred its 'us/them' categories still further by blending cartoon images of British and US political leaders – Blair, Clinton, Thatcher – with those of monstrous murderers – Pinochet, Milošević, Saddam Hussein, Pol Pot. Sometimes these were ambiguities focussed on military strategy: the *Daily Mirror*, for instance, favoured a follow-up to the bombing with a ground war. Yet even within the pages of the *Mirror* there were articles like Parsons' challenging the morality of a ground war.

It was images of Račak circulating internationally that had a profound effect in fixing the stamp of 'ethnic cleansing' on the picture of Kosovo. Yet we have seen that British newspaper debate, including cartoons, negotiated with this initial impact from Račak. Arguably Tony Blair's Chicago speech in April 1999 was a direct intervention in another public sphere to extend the power of 'Račak'. Equally, what these images meant was being debated among public intellectuals and academics, whose arguments we turn to next.

Images of 'virtual war'

Historian, broadcaster and Canadian politician Michael Ignatieff argued in his book *Virtual War* (2000) that the Kosovo War was a virtual war. It was virtual because US-NATO Commanding General Wesley Clark's contact with war was 'virtual rather than visceral' (p. 102): via video teleconferences and gun camera footage; via email on secure internet systems; and because NATO avoided being the Kosovo Liberation Army's air force by denying them the ground communication equipment necessary for effective forward air control of the NATO planes overhead. It was also virtual morally and strategically because it was war without risk on one side. Precision-violence, Ignatieff observes, was now 'at the disposal of a risk-averse culture' in the US, as represented by President Clinton. It was fought by a virtual war alliance since in reality the US did most of the fighting, and denied allies the military intelligence behind all targets hit by US planes or missiles. Therefore, at the military level, Ignatieff claims, alliance cohesion was a myth. The alliance held together by becoming virtual, via public displays of political unity. And it was a war of virtual values and virtual resolution because it reflected a conflict within the allies' own principles: between commitment to the human rights of Kosovo's citizens and the self-determination of Kosovo as an independent state. Ignatieff argues that the Kosovo virtual war led on to virtual victory. There was no unconditional surrender and immediate regime change, but instead an ambiguous 'end state'. Thus, the Serbs withdrew and NATO entered Kosovo, with its future juridical status entirely undefined.

Most particularly this was a war of virtual consent. Ignatieff argues that the Kosovo war was new in that it closed off a 200-year history of conscription and mass mobilization of the populace on behalf of national survival. Further, as a result of the exponential growth of the modern economy, war no longer draws on the entire economic system. Thus, virtual war only enlists societies in virtual ways:

> [. . .] it is no longer a struggle for national survival; with the end of conscription, it no longer requires the actual participation of citizens; because of the bypassing of representative institutions, it no longer requires democratic consent; and . . . [t]hese conditions transform war into something like a spectator sport . . . War affords the pleasures of a spectacle, with the added thrill that it is real for someone, but not, happily, for the spectator.
>
> (Ignatieff 2000: p. 191)

Since a virtual war is a spectator sport 'the media becomes the decisive theatre of operations' (p. 191). Thus, Ignatieff notes, Milošević, unable to fight militarily because of an outdated air-defence system, fought a media war. His goal was to sow doubts in the minds of the Western electorate. Ignatieff says that by the end of the Kosovo war public opinion polls showed that support had slipped below 50 per cent. Virtual war, he suggests, 'is won by being spun' (p. 196).

Thus, Ignatieff maintains that the targeting of the Belgrade TV station became a key image. Because of the media transparency of this virtual war, journalists reported the suffering in Serbia, television showed the stunned survivors of the TV station bombing, and emails between friends (now virtual enemies) flowed between Serbia and the US/UK, predicting the next 'precision-bombing' site. This in turn had an effect on Serb resistance; for example if bridges were predicted as the next site of attack Serb civilians massed there to stop the bombing.

Ignatieff's Baudrillard-style analysis offers a layered and powerful argument for 'virtual war' over Kosovo; and his understanding of the images used in this media war for 'virtual consent' responded to this argument. Images circulated to the media by Milošević's regime related directly to the media war in the West and within Serbia. The 'collateral damage' caused to Kosovar civilians could be used against the 'virtual alliance'. And the images from Račak were used to start the virtual war in the first place. As Ignatieff sees it, Milošević miscalculated at Račak. Without the international circulation of these images by a strong

Kosovar-Albanian diaspora – especially in New York City – 'air strikes would never have happened' (p. 58).

New wars theory

From a different perspective, 'new wars' theorists such as Mary Kaldor, Mark Duffield and Michael Humphrey have described a changed era in international politics that has its roots in the period of national instability after the break-up of the Soviet Union. These academics do not conceptualize the new wars via the 'September 11 changed everything' discourse of surveillance-security theory (Chapter 6). Rather, they see new wars emerging rhetorically out of earlier, post-Cold War debates about tragic non-intervention (in the 1990s in Africa) and actual military 'humanitarian intervention' (beginning with Kosovo).

After Blair's Chicago speech, terms like 'ethnic cleansing', 'genocide' and 'terrorism' were used systematically to legitimize new military interventions, which were variously justified as 'humanitarian war', 'militaristic humanism', 'war against terror' and, in the case of Iraq, 'pre-emptive war'. Key to new wars theory was the notion that these 'humanitarian wars' were distinct in not being inter-state wars, but rather were focussed on civilians as the primary targets of atrocities designed to injure, kill and traumatize entire populations into submission or flight – precisely the humanitarian Western media discourse and images surrounding the 1999 Kosovo War.

However, Mary Kaldor has argued that rather than being explained by specific causes like 'ethnic conflict', these new wars marked the erosion of state monopoly over legitimate violence. Mark Duffield (2001) notes that this erosion has partly come from above, as new war emergencies led to international war networks of militaries, UN agencies, donor governments, NGOs and the corporate sector. But, given the privatization of violence by paramilitaries, breakaway groups from regular armies, local warlords, insurgency organizations, mercenaries and criminal gangs, the erosion also comes from below. 'Terrorism' can then, in Michael Humphrey's new wars analysis, be understood as an extension of privatized violence in the new post-Cold War discourse of 'periphery states', 'failed states' and 'rogue states'. These 'networked' wars over 'rogue states' mark a new phase of surveillance whereby states (most recently the case in Libya) 'find themselves increasingly under the observation and subject to the criticism of other nations' and their media (Assmann and Conrad, 2010: 4–5; see also Arquilla and Ronfeldt 2001: 6).

New wars theorists differ in the degree to which they are sanguine about these changes from above and below. Kaldor emphasized the significance of democratic 'cosmopolitanism' in the face of the privatized barbarism of sectarian nationalists like Milošević.

Other new wars theorists, however, have a more pessimistic view. For example, Michael Humphrey emphasizes that the focus on the victims of ethnic violence is a 'therapeutic strategy' by the state designed to recover major power sovereignty (as, for example, in the case of US neo-imperialism in Iraq). But this focus on individual well-being and healing 'through victim centred truth politics or conflict prevention through behavioural and attitudinal change . . . is no substitute for the reconstruction of an inclusive political community' (Humphrey 2005: 203). Humphrey argues that failure to win a stable peace after war, as in Iraq and Afghanistan, can then easily lead to 'a new imperium in which terms like "protectorate" gain a renewed legitimacy' (nearly a century after its earlier use) in the quest for 'world peace'. He adds that 'Rather than the recovery of sovereignty of weak states we are witnessing the extension of sovereignty of strong states, or "empire"' (2004: 9); and 'intervention, while aimed at conflict prevention, is not primarily focused on the recovery of sovereignty through social re-integration but on the control and containment of violence' (p. 10).

Kaldor also draws attention to the perils of this post-conflict situation, where 'standard formula' of formal elections and the privatization focus of neo-liberalism replace the search for 'meaningful institutions through which genuine debate and participation can take place' in post-conflict reconstruction. She argues that 'in situations where the rule of law is weak and where trust and confidence is lacking, this standard formula can exacerbate the underlying problems, providing incentives for exclusivist politics or for criminalization of formerly state-owned enterprises' (Kaldor 1999b: 133).

Mark Duffield also expresses concern over what he calls the development–security paradigm of 'global liberal governance' (2001: 34). He argues that networks of intervention and dependence are established early between militaries, major international institutions like the UN, OSCE, OECD, World Bank, NGO and donor organizations. The aim of these assemblages is not the recovery of national sovereignty in 'failed states' but rather a new global interventionism on behalf of 'democratization', stability through 'reconstruction' and the 'free market'. New wars political rhetoric thus became, in Duffield's analysis, a key motor force in the neo-liberal globalization ideology (see Chapter 7) keenly mobilized by Bush and Blair.

Duffield argues that the concepts of 'liberal peace' and 'new wars' resemble each other in their networked character, in so far as they are both privatized networks of state and non-state participants operating transnationally and outside the competence of any single state government. In a series of case studies, Duffield notes the networks of local warlords, military, aid agencies, financial institutions and multinational corporations that enable the new wars, a pattern that was clearly evident in Afghanistan after the removal of the Taliban by Western alliances, and equally clearly perceived by the resurgent Taliban in Afghanistan in 2008 when aid workers were targeted for assassination as 'soft targets' in the western alliance. The development security paradigm, Duffield argues, with its 'project of liberal peace' constructs the world's poor as victims, denying them the right to express their grievances through resort to violence, while vilifying and criminalizing the leaders of violence (Duffield 2001).

In the light of new wars theory, we can examine images from both the Kosovo War and the 2004 riots in Kosovo to see to what extent the complexity of these new wars was represented in the media.

As we have seen, there was direct exposure to the new wars ideas of Mary Kaldor in *The Observer* and *The Guardian*. But in the media her emphasis on civil rights organizations and the danger of the war spreading to other ethnic Albanian states tended to be at the expense of a more detailed focus on the centrality of neo-liberal economics to the military interventions which she approves. Hence, she overplayed the relevance of her concern for a land war (which she supported) at the expense of analysis of the expansion of organized crime activities (which she also clearly recognized).

A key part of UNMIK's 'standards before status' six-year governance of Kosovo had been the neo-liberal 'market' consensus that had by then controlled international politics for two decades. In Kosovo, this consensus has overseen the sell-off of socially-owned assets to dubious buyers linked to corrupt politicians and organized crime. In their study of Kosovo, Bideleux and Jeffries attack the failure of the US-led coalition in the 1999 war to include major ground force action. 'Organized criminal networks and supporters of the KLA' took advantage of the 'law and order absence' of international military, civil and police forces and imposed 'their own coercive and intimidatory forms of organization at street level in towns and villages across Kosovo' (2007). The internationals failed in the war and failed in the reconstruction, Bideleux and Jeffries argue, through 'simply relying on the American strategy of smashing Kosovo's economic and societal infrastructure to smithereens through colossal aerial bombardment and then naively hoping that the liberated province would be administered by law-abiding liberals rather than by thugs' (p. 561).

Understanding of this continuing link between current KLA politicians and organized crime positions our interpretation of 'Račak' very differently. In Bidelux and Jeffries' analysis, the Kosovo War and its following 'reconstruction' (conventionally seen in the media as one of Blair's 'humanitarian war' success stories) looked uncomfortably similar to the failure in Iraq. Further, the unpopularity of UNMIK in Kosovo in 2004 (imaged via photographs of burning UN vehicles) was, among other things, much to do with their failure in the face of Serbian opposition to further 'liberalize' the economy from which organized criminal networks could expect further benefit. Neo-liberal economic consensus – forcing the state providers of water, education, communication, heating and power into private hands – has been (until the 'credit crunch' crisis of 2008) systemic and world-wide. But an economic ideology is not easily conveyed in a photograph. It is easier to describe images of violence keyed by Račak in Kosovo as 'ethnic cleansing'.

Old imperialism

A strong challenge to the rhetoric of military humanism comes from Noam Chomsky's *The New Military Humanism. Lessons from Kosovo* (Chomsky 1999). He argues that the 'New Humanism' is, in fact, an old wolf in sheep's clothing and he challenges centrally new military humanism's claim to be supporting the fight against ethnic cleansing. Chomsky cites President Clinton's television address in 1999: 'We cannot respond to such tragedies everywhere, but when ethnic conflict turns into ethnic cleansing where we can make a difference, we must try, and that is clearly the case in Kosovo' (Clinton 1999, cited in Chomsky 1999: 3).

In contrast, Chomsky examines in detail those times when the US did *not* 'respond' to ethnic cleansing elsewhere: e.g. Turkey's ethnic cleansing of Kurds, because in this case Turkey was a key ally of the US, and Indonesia's ethnic cleansing in East Timor, where, in spite of Robin Cook's claimed 'ethical' foreign policy, there was extensive sale of British military equipment to the Indonesian government. Chomsky quotes the Indonesian Ministry of Defence attaché reporting on British television that British armaments were used to crush dissent in East Timor (p. 45).

Chomsky's book, although 'about Kosovo', in fact represents a world in which the US has been involved in helping crush democratic local movements, often at the cost of massive killings: in Africa, Colombia, East Timor, El Salvador, Nicaragua and Southeast Turkey. His is a comparative political method: comparing policy, comparing numbers of dead as crimes against humanity, and comparing, as Paul Rutherford put it, 'differences between the ways the media reported the global activities of the American state and of America's enemies' (2004: 185).

Chomsky's argument – that the 'new military humanism' in Kosovo provoked far more ethnic cleansing than there was before the war – is not in defence of Milošević. Indeed he says the indictment for war crimes of Milošević and his associates at the International Tribunal at The Hague was 'long overdue' (1999: 85). Rather, Chomsky is arguing that the widely-held view (by the international media, by the UN Secretary General Kofi Annan and by Ignatieff) that the massacre at Račak in January 1999 was 'the decisive event that impelled Washington and its allies, horrified by the atrocity, to initiate preparations for war' (p. 33) is a fallacy.

His emphasis here is not that the Račak photographs did not lead directly to war. Rather, he denies that it was US 'horror' over the atrocity that was the cause of the bombing in March 1999. Chomsky notes that the reporter of the Račak massacre, US diplomat William Walker, leading the OSCE war crimes verification team, was an unlikely player in this tale of being horrified by atrocity because it was Walker who, as US Ambassador in El Salvador

> administered the US support that allowed the government to carry out extreme state terror, peaking . . . in November 1989 in an outburst of violence that included the murder of six leading Salvadoran dissident intellectuals, Jesuit priests, along with their housekeeper and her daughter. Their brains were blown out by the US-trained Alacatl brigade, which had compiled a remarkable record of shocking acts. These were much the same hands, with the same guidance, that had murdered Archbishop Romero to open the terrible decade of US-guided atrocities in El Salvador, in large measure in a war against the Church, which had violated the norms of good behaviour and infuriated the leading enlightened state by adopting 'the preferential option for the poor'.
>
> (Chomsky 1999: 41)

Chomsky continues that in January 1999:

Walker received great praise for his heroism at Račak, inspired by his recognition that 'he may not have done enough to stop past atrocities' (Ted Koppel, *Nightline*) and by his regret for his 'silence' on the assassination of the Jesuits, when he was 'speechless' (*Washington Post*).

(p. 42)

This exploration of the Račak images by Chomsky is typical of two aspects of his analytical style. First, it shows his symptomatic methodological use of evidence and admissions in the public record, where the voices of the people under analysis – in this case, Walker – can be made to speak against themselves. Second, it illustrates Chomsky's comparative approach, and his refusal to confine that analysis to a post-2001 (or indeed post-1999) scenario. For him, the Kosovo War was part of a long history of US complicity with state terror.

In contrast to Ignatieff, who focuses particularly on Milošević's use of images of the carnage at Belgrade's TV station in a media war for 'hearts and minds' in the West, Chomsky focuses on Western media *response* to the television station destruction in the shift to bombing Serbia:

Recognizing that 'depriving Serbia of electricity, and disrupting its water supplies, communication, and civilian transport are part of the program,' liberal columnist William Pfaff [in the *Boston Globe*] concluded that it is a mistake to describe NATO's war as 'being in conflict only with Serbia's leaders', Milošević and his cronies. 'Serbia's leaders have been elected by the Serbian people' . . . We should therefore not misdescribe Milošević as a dictator; he is a true representative of the Serbian people . . . They, too, must now be demonized, not just their elected leader, if the attack on the civilian society is to be portrayed as an exercise of the New Humanism.

(p. 93)

Chomsky's might have added that Pfaff's 'liberal' response in justifying state terror against civilians is of the same order as the 7/7 terrorists' justification of their attack on the population of London. For Chomsky, the 'innovative extension of international law' (p. 152) in relation to Kosovo was devised by the powerful to serve their own economic and geopolitical interests. To make his case he cites '"humanitarian intervention" by bombs in Kosovo, but no withdrawal of a huge flow of lethal arms for worthy ethnic cleansing and state terror within NATO itself' as simply one of its 'most dramatic' illustrations (p. 52).

Conclusion: Imaging Kosovo

The different theories during the last decade about the Kosovo War and reconstruction have edited their own key images into the frame, according to their particular master narrative. Ignatieff focuses on the images of the bombed TV station in Belgrade as part of his thesis about 'virtual war' and 'virtual consent' via the media. New wars theorists moved away from hegemonic images of 'ethnic cleansing' into their more complex theories of linked assemblages and the erosion of state monopoly over violence, while not engaging clearly with the implication of that theory for images like Račak. Chomsky focuses on Račak as a case study in his attempt to demystify the 'new military humanism' as an old US ideology of control.

In revising the ideas of her earlier book *On Photography*, Susan Sontag says in *Regarding the Pain of Others* that:

> Nonstop imagery (television, streaming video, movies) is our surround, but when it comes to remembering, the photograph has the deeper bite. Memory freeze-frames; its basic unit is the single image. In an era of information overload, the photograph provides a quick way of apprehending something and a compact form for memorizing it. The photograph is like a quotation, or a maxim or proverb.
>
> (Sontag 2003: 22)

Her comment, if we take it a little further, is an apt one for this chapter. Single photographs are, indeed, like quotations or maxims or proverbs for each of the theories (of 'virtual war', 'new war' and 'old imperialist war') we have been looking at in this chapter.

What different theorists find to be profoundly iconic is tied closely to the narrative that embeds it: the multi-layered 'virtual war' of Ignatieff's analysis, the comparative historical (US-backed) atrocities in Chomsky's story.

And this 'quoting' of images is equally true of Sontag's own account. She says:

> The practice of representing atrocious suffering as something to be deplored, and, if possible, stopped, enters the history of images with a specific subject: the suffering endured by a civilian population at the hands of a victorious army on the rampage. It is a quintessentially secular subject.
>
> (p. 42–3)

We might think that Sontag was talking here about Serbian military atrocities in Kosovo in 1999. But she wasn't. When Sontag does mention Kosovo, it is in the context of her analysis of images from postcolonial Africa. She describes these African atrocities as a:

> succession of unforgettable photographs of large-eyed victims, starting with figures in the famine lands of Biafra in the late 1960s to the survivors of the genocide of nearly a million Rwandan Tutsis in 1994 and, a few years later, the children and adults whose limbs were hacked off during the program of mass terror conducted by the RUF, the rebel forces in Sierra Leone.
>
> (p. 71)

Then she adds:

> That there could be death camps and a siege and civilians slaughtered by the
> thousands and thrown into mass graves on European soil fifty years after the
> end of the Second World War gave the war in Bosnia and the Serb campaign
> of killing in Kosovo their special, anachronistic interest. But one of the main
> ways of understanding the war crimes committed in south eastern Europe in
> the 1990s has been to say that the Balkans, after all, were never really part of
> Europe.
>
> (pp. 71–2)

We know that this was not a 'main way of understanding' shared by Susan Sontag.
Yet the comparison does lead her straight back to her theme: that generally

> the grievously injured bodies shown in published photographs are from
> Asia or Africa. This journalistic custom inherits the centuries-old practice of
> exhibiting exotic – that is, colonized – human beings . . . The exhibition in
> photographs of cruelties inflicted on those with darker complexions in exotic
> countries continues this offering, oblivious to the considerations that deter
> such displays of our own victims of violence; for the other, even when not an
> enemy, is regarded only as someone to be seen, not someone (like us) who
> also sees.
>
> (p. 72)

Yet the iconic images from Račak *were* all about European 'grievously injured
bodies'. Sontag's is a powerful analysis of photographic images in the tradition of
post-colonial theory, which we return to in Chapter 10. For the moment, though,
we refer to it to indicate how any theoretical account will edit its iconic images and
limit its discourse – so that in *Regarding the Pain of Others*, Kosovo 1999 slips in and
out of Sontag's text. 'Račak' is not really the quotation or maxim she wanted.

6 Did 9/11 'change everything'?

Icons out of a clear blue sky

A jet airliner is lined up on one of the World Trade Center towers in New York, Tuesday
September 11 2001 © Press Association

We all remember the images of 11 September 2001; those of us who saw them live on TV or endlessly recycled on television channels for days. Paul Virilio says of these images that the attack on the Pentagon in Washington, DC was of little consequence compared to 'what exploded in people's minds' in seeing the destruction of the World Trade Center (2002: 82). Because there were two towers, two images remain with us: a fiery explosion in one of the World Trade towers, high up; and then a momentary sighting of an aircraft flying low from behind the second tower, and, as it disappeared, a terrible fire ball exiting the front of the tower.

W.J.T Mitchell says, 'The destruction of the World Trade Center was a symbolic destruction of an iconic object designed as the production of a spectacular image calculated to traumatize a whole society' (2011: 12–13). As sociologist Stuart Hall described it:

> suddenly . . . two planes fly into what is the most obvious symbol that any Hollywood producer could ever have selected to symbolize global capitalism at work and play – the twin towers of the World Trade Center. And we say, hands on our hearts, 'we don't know where they come from. They seemed to come out of a clear, blue sky'.
>
> (Hall 2001: 15)

Many other unforgettable images followed: 'the jumpers' escaping the conflagration in the towers, falling to their deaths from unimaginable heights; one tower, then the other collapsing inwards, upon itself; the shocking fog of dust, smoke, panicking people, firefighters running to and from the disaster scene; the stark, skeletal metal remains at 'ground zero', surreal fingers pointing upwards; the impromptu hoardings of photographs of the missing, first a desperate sign of fear and absence of loved ones, then a human-sized memorial to a giant-sized crime.

Finally, there was the visual absence of the towers themselves on the New York City skyline; the gap in the air displaying clear blue sky and offering as much offence as the planes themselves. What happened in New York, between experiencing 11 September, keeping it in memory and memorializing it for a different future amounted to an attempted rebuilding of the iconic power of those towers. To the terrorists they had been an icon to trade, capital and western commodity values. Rebuilding this space, materially, spiritually and ideologically became a new war of icons.

This was '9/11', as it quickly came to be called. Stuart Hall's 'clear blue sky' is not simply a description of space, but also of time; suggesting that this attack could not be imagined in terms of anything that had gone before. The war of icons and discourses around that spatial-temporal notion of 'a clear blue sky' itself generated the most powerful of all 9/11 discourses in the West: that 'September 11 changed everything'.

In this chapter we will explore both state-centred and critical discourses around 9/11 and the Twin Towers to examine industry, political and academic construction of its most iconic images. We recognize from the outset that many scholars, journalists and public figures have written about 9/11 and its aftermath and it is not our goal here to survey this vast literature (see, for example, the edited volumes by Zelizer and Allan 2002 and by Kavoori and Fraley 2006). Our guiding question is: did 'September 11 change everything?'

Security discourses

Certainly many thought so at the *Transport Security World* international conference for senior aviation, shipping and government executives in Sydney which we monitored in November 2003. In his early address, Alfred Rollington, CEO Janes Information Group, told the conference that his American colleagues viewed the attacks as a passage from 'New World innocence into an Old World insecure experience', and it was 'clear our world was going to change' (Australian Transport Security World Conference 2003: 15–16).

Perhaps more than most other corporate/government areas, the transport industry's world did change after 9/11. One CEO after another spoke of the need for 'culture change' in their industry. Brian Lovell, CEO Australian Federation of International Forwarders, told the conference of the need to overcome 'culture shock' and move beyond simple 'theft protection' of cargo to face 'The NEW threat . . . about . . . covert infiltration . . . of cargo, with the purpose of causing harm or damage on board aircraft carrying passengers and crew' (p. 31).

Speakers emphasized that the corporate sector could no longer put profit as the first priority. Security came first now; not least because successful terrorist attacks had an enormously negative impact on national and corporate economies. Thus Stephen McHale, Deputy Administrator of US Homeland Security Transport Administration, explained that 9/11 was not only an attack on the military and finance but also on transportation:

> freedom of movement is the key to our culture. Destroy confidence in moving people and goods, and you bring the economy to its knees. In a global economy, where goods can circle the globe in half a day, economies are interdependent, as is security.
>
> (Australian Transport Security World Conference 2003: 70–1)

The conference heard sobering worries about risk to shipping, which needed workplace consciousness-raising and systemic supply-chain monitoring. The Unisys conference document, 'A Global Safe Commerce Blueprint', noted estimates that the cost of a terrorist attack on shipping could be one trillion dollars:

> It's a global risk of daunting odds . . . An act of terrorism targeted at a commercial container or port would have a global economic impact many times larger than that of September 11.
>
> (Australian Transport Security World Conference 2003: p. 2)

This comment reflected the dominant theme of the conference: the need for new integration between the commercial transport sectors, governments and surveillance agencies; between the different parts of the commercial supply chain; and between the physically separated spaces within airports, ports and other transport systems.

But not everyone believed that September 11 changed everything. We look next at discourses which challenge this 'state-centric' emphasis, taking two examples of academics associated with the journal *Critical Studies on Terrorism*.

Lee Jarvis: temporality and legitimation of 'War on Terror'

Jarvis engages directly with the assertion that September 11 definitively shifted time (2008: 245). He itemizes three theoretical frames in dominant US political discourse: 'writing 9/11' as temporal rupture, as temporal linearity and as timelessness (p. 246); and he draws on systematic discourse analysis to explore these distinct temporal narratives 'that were persistently invoked within early governmental texts'.

The most obvious of the temporalities in political rhetorical framing, he argues, was 'writing 9/11 as temporal rupture'. This represented a 'new era of radical insecurity' (p. 247) exemplified by US Attorney General John Ashcroft's warning that 9/11 was a harbinger of future terrorist events demanding international political action to dismantle terrorist organizations. He spoke of a future not only of uncertainty, but of proliferating enmity against the USA. As Paul Wolfowitz expressed it, 'We must prepare ourselves for the virtual certainty that we will be surprised again' (Wolfowitz 2001, cited in Jarvis 2008: 248).

This discourse of sudden transition marked by 9/11 shifted political perception from the relatively stable Cold War world of nuclear deterrence to a new security environment of unexpected attacks from 'out of a clear blue sky'. In Jarvis' analysis, the Bush administration positioned 9/11 as a moment of abrupt temporal discontinuity, a warning or lesson of 'a new vulnerability marked by global terrorist actors and their unknowable equivalents' (p. 248).

A key part of this political rhetoric of temporal rupture was President Bush's assertion that an act of war had been declared against the USA because 'these people can't stand freedom' and 'hate our values' (Bush 2001, cited in Jarvis 2008: 248). As Jarvis argues:

> Motivated by an apparent rejection of freedom, 9/11 emerges here as an instituting moment of origins catapulting the United States and its allies into an entirely unprovoked and unseen conflict.
>
> (p. 248)

Bush bolstered this political discourse of temporal discontinuity by asserting that whereas the terrorists had hoped the US would disintegrate, a new era of political, religious and social responsibility had emerged; 'After the attacks, moms and dads held their children closer' and 'Millions have gone to synagogues and churches and mosques . . . to be reminded of the true values of life' (Bush 2001, cited in Jarvis 2008: 249). Thus, Jarvis argues, out of three related accounts of temporal discontinuity – 'writing "9/11" as warning/lesson', 'writing "9/11" as declaration of war' and 'writing "9/11" as self-transformation' – the statement 'September 11 changed everything' was forged as a coherent discourse.

Yet this dominant political theme of 9/11 as temporal discontinuity was supported by two other rhetorical discourses which logically contradicted it. One, which Jarvis calls 'writing temporal linearity', was the assertion that this was not the start of a new war; and he quotes Secretary of State Colin Powell and Defence Secretary Donald Rumsfeld:

> It just wasn't what happened on 9/11. It was the terrorism that has been going on before 9/11 and would continue to afflict the world.
>
> (Powell, cited in Jarvis 2008: 251)

> If you recall, the World Trade Center was attacked by terrorists the first time . . . in . . . 1993. It was followed by attacks on: the Khobar Towers in 1996; the embassies in Kenya and Tanzania . . . in 1998; and the USS Cole just about six years ago.
>
> (Rumsfeld, cited in Jarvis 2008: 251)

The other logically contradictory discourse among the US political leadership was 'writing timelessness'. Deeply premised on President Bush's Christian fundamentalist beliefs, 9/11 'was reduced to one moment within a perpetual Manichean struggle' (p. 254). On one hand, there was the eternal need for us 'to know that evil like goodness exists' (Bush, cited in Jarvis 2008: 254). On the other was Bush's understanding of history as a series of repetitions of this eternal struggle. Thus the 'first war of the twenty-first century' was positioned as a conflict against 'history's latest gang of fanatics trying to murder their way to power' (ibid. : 255). A similar conception of temporality as a static, unchanging horizon of politics was the President's account of the conflict as a continuing struggle between freedom and fear. As Bush put it, 'freedom and fear, justice and cruelty have always been at war and we know that God is not neutral between them' (ibid.).

Jarvis emphasizes that while the three separate strands of government rhetoric – of temporal rupture, linearity and timelessness – were conceptually contradictory, they were enormously powerful working together as rhetorical agency. In the context of the increasing evidence of the failure of reconstruction in Iraq, Jarvis argues that Bush's discourse of timelessness offered a particularly powerful mechanism for pre-empting possible objections to this unfolding 'war' (p. 257). Bush spoke of the 'civilized world' knowing that other fanatics throughout history – from Hitler to Stalin to Pol Pot – had consumed nations in war and genocide: 'Evil men, obsessed with ambition and unburdened by conscience, must be taken very seriously – and we must stop them before their crimes can multiply' (Bush, cited in Jarvis 2008: 257).

By identifying and tracing the discourses of rupture, continuity *and* timeless repetition within the Bush's administration's discourses of 'war on terror' Jarvis contributes to the analytical power of critical terrorism studies in challenging conservative security paradigms.

That this apparently persuasive discursive formation was capable of sustaining three radically distinct conceptions of temporality should alert us to its contingent, constructed, and ultimately, political existence.

(p. 258)

Richard Jackson: *Writing the War on Terrorism*

Richard Jackson, editor of *Critical Studies on Terrorism*, identifies four meta-narratives repeatedly drawn upon by the Bush Administration in post-9/11 discourse in his 2005 book *Writing the War on Terrorism*: comparisons between 9/11 and the Second World War; the struggle against communism during the Cold War; the battle between civilization and barbarism; and the threat posed by terrorism to the 'progressive benefits of globalization' (pp. 40–58). For example, the label used to identify the site of the Twin Towers collapse – 'ground zero' – would be known to many readers as the site where the US detonated the atomic bomb over Hiroshima during the Second World War. Jackson writes:

> it is singularly ironic that America's greatest crime against humanity is discursively remade as a crime against America: where it once represented the incineration of more than 90,000 Japanese civilians.

(Jackson 2005: 43)

Jackson argues that with the US positioned as victim, the historical analogy with Hiroshima could not be acknowledged (pp. 43–4). To do so would be to admit to an earlier form of terror perpetrated by the US. Yet there is, as Jackson identifies, another meaning to 'ground zero'; that of starting anew. For Jackson this is a 'chilling reminder' of the Khmer Rouge's 'year zero' in Kampuchea. Not only is Hiroshima hidden in the new 'ground zero' discourse, but so too is the US's controversial and aggressive role in the Kampuchean conflict. Jackson notes that use of the term 'ground zero' is tied discursively to the notion that 'everything changed after 9/11' (pp. 43–4). This meaning taps into a dominant cultural and political myth about the way Americans see themselves – the founding fathers of America 'designed a new political system rooted in Nature and God that transcended the particularities of time and space, and which owed no debt to history or culture'. Thus, Jackson writes:

> the notion of 'ground zero' is a crucial discursive strategy in establishing the attacks as a special kind of war, and in historically and politically decontextualizing them from concrete political events.

(p. 44)

What the journal editors call 'state-centric' terrorism studies is challenged by these *Critical Studies on Terrorism* articles and books in two ways: (i) rejecting the state's 'common-sense' notion that 'September 11 changed everything', revealing it, rather, as politically motivated construction; and (ii) claiming the iconic power of the 'ground zero' created by the Twin Towers' collapse as a rewriting of earlier US military history, thus converting ideologically the US from aggressor to victim (see also Bacevitch 2005).

Spectres and spectacles of the real: Young, Hall, Kellner and Žižek

Critical Studies on Terrorism is a new journal but critical studies of the images and discourses around 9/11 have been circulating since the event itself. We look next at some of the more important of these, focusing on their different emphases and epistemologies in considering its iconic images.

Alison Young: ground zero's spectral walls

Academic law professor Alison Young argues that when the Twin Towers came down New Yorkers experienced viscerally today's pitilessness against the human body. The initial trauma of the falling bodies was quickly replaced by the visual absence of the towers in the midst of olfactory horror: the stench of death across the city, microscopic body parts filling the air.

> From the items and body parts collected by landfill workers to the microscopic fragments that passed into people's lungs, body parts and belongings were turned into *relics* . . . Ground Zero is similarly regarded: it is the appalling gravespace of the dead, every crevice and seam filled with their reliquary dust.
>
> (Young 2005: 129)

What to *do* with that space, how to refashion it as monument, became, as Young describes, a conflict between *prospective* icons. Some wanted an exact replica built, deriving 'from the wish to return to the last place of the loved one, to deny the existence of the gravespace of the beloved's death, to cover over the wound in the city' (p. 132). Others wanted the image of a grave articulated; Japanese architect Tadao Ando suggesting 'an earthen mound about 30 metres high . . . reminiscent of the ancient burial mounds' (Ando, cited in Young 2005: 132). Still others wanted a bellicose 'US rules' statement: 'Build the tallest building in the world on the site. Let the terrorists know that we can't be pushed around' (p. 132). As well as aesthetic statements (centred on repressing the 'ghost' of 9/11) and pragmatic considerations (should the new buildings be for trade, as the last ones were, or for people, with restaurants, trees and parks?), Young emphasizes the key question: 'What form should a public memorial take? How can an image – a building, a monument – provide a space for mourning and memory?' (p. 133).

Young describes an interim memorial of two light beams, forming pillars in the night sky as 'spectral evocations of the vanished towers, mere hints and memories, without substance or permanence' (p. 139). In constituting the spectral, they invoked the media response to 9/11 where the towers now became one of the most unsettling cultural images. Film and television programmes that featured scenes shot near or at the World Trade Center were edited or their release date delayed.

> In some ways, it is as if the image of the World Trade Center has become unbearable . . . Yet at the same time, images of the lost World Trade Center seem to have endlessly replicated and reproduced themselves . . . Baudrillard notes: 'Although the two towers have disappeared, they have not been annihilated. Even in their pulverized state, they have left behind an intense awareness of their presence. No one who knew them can cease imagining them and the imprint they made on the skyline from all points of the city. Their end in material space has borne them off into a definitive imaginary space (Baudrillard 2002: 52)'.
>
> (p. 139)

While waiting for the memorial to be built, people in New York had pasted hundreds of photographs and postcards on the grey walls around the gaping hole of ground zero.

> Trembling between the past that has been lost and the site of redevelopment for a building whose shape is yet to come: each performs the twin processes of memory and counter-memory, of art in the remnants of disaster, image in the place of ruin
>
> (p. 140)

Both in this visual response from traumatized New Yorkers and in various divergent architectural plans for replacing the lost Twin Towers, Young discovers popular counter-voices and images to those of their government in power.

Stuart Hall: from behind invisible walls

For Stuart Hall, a 'secular left' critical-realist thinker, 9/11 contained new elements but was not an entirely new phenomenon. He approached the temporal rupture/temporal linearity contradiction that Jarvis describes as a conceptual tension.

> So there is this curious effect of something which is both familiar and strange, both an event – a rupture – and a kind of unraveling of some of the huge consequences of long-running processes that were always-already in place.
>
> (Hall 2001: 9)

First, Hall points to the unique disparity of international power following the collapse of the Soviet Union in the late 1980s. In a new global system the US had emerged as having the unilateral 'capacity for forceful intervention', creating a 'new world disorder' (p. 10). He notes that suicide-terrorism is one way that weak peoples can strike out at a system they define as oppressive: 'the means of delivery of violence without cost, combined with the messianic capacity to mobilize around a kind of absolute, is a very dangerous combination' (p. 10).

Hall, like many politicians left and right, argued that that the US military response to 9/11 was itself a dangerously missed opportunity to appeal to international law through the United Nations, the International Court of Human Rights or the International Court of Justice. Instead responses, he argues, took the form of ad-hoc coalitions of the powerful that were in keeping with American self-interested policy, and a steadfast refusal to join the project to construct an international court of justice which has weakened the UN (p. 11). This deliberate weakening by the US of international legal and diplomatic systems was ongoing, not new after 9/11.

Secondly, Hall foregrounds the invisible walls of an economic system, neoliberalism, which had been emerging as a hegemonic force for more than two decades. He argues that the power of the transnational corporations had combined with US power to constitute new forms of sovereignty for the stabilization of global power, through organizations such as the IMF and WTO. To illustrate the point, Hall draws on his own region of birth, the Caribbean, where Jamaica once had a small indigenous dairy industry (p. 4). But Jamaicans now drink American powdered milk and the local dairy industry has been destroyed because the US dumped powdered milk into this market simply to change habits via savage cost-cutting. No distinctions are made, Hall argues, between the needs of the local culture, the rules of the IMF and the interests of American global corporations (p. 14).

For Hall, therefore, the attack on 9/11 was 'the first crisis of a new world disorder' (p. 12), which had been gathering momentum for a long time. He cites as another example of neoliberalism the electricity blackouts in several majority-world cities – Jaipur, Kingston, Salvador in Brazil – resulting from systematic pressure by international forces to privatize public utilities and sell them to utility corporations in the US, who then drive up the unit costs of electricity and deregulate supply.

In Hall's analysis, the 'distortions of wealth, opportunity, goods, symbolic power, culture, between the South and the North . . . has been growing steadily over this whole period' (p. 13). On one hand this has generated in the US the sense of a 'homeland' invulnerable to the rest of the world – which is why, Hall says, the falling of the Twin Towers was such a traumatic experience. On the other hand, there had been a deepening sense of exclusion, desperation and rage elsewhere in the world at the multiple ways power is exercised against people located behind the invisible walls of global economics.

At the same time, Hall argues, the world has seen the US support 'some of the most corrupt and dictatorial political regimes ever seen' and, in the 1990s post-Cold War reality, this synergy of political, military, economic, cultural and symbolic power has been enhanced by the ideology of neoliberalism (p. 15). He argues it is this reality which the 9/11 attack signified in its careful attention to the symbols of that power: the economic in the two towers, the political at the White House, the military at the Pentagon, the cultural in being presented as a television event.

Douglas Kellner: terror as spectacle

Critical realist Douglas Kellner notes that spectacle is a crucial part of terrorism, and al Qaeda has systematically used the spectacle of terror to promote its agenda. Previous al Qaeda attacks – the 1993 World Trade Center bombing, at embassies in Kenya and Tanzania and the USS Cole – combined surprise and detailed planning to create a 'high concept terror spectacle'.

In that sense 9/11 was not new as strategy. Terror spectacle, Kellner argues, catalyzes unexpected events to spread further terror through the targeted population. It aims at economic and cultural effects by disrupting and wounding urban and economic life. He notes that the Twin Towers and other targets were partly symbolic (global capital and American military power) and partly material (the intention to disrupt the airline industry, business and perhaps the global economy itself by paralyzing the world's largest financial centre). An unparalleled shutdown did occur across the US after the attacks: government and businesses closed, airlines cancelled all flights, Wall Street and the stock market were inoperative for days, baseball and entertainment events were postponed, McDonalds locked up its regional offices and most major US cities became eerily quiet (Kellner 2003a: 2).

Consequent to this media construction of terror-spectacle, Kellner notes that a series of unforgettable images quickly became iconic.

> The images of the planes striking the World Trade Center, the buildings bursting into flames, individuals jumping out of the window in a desperate attempt to survive the inferno, and the collapse of the towers and subsequent chaos provided unforgettable images, much like the footage of the Kennedy assassination, photographs from Vietnam or the Challenger space shuttle explosion.
>
> (Kellner 2003a: 2)

These images were the intentional strategy, as Kellner sees it, of the terrorist challenge to US military-industrial-economic power, and he discusses how that complex of US agencies hit back systematically. For example, Kellner emphasizes that mainstream US media promoted war fever and retaliation rather than initiating public debate about wider issues of terrorism. The media discourse privileged the 'clash of civilizations' model (the meta-narrative of civilization versus barbarism (Jackson 2005: 47)) and established a binary dualism between Islamic terrorism and civilization.

Thus, Kellner asserts that there were similarities between Bush Administration discourses and those of bin Laden and radical Islamists in that both were 'fundamentally Manichean, positing a binary opposition between Good and Evil, Us and Them, civilization and barbarism' (2003a: 5). In Kellner's view, US broadcast television 'allowed dangerous . . . zealots to vent and circulate the most aggressive, fanatic . . . views, creating a consensus around the need for immediate military action and all-out war' (pp. 7–8). Behind this zealotry, Kellner sees another level of intentionality, a 'deep structure', representing the economic realities of power, especially among the experts called to speak on television. Henry Kissinger, James Baker and other long-time advocates of the military-industrial complex, instantly demanded an immediate military response and dramatic expansion of the US military. But, Kellner observes, people like Kissinger and Baker were tied to the defence industries thus 'guaranteeing that their punditry would be paid for by the large profits of the defence industries that they were part of'. This was rarely discussed on television and was left to alternative media and the internet to elaborate (p. 8).

Kellner's analysis of the visual spectacle of 9/11 is political-economic in orientation, providing a deep-structural explanation of the iconic images and of television's own response. For Kellner, the 'deep structure' is the continuing embedding of neo-liberalism within a political-military-industrial complex that ruled US foreign policy long before the 'neo-liberal turn' (see Chapter 8). Other commentators, however, while adopting similar military-technological and 'neoliberalism'-based explanation of 9/11, focused more on the psychoanalytical sense of the dual identity of US 'play' and 'work' to which Stuart Hall alludes.

Slavoj Žižek: spectres of the real

In his book *Welcome to the Desert of the Real*, Žižek writes that in the days following 11 September we in the West were transfixed by the image of the plane hitting the tower (2002). We wanted to see the image again and again:

> the uncanny satisfaction we got from it was *jouissance* at its purest. The authentic twentieth-century passion for penetrating the Real Thing . . . through the cobweb of semblances which constitute our reality thus culminated in the thrill of the Real as the ultimate 'effect', sought after from digitalized special effects, through reality TV and amateur pornography, up to snuff movies.
>
> (p. 12)

But despite this obsession with seeing the plane hit the tower, there was also, Žižek adds, a strange 'derealization' of the images in that we did not actually see dying people or carnage:

> in clear contrast to reporting on Third World catastrophes, where the whole point is to produce a scoop of some gruesome detail: Somalis dying of hunger, raped Bosnian women, men with their throats cut . . . Is this not yet further proof of how, even in this tragic moment, the distance which separates Us from Them, from their reality, is maintained: the real horror happens *there*, not *here*.
>
> (p. 13)

This is similar to Sontag's point (Chapter 5); though Young's answer to Žižek might be that there *were* no gruesome details. The victims of 9/11 were reduced mainly to dust.

But that does not quite answer Žižek. There were 'the jumpers', never seen in 'gruesome detail' either, and even the long distance shots of them falling were quickly removed from the media. There were also the 'desperate faces of dying people' at the Twin Tower windows, represented by distant images. Žižek thus poses a different question in answer to his first one: where have we seen this before?

> The fact that the September 11 attacks were the stuff of popular fantasies [in the cinema] long before they actually took place provides yet another case of the twisted logic of dreams: it is easy to account for the fact that poor people around the world dream of becoming Americans – so what do the well-to-do Americans, immobilized in their well-being, dream about? About a global catastrophe that would shatter their lives.
>
> (p. 17)

'Dreams' are about fantasy, displacement and repression; thus Žižek's analysis advances on Kellner's in a significant respect by adding a psychoanalytical analysis of the meshing of 'dream' with 'reality', while still emphasising 9/11's long history. In particular, he offers an interpretation of the importance of iconic images which 'will hegemonize a field, and function as the paradigmatic embodiment of an idea, a regime, a problem' (Žižek 2004: 3). To flesh out this relationship of dream with reality, and of icons with ideological narrative, Žižek recalls the image of Jessica Lynch as she was elevated by the media 'into the paradigm of the US soldier' in Iraq (p. 3). For Žižek, Lynch's story can be read at three levels corresponding to the French psychoanalyst Jacques Lacan's triad of Imaginary-Symbolic-Real (ISR):

> First there was the imaginary spectacle: the ordinary all-American girl-next-door, tender and fragile, the very opposite of the brutish soldier of our imagination . . . Then, of course, there was the underlying ideological background, the symbolic level of media manipulation. And, last but not least, we should not forget the 'vulgar' economic aspect: Jessica enlisted in the US Army in order to be able to pursue her studies, to *escape* the small-town, lower-class life of a rural community in crisis.
>
> (p. 3)

Žižek matches these three personal ISR constituents of Lynch's image with broad national/social ones by asking the question: 'What . . . was the real reason for going to war?' He argues that the three reasons were a sincere ideological belief that the USA was bringing democracy and prosperity to another nation; the urge to brutally assert and demonstrate unconditional US hegemony; and economically to control Iraq's oil reserves.

> Each of the three levels has a relative autonomy of its own, and should not be dismissed as a mere deceptive semblance . . . The three 'true' reasons for the attack on Iraq . . . should be treated like a 'parallax': it is not that one

is the truth of the others; the 'truth' is, rather, the very shift of perspective between them. They relate to each other like the ISR triad mentioned above: the Imaginary of democratic ideology, the Symbolic of political hegemony, the Real of the economy, and, as Lacan would have put it . . . they are knotted together.

(pp. 6–7)

This psychoanalytic 'knotting together' of the ISR triad in contrasting iconic images is important to Žižek, especially because he is quite positive in his belief in the potential of the Imaginary. There is, he believes, something 'true', something empowering in imagining the face of Jessica Lynch as the opposite of brutish militarism; and Žižek is equally keen to emphasize the 'sincere' ideological belief in expanding freedom and democracy. This is not a 'deceptive semblance'.

But this kind of 'naïve benevolence' gets caught up in the realities and symbolization of history. This, for Žižek, is what happened after 9/11, when

the USA basically wrote off the rest of the world as a reliable partner: the ultimate goal is therefore no longer the . . . utopia of expanding universal liberal democracy, but the transformation of the USA into 'Fortress America', a lone superpower isolated from the rest of the world, protecting its vital economic interests and securing its safety through its new military power.

(pp. 6–7)

Žižek also offers his challenge to the phrase he says reverberates everywhere: 'nothing will be the same after 11 September'. This is, he says, an empty gesture because we have nothing new we want to say:

What if, precisely, nothing epochal happened on September 11? What if – as the massive display of American patriotism seems to demonstrate – the shattering experience of September 11 ultimately served as a device which enabled the hegemonic American ideology to 'go back to basics', to reassert its basic ideological co-ordinates against the anti-globalist and other critical intentions?

(Žižek 2002: 46)

Žižek, like the other critical realists we have discussed here, Hall and Kellner, offers a 'deep structure' behind the powerful icon of the Twin Towers under attack and, like them, he doesn't believe September 11 'changed everything'. But by offering an analysis that 'knots together' the realities of power interest, media representation and unconscious symbol displacement, he avoids reducing our understanding of the most powerful images of 9/11 to just one underlying (economic) cause. He is a critical realist nonetheless. The Other, in his analysis, returns from behind those globalized walls from a real, impoverished world of its own. As we will see next, Jean Baudrillard offers a similar but different reading (and for an alternative analysis of 9/11 images using Lacan and Freud, see Pollard 2011).

Jean Baudrillard: 9/11 and the 'resurgence of the real'

Baudrillard was publicly controversial at the time of the 1991 Gulf War and was controversial again soon after 9/11, when he wrote that all of us had fantasized this event.

> The fact that . . . everyone without exception has dreamt of it – because no one can avoid dreaming of the destruction of any power that has become hegemonic to this degree – is unacceptable to the Western moral conscience. Yet it is a fact, and one which indeed can be measured by the emotive violence of all that has been said and written in the effort to dispel it.
>
> (Baudrillard 2002: 5)

Baudrillard appeals to his readers to preserve 'intact the unforgettable incandescence of images' (p. 4). These opening comments in his book *The Spirit of Terrorism* lead us immediately to his privileging of 'symbolic' images and, with them, particular 'slower' modes of analysis. Before 9/11, he says, 'banal' images – of World Cups and Princess Diana – circulated the world. But 9/11 instantly changed this 'stagnation' of symbolic images during the 1990s. Suddenly world media coverage revealed 'a setback for globalization itself' (p. 3). We need, he argues, a longer, slower history that explains why it is that 'the collapse of the Twin Towers . . . much more than the attack on the Pentagon – had the greatest symbolic impact' (pp. 7–8) in generating the iconic images.

Baudrillard believes that resistance to globalized hegemony is inevitable and universal and adds that 'if Islam dominated the world, terrorism would rise against Islam, *for it is the world, the globe itself, which resists globalization*' (p.12). So, as well as representing all those external to the US who have been exploited by its globalizing system, terrorism is deeply embedded in the Western psyche itself. He says there is within the populations of the West a 'deep-seated complicity' (p. 6) with terrorism:

> At a pinch, we can say that [the terrorists] *did* it, but we *wished for* it. If this is not taken into account, the event loses any symbolic dimension. It becomes a pure accident, a purely arbitrary act, the murderous phantasmagoria of a few fanatics, and all that would remain would be to eliminate them.
>
> (p. 6)

For Baudrillard the appeal of countless disaster movies bears witness to this Western fantasy of self-destruction (pp. 5–6). Many people after 9/11 said they initially thought they were watching a disaster movie on television. But Baudrillard's 'slower' analysis goes beyond this to argue that these cultural-psychological manifestations within the 'Hegemon' power itself reflect an inner, terroristic 'object of desire' among entire populations. This is why the 9/11 icons of the Twin Towers were so powerful symbolically.

When, Baudrillard argues, a global 'Hegemon' exerts unilateral monopoly power, and when alternative forms of thinking are not allowed, 'what other way is there but a *terroristic situational transfer*':

It was the system itself which created the objective conditions for this brutal retaliation. By seizing all the cards for itself, it forced the Other to change the rules. And the new rules are fierce ones, because the stakes are fierce.

(pp. 8–9)

Baudrillard is saying here that the more powerful a single superpower becomes in controlling the world, the more prone it is to assault. The attempt to export liberal democracy can only achieve absolutism and monopoly power via its 'virus' of globalization (p. 10). After 9/11 every time someone in the West thought or said the 'US had it coming' – and there were many who did – the alternative virus of terrorism was found within us.

But he also said that the 9/11 terrorists gave back to the 'Hegemon' their own gift. Baudrillard drew here, as he did throughout his writing career, on French anthropologist Marcel Mauss' notion of potlatch (or exchange of gifts). Mauss argued that potlatch in Native American and Polynesian societies, while apparently being voluntary, was in fact part of a structured *communication* system where exchange was obligatory. For Mauss, the exchange of gifts marked the totality of societies, the *connected* nature of social phenomena. Other cultural theorists have extended this notion of exchange to modern societies, including the contemporary 'market economy'. Mauss saw potlatch exchange as both obligatory – a gift had to be paid back in archaic societies or else honour would be lost and the wholeness of society broken – and multi-dimensional, since the gift was at one and the same time economic, moral, religious, militaristic, judicial, aesthetic and mythological. In analyzing 9/11, Baudrillard draws on all these dimensions that form the principle of gift exchange, even if the initial exchange between 'Hegemon' and terrorist was militaristic.

Yet, Baudrillard goes beyond Mauss. For him 9/11 was a symptom of the complete *breakdown of the communicative structure* in the dominant society, partially as a symptom of the psychic resistance in its own people. The terrorists' 'gift', in Baudrillard's analysis, is death through suicide. He quotes Osama bin Laden: 'Our men are as eager to die as the Americans are to live!' (p. 16). The hegemonic power, the liberal democracy of the USA, has, Baudrillard argues, erased death from consideration as it enjoys the everyday pleasures of simulation and commoditization. But for the terrorists death is their main weapon, which rides beneath the very belly of liberal democracy's globalized achievements: its technology (aeroplanes), its powerful communication (its media), its mighty buildings (the Twin Towers): 'Defy the system by a gift to which it cannot respond except by its own death and its own collapse' (p. 17).

Baudrillard says that *every* aspect of Western 'hyperefficiency' – from its television and its airplanes to the banality of its suburban daily life – is sucked into this 'terroristic situational transfer' (p. 18). The terrorists have taken over the weapons of the dominant technological power (money, stock market speculation, computer technologies, aeronautics and media spectacle). Further, as terrorists emerged out of the suburbs of the US, they captured its innermost spaces. The 'faultless mastery of this clandestine style of operation is almost as terroristic as the spectacular act of September 11, since it casts suspicion on any and every individual' (p. 18).

Thus, the US media circulated both technological and spatial fear of the attack, and by repeated replay increased that fear exponentially. Simultaneously they were complicit in the move to militaristic excess, with the US acting in revenge mode. As Kellner writes of Baudrillard:

> For many of us, the Bush administration did what Baudrillard said the terrorists would want them to do, in terms of overreaction to the 9/11 attacks that would melt the initial sympathy for the US and that would win recruits for the terrorists reacting against the excess violence and aggression of the US response.
>
> (Kellner 2005)

Kellner makes an important point about a new emphasis in Baudrillard's post-9/11 analysis of the 'real' (ibid.). Before 9/11, Baudrillard saw globalization and technological development producing standardization and virtualization that was erasing individuality, social struggle, critique and reality itself. But the symbolic-real has reappeared in Baudrillard's writing along with the reappearance of multiple forces of resistance to the global 'Hegemon'. As Baudrillard wrote in *The Spirit of Terrorism*, the attacks on the World Trade Center radicalized both the world situation and the relationship of image to reality: 'Whereas we were dealing before with an uninterrupted profusion of banal images and a seamless flow of sham events, the terrorist act in New York has resuscitated both images and events' (2002: 27–8). That is what Kellner describes as Baudrillard's 'resurgence of the real'.

So, for Baudrillard, at one level 9/11 did change images significantly. But at another, its icons represented a much longer history. To recognize the full significance of the 'resuscitated' images of the Twin Towers, Baudrillard suggests that we remember the slow, long history of potlatch which aimed, above all, to avoid, via minimal exchange, cultural humiliation:

> To understand the rest of the world's hatred of the West, we have to overturn all our usual ways of seeing. It is not the hatred of those from whom we have taken everything and given nothing back; it is the hatred of those to whom we have given everything without their being able to give it back. It is not, then, the hatred bred of deprivation and exploitation, but of humiliation . . . . And it is to humiliation that the terrorism of September 11 was a response: one humiliation for another. The worst thing for a global power is not to be attacked or destroyed, but to be humiliated. And it was humiliated by September 11 because the terrorists inflicted something on it that it cannot return. All the reprisals have merely been a system of physical retaliation, whereas the global power was defeated symbolically.
>
> (Baudrillard 2002: 100–1)

We note that Baudrillard rejects here the critical-realist interpretation of 9/11 that this was the response of economically and culturally impoverished people. Rather, he argues, it was a strategic breakdown in the very system of symbolic exchange in

communication itself – an example of Baudrillard's emphasis on globalized simulation and the social reproduction of communication (Chapter 4). In his analysis, it
is finally the Western (and especially US) inability to return the 'gift' which marked
its ultimate symbolic humiliation.

William Merrin takes our analysis further via Baudrillard's discussion of 9/11 as a
new kind of 'absolute event'. Baudrillard, Merrin argues, developed in the 1970s and
1980s the notions of 'deterrence' and 'dissuasion' to explain wider processes operating in western society. Following his controversial analysis of the Gulf War, Baudrillard argued that the deterrence of the real by simulacral programming ensured that

> the playing out of a programmed event cannot constitute its occurrence . . .
> As Baudrillard says, whereas 'in earlier times an event was something that
> happened – now it is something designed to happen. It occurs, therefore, as a
> virtual artefact, as a reflection of pre-existing media-defined forms' (Baudril-
> lard 1993: 41).
>
> (Merrin 2005: 67)

Both the visually aestheticized television coverage of air attacks on Baghdad in the
Gulf War and the 'Shock 'n Awe' television coverage that began the Iraq War (after
endless advance notice of its power in the media) were imagistic media-defined
forms of this kind. Hence, Baudrillard argued, they were non-events with no signs
of symbolic resistance available to the viewer. Hence, Merrin argues, Baudrillard
turned to the 'event-strike' of provocative concepts like 'the Gulf War did not take
place'. This allowed his 'theory to become an *event* in the world to challenge the
latter's non-events' (p. 99).

In contrast, in his book about 9/11, *The Spirit of Terrorism*, Baudrillard called the
attacks 'the absolute event' (2002: 4). For Merrin:

> The event strike he had theorized through the 1990s was over (Baudrillard
> 2002: 3) Sharing the surprise at that day he not only reversed his theory but
> also his methodology, arguing a slower thought was required to deal with the
> 'speed' of such events (2002: 4). For him the [9/11] attacks were marked by
> a spiralling of semiotic and symbolic, with the western response – the 'war on
> terror' and the Afghan War – representing a further spiralling as the simulation
> of security and war was employed against the symbolic threat of terrorism.
>
> (p. 101)

Merrin's analysis is valuable here in tracing the *stages* of 'the survival of the symbolic and its "demand" within semiotic societies' in Baudrillard's theory (p. 100).
Initially, Baudrillard understood the symbolic as a site of resistance, a memory of
the past against the contemporary semiotic society of signs and simulacra. Later,
his interest shifted to understand the form of the symbolic as

> creative reversive forces within the semiotic system . . .This leads to a new
> strategy: not of opposition but of *exacerbation* – 'things must be pushed to the

limit where, quite naturally, they collapse and are inverted' (Baudrillard 1993: 4) – and Baudrillard's own theory attempts . . . to produce exactly this escalation in its potlatch with the world.

(Merrin 2005: 100)

This is the stage of Baudrillard's 'event strike' statement that the Gulf War did not take place – Baudrillard's own 'gift' to the system of simulation in the absence of other overt 'reversive' forces. But, Merrin adds, these 'other' forces then do appear in Baudrillard's writing. 'The final mode of resistance emerges in his later work in his discussion of the surviving symbolic cultures of the world, such as Aboriginals and Islam, whose vitality and beliefs pose an external threat to the west' (p. 100).

This final stage, focussing on Islamic cultures, becomes the central theme of Baudrillard's reading of the 9/11 attacks on the World Trade Center and Pentagon in 2001. But, equally important in Baudrillard's description of the new 'symbolic' is that in addition to the Islamic attack – the terrorists' external symbolic challenge – he argues that without the complicity of the western public, the attacks could not have achieved their 'full symbolic dimension' and 'resonance' (Baudrillard 2002: 5–6). This was '"a terrorism of the rich", Baudrillard says: of those who had assimilated modernity and globalism, and still wanted to destroy the west' (Merrin 2005: 103–4). The deaths of the Islamic terrorists were multiplied 'to infinity' via these 'modern resources' of the west (p. 104).

On one hand, Baudrillard describes the 'enormous visible power of the west': 'the purest form of spectacle' (2002: 21), the mode in which 9/11 was covered live on US and then world television. This was, in Baudrillard's term, a spectacle of non-event.

Despite the audience's extension into the heart of the event – the real-time montage of close-ups, long shots, multiple angles and ground images, edited and replayed and mixed with commentary, speculation, political reaction, and the apprehension and adrenalin of the live moment – no event was 'happening' for them . . . As in the Gulf War, *they* did not risk their lives that day.

(Merrin 2005: 102)

Merrin adds to this the 'pornographic' television images, exemplified by the helicopter-cam of 'people waving at the windows and tracking shots of bodies in freefall down the tower's side' (2005: 102). Baudrillard emphasizes here the visual 'obscenity', which was extended far beyond 9/11 and is alive and well, Merrin argues, in the consumption of 'real-life pain and humiliation' (p. 102) via real-life television, game shows, viewer footage clip shows and news coverage of disasters and wars.

September 11 was the continuation of this scheduling by other means. In the mediated consumption of another's pain there is a direct line from the smart-bomb's view of the Gulf War, to the impotent copter-cam close-ups of 9/11: *you've been maimed.* In 1978 Baudrillard claimed terrorism was 'our theatre of cruelty' (*In the Shadow of the Silent Majorities*, 1978: 114). By 2001 it was part of a wider media experience.

(p. 102)

But on the other hand, spiralling within this 'purest form of spectacle' at 9/11, there was also, for Baudrillard, the countervailing 'purest symbolic form' (Baudrillard, cited in Merrin 2005: 21, 22, 29–30). It was thus that 'The whole of visible power can do nothing against the tiny, but symbolic, death of a few individuals', the 'infinitesimal point' of their deaths creating 'a gigantic suction or void, an enormous convection' (Baudrillard 2002: 19, 18), provoking a hyper-reaction as the US military/media systems swung into fear and repression modes of 'security'.

> Once the system has terrorized its own population with a fear of terrorism, all natural, accidental and reversive forces are experienced as terroristic – so the anthrax attacks in October 2001, the plane crashes in New York in November 2001, in Florida in January 2002 and in Milan in 2002, as well as the American-Canadian blackouts in August 2003 were all immediately seized on as Bin Laden's work (Baudrillard 2002: 33).

(Merrin 2005: 104)

And so the semiotic/symbolic struggle of images spiralled on, entwined within the contemporary war of images. Merrin is acute in his discussion of the Afghanistan and Iraq Wars as a further turn of the spiral, when the US 'system' sought *symbols* to extinguish those of 9/11. Beginning in October 2001, Merrin says, there was the cruise missile bombing on Kabul; but the war 'would always suffer from being a TV repeat of the Gulf War', appearing as 'an impoverished act' (p. 107). It was what Baudrillard considered a 'repetitive, rehashed pseudo-event', in which the semiotic model of presentation preceded, dominated, could not substitute 'for a real and formidable, unique and unforeseeable event' like 9/11 (Baudrillard 2002: 34, cited in Merrin 2005: 107). And so the images from the Afghan War could not easily become iconic. 'Northern Alliance fighters, televisually indistinguishable from the Taliban they opposed (and often had once been), came a poor second to the real-time, hypervisible spectacle of the imploding Twin Towers' (Merrin 2005: 107).

Hence, Merrin argues, came the US turn to war in Iraq in early 2003.

> Though it offered little advantage in the fight against terrorism, it promised a more tangible target amenable to western military power, the opportunity to repeat the global spectacle and ratings success of the 1991 war, a more certain, visible and traditional victory than any in the 'war on terror', and the chance to settle old, familial geopolitical scores against an enemy whom many Americans believed anyway to be behind the World Trade Center attacks.

(p. 107)

Yet the US quest for the visually symbolic failed miserably again, Merrin asserts, as emblematized by the stage-managed 'half-toppling' of Saddam Hussein's statue in Baghdad on 9 April 2003. It was, Merrin says, a too obvious and weak symbolic counterpart to the fall of the Twin Towers. With Saddam's disappearance, all that was left was a non-event produced and framed for our consumption as the definitive and predictable sign of the regime's end.

(p. 109)

In any case, he adds, the 'liberated' Iraqi people in this spectacle, surrounded by US tanks, did not understand the primacy of the Western audience, the time constraints even of rolling news, and the networks' fear of a drifting audience, and their need to deliver that 'Kennedy' moment ('where were you? . . . watching television'). So the Iraqis were excluded from this act, in an implosion of media and military with the event that neutralized and short-circuited the people's efforts, replacing them with that demanded, semiotic image of the statue's fall. The US military stepped in to finish the job of pulling the statue down.

> Believing they were the centre and meaning of the act, the Iraqis did not see that they were only the extras, providing local colour and a guarantee of authenticity and legitimacy for the western audience for whom the event really occurred. This forced, final act exposed the paucity of the war's spectacle, rushing the end of the war for the television public.
>
> (p. 109)

Merrin's Baudrillard-style analysis of the US attempt to re-capture the symbolic, to return the terrorists' 'gift' of 9/11, is convincing in clarifying Baudrillard's 'spiral' conceptualization of the war between the symbolic and the semiotic image, and in emphasising his complex stance on the relation between old and new histories of symbolisation. As Merrin puts it:

> For Baudrillard, therefore, the American response to 9/11 represented a further spiral of the semiotic and symbolic processes within those events and an attempt to employ simulation as a means of global control and homogeneity. His claim that the unilateral, simulacral model of non-war was employed by the west to eradicate globally resistant forces finds support in the operations of Afghanistan and Iraq and their aftermath. These were not just conducted in order to defeat terrorists or a future terrorist threat but also to integrate these outlaw zones and their symbolic cultures within a western model of democracy and a controlled, global system.
>
> (p. 111)

Baudrillard's and Virilio's 'accident'

The theme of this chapter has been to focus on iconic images of the Twin Towers and on key critical challenges to state-centric discourses around temporal and spatial discontinuity. But these critical discourses are themselves as much a matter of social construction as the US government's '9/11 changed everything' discourse. This recognition inevitably leads us to epistemological questions, as in comparing definitions of the 'iconic' as between the structural 'real' of some theorists represented here and the constructivist 'communication exchange' of Baudrillard.

We conclude that any concept within these epistemologically loaded debates – such as Baudrillard's use of the term 'accident' as 'a purely arbitrary act, the murderous phantasmagoria of a few fanatics' quoted in his critique of realism above – is equally loaded. If, for example, we compare Baudillard's use of the term 'accident' with its central usage by Paul Virilio, the social theorist quoted at the beginning of this chapter, we would need to compare Baudrillard's long development within radical and constructivist sociology (Chapter 4), with Virilio's on-going Christian-humanist critique of modernist/postmodernist art forms, surgical techniques and 'integral accidents' which, for him, are the hidden face of 'progress'.

There are similarities between Baudrillard's historical stages (which move from the 'disappearing object' of class values and humanism to the 'integral-reality' of globalization) and Virilio's history of the shift from 'the era of class-based communitarism to that of instant and simultaneous globalization of affects and fears'. Consequently, there are some similarities in their view of the mass media after 9/11. Virilio described 9/11 as the 'accident of accidents' because it was a world-integrating accident which appeared in images live on television and the internet everywhere at the same time.

But the conclusion of Virilio's book *Ground Zero* (2002) confirms that his analytical story takes a different direction from Baudrillard's. Whereas for Baudrillard a global 'accident' is a purely arbitrary act, for Virilio it is systemic, historical and motivated. Virilio had begun focusing on the technological aspects of speed from the late 1970s when he argued that real time superseded real (organic) space. An aeroplane, he notes, can enable us to travel quickly across the Atlantic. But it can also be used in a terrorist suicide attack. This is an 'integral accident' that is built into the very design and speed of the vehicle. Technology cannot exist without this potential for accidents to happen through speed; and terrorism has co-opted this technology.

Much of *Ground Zero* tells a tale whereby 'the techno-scientific imagination has structured itself for some six hundred years around the *concept of disappearance* – of the inexorable enactment of a stripping down of the World, of the substance of the living world' (Virilio 2002: 12–13). Whereas for the radical Durkheimian Baudrillard that loss is of the human-symbolic *communication system*, the disappearance for Virilio is of the Christian-human *body* originally imaged by the 'oneness' (as human being and God) of the iconic image of Christ on the Cross. Virilio has said 'as a Christian I reject nuclear faith', and he has castigated the 'idolatrous belief: the missile, no longer the Messiah' (Virilio and Lotringer 1983: 122, cited in Oventile 2003).

This Christian-humanist foundation of Virilio's theory of war and the image brings him into critical confrontation with contemporary medical and artistic trends that combine machine and bodily functions. It also brings him into conflict with postmodernism's interest in hybridity (Chapter 10). For Virilio 'Humanity's being inheres in a oneness' which 'biotechnology may dismantle by breaking humans into the genetically enhanced and underprivileged, and even by hybridizing humans with non-humans' (Oventile 2003). Virilio argues that while the West is always somewhere else – in the accident-prone, speed-obsessed world of the mediated integral accident, via stock exchange crashes, automated warfare, and mass television's pitiless images – so, ironically, is the terrorist offered power by the very 'freedom to move' in the little organic and suburban spaces we have left to us.

Virilio and Baudrillard agree that, of all the images of 9/11, 'what exploded in people's minds was the World Trade Center' rather than the destruction of the Pentagon (Virilio 2002: 82). But the profoundly different intellectual narratives behind this apparent agreement underline the central theme of this chapter: that the choice of images of the 'iconic' as well as the notion that '9/11 changed everything' is theory driven, whether among transport executives, politicians or public intellectuals and academics. A critical approach to terrorism and its images must always be aware of this.

Conclusion

Baudrillard does not use the word 'iconic' in relation to the images of the Twin Towers. Instead he speaks of the 'incandescence' of the image. To us this indicates what we began to speak about in the previous section: that the use of words, whether 'accidents' or the word 'iconic' itself, depend on the conceptual and theoretical ground of the argument.

It seems odd that Baudrillard, who finds in the 9/11 attack an 'absolute event', replacing the non-events of contemporary history and marking the return of the symbolic, should not also see these 'incandescent' images as iconic. But it is one which is conceptually driven.

Merrin discusses tensions between two separate histories, or 'genealogies', within Baudrillard's early and later work as he developed his theory of 'the transformation of the lived symbolic into the semiotic production' (2005: 32). First, there was the discussion of an 'abrupt division' between symbolic and semiotic orders in the Renaissance; and here Baudrillard spoke of the iconoclasts, breakers of holy images during the Reformation. Iconolasts, he believes, 'saw that, incarnated and multiplied, God did not remain God but was volatized in images which henceforth 'alone deploy their pomp and power of fascination'. This, for Baudrillard, was an early recognition of the 'omnipotence of simulacra . . . erasing God from the conscience of men' and 'annihilating truth' in revealing that only the simulacrum of God existed (Baudrillard 1978: 4–5)' (Merrin 2005: 32). What was at stake in the destruction of icons, Baudrillard argued, was their 'power to murder the "real" by murdering "their own model" in favour of their own full reality (Baudrillard 1978: 5' (p. 33). Iconoclasm was humankind's 'metaphysical despair', Baudrillard said, over the recognition that the icon had more 'fascination', more 'reality' in the world than God. (Baudrillard 1978: 5, cited by Merrin 2005: 3).

Later, Merrin notes, Baudrillard came up with a different genealogy of simulation which emphasized 'the transition from signs that dissimulate something to signs that dissimulate that there is nothing, a passage from "a theology of truth and secrecy" to the simulation marking our own contemporary era' (Baudrillard, 1994: 6–7)' (p. 33). Without any precise historical location in Baudrillard's analysis, this shift – which Merrin argues 'simultaneously develop and contradict his earlier discussion of simulacra' (p. 33) – may have been a significant reason for Baudrillard's widespread reputation for nihilism.

Moreover, when Baudrillard turned in his late career to photography himself, as Merrin says, he rejected the views of many photojournalists and academics like McLuhan and Sontag that iconic images have 'a demonstrable power to move us, and to change our behaviour and responses' (p. 148). Instead,

> He emerges from his discussion of photography as even more implacably opposed to the semiotic media's use of the image for new, entertainment, information, communication, signification, and ideological, political and aesthetic effects, and for moral testimony as a banal witness to the real.
>
> (p. 149)

And this is despite the fact that in his photographic writing 'Barthes is specifically employed to support Baudrillard's critique of contemporary images and to evoke the possibility of another – symbolic – mode of experience, relations and meaning with and through the image' (p. 146). John Berger, drawing on his socialist analysis, did deploy Barthes for precisely this valuation of certain photographers in seeking a 'radial system . . . around the photograph so that it may be seen in terms which are simultaneously personal, political, economic, dramatic, everyday and historic' (1980: 64, 67). Baudrillard did not.

For Merrin, this conundrum about Baudrillard and the image requires the more detailed history of Baudrillard's use of iconicity. For us, it is a clear example of the fact that use of the term 'icon' depends on theory and even on contradictions within that theory.

7 Shock doctrine in Iraq

The 'Marlboro Marine' and 'Shock and Awe'

James Blake Miller, the 'Marlboro Marine', during the US assault on Fallujah, Iraq, November 2004. Photograph taken by Luis Sinco © 2007. Los Angeles Times. Reprinted with permission.

A US Marine is photographed in close-up during the November 2004 attack on Fallujah, Iraq. It is a shot of an exhausted, bloodied soldier, cigarette in mouth, one mission completed, others to follow. His eyes are steely and unfocused. Though looking towards us he is not looking at us. His exhaustion denies us any direct address.

During this moment of smoking his cigarette, he seems distanced from what he has seen, where he has been, what he has done. The cigarette clamped tight in his mouth is jaunty, yet relaxed in its gesture over his helmet chinstrap and down to the bottom of the frame. This cigarette is an important public signifier. 'Smokin' is the front page headline of the *New York Post* and the photograph fills the front page. Below is the newspaper's subsidiary headline: 'Marlboro men kick butt in Fallujah'. The cowboy-Western association of Marlboro cigarettes' original 'Marlboro man' advertisement, which this image and these headlines recall, convey the sense of US manifest destiny in Iraq. This is a man of the Western, steely hard, laconic, physically strong, speaking no words but 'getting the job done'. He is the human embodiment of militaristic 'Shock and Awe'. This new 'Marlboro Marine' became a national icon in the United States, representing its ideals and dreams in the invasion of Iraq.

Photographer Luis Sinco, in a reflexive news feature written some years later, described his image:

> The young Marine lit a cigarette and let it dangle. White smoke wafted around his helmet. His face was smeared with war paint. Blood trickled from his right ear and the bridge of his nose . . . His expression caught my eye. To me it said terrified, exhausted and glad just to be alive. I recognized that look because that's how I felt too. I raised my camera and snapped a few shots. With the click of a shutter, Marine Lance Corporal James Blake Miller, a country boy from Kentucky, became an emblem of the war in Iraq.
>
> (Sinco 2007: 6)

Within days Sinco's photograph was iconic, appearing on the front pages of more than 150 newspapers. Sinco describes how the American public, including President George Bush, wanted to know about this 'brave young man' and hundreds sent 'care packages'. At one level the iconic reception of the 'Marlboro Marine' derived from the 'Shock and Awe' militarized images from the Iraq War. For example, Fox News, a major newsfront for the Murdoch media empire, supported the invasion wholeheartedly and positioned itself quite precisely during the initial bombing of Baghdad. It saw the war from the eyes of the aircrew. For example, from 'Tiger,' a squadron commander who served in Desert Storm: 'I think the enemy's eyes are going to be opened wide when he sees the ferocity that we can bring to bear, and the shock and awe that he's going to have to withstand' (Fox News 2008).

At another level, Naomi Klein suggests that Sinco's icon derived from a longer warlike history:

> In truth . . . it's a straight-up rip-off of the most powerful icon in American advertising (the Marlboro man), which in turn imitated the brightest star ever created by Hollywood – John Wayne – who was himself channelling America's most powerful founding myth, the cowboy on the rugged frontier.
>
> (Klein 2004: 27)

Klein speaks of an immediate 'politically correct' debate in the US media about the image. One issue concerned the potential of young children to copy or imitate Miller's cigarette smoking habit. As one scolding letter to the *Houston Chronicle* complained, the iconic message was that the way to relax after battle is to smoke. Klein commented: 'letter writers across the nation are united in their outrage – not that the steely-eyed, smoking soldier makes mass killing look cool; but that the laudable act of mass killing makes the grave crime of smoking look cool' (Klein 2004: 27).

But, Klein says, there is another context of the 'Marlboro Marine' as icon that we need to consider – the era of 'supercharged American impunity':

> Because, outside US borders, it is, of course, a different marine who has been awarded the prize as 'the face of Falluja': the soldier captured on tape executing a wounded, unarmed prisoner in a mosque. Runners-up are a photograph of a two-year-old Fallujan in a hospital bed with one of his tiny legs blown off; a dead child lying in the street, clutching the headless body of an adult; and an emergency health clinic blasted to rubble. Inside the US, these snapshots of lawless occupation appeared only briefly, if they appeared at all. Yet Miller's icon status has endured, kept alive with human interest stories about fans sending cartons of Marlboros to Falluja . . . Impunity – the perception of being outside the law – has long been the hallmark of the Bush regime.
>
> (p. 27)

In this chapter we look at theories among photojournalists and academics about what Klein calls 'supercharged American impunity' and its militaristic images of 'Shock and Awe', the 'Marlboro Marine' and Iraq.

Embedded photojournalism in the Iraq war

Photographer/academic Julian Stallabrass has written about the Pentagon's practice of embedding journalists with particular troop units. The practice gave journalists good access to the fighting but encouraged them to take a positive view of what they witnessed, and fostered a strong identification with the unit (2008: 5).

At the same time Stallabrass comments on the disadvantages of the embedded system, citing David Zucchino who worked for the same newspaper as Sinco, the *Los Angeles Times*. Zucchino noted that embedded access could suffocate and blind journalists because they were denied a full picture of war. 'I could not interview survivors of Iraqi civilians killed by US soldiers or speak to Iraqi fighters trying to kill Americans . . . I had no idea what ordinary Iraqis were experiencing' (Zucchino, cited in Stallabrass 2008: 5–6).

Stallabrass adds that embedded photography led to perspectives from the 'centre', not the 'margins'; that is, a narrow perspective focused on the experiences of the troops and not broader issues.

> Embedding fitted the demands of the news organizations in the US and the UK, for spectacular, live or at least up-to-the-minute reports, high on affect and low on analysis, and likely to stiffen patriotic sentiment.
>
> (Stallabrass 2008: 6)

His view is supported by a number of photojournalists who observed the process of embedding in Iraq. The internationally respected Vietnam War photojournalist Philip Jones Griffiths noted that embedded journalists had to sign a contract giving the military control over their stories, and they underwent rigorous basic training.

> Once in Iraq, these 'trained' reporters became cogs in the military machine . . . Being embedded means that objectivity is easily abandoned. Ties and relationships are soon formed, and that is to be expected; bonding is an essentially human trait.
>
> (Griffith 2005: 2)

Andrew Hoskins also agrees, adding that:

> the discourse of the embeds often reflected the power of the military machines and the desert landscape through which they raced . . . their description evoking Hollywood, the Wild West (very much like the experience of travels through *America* that Jean Baudrillard describes).
>
> (Hoskins 2004: 64)

It is clear from Sinco's article that all the features of embedded journalism described by Stallabrass, Griffiths and other photojournalists were evident in his reflection about the 'Marlboro Marine' image-event. His photograph of Miller generated enormous patriotic sentiment. Sinco was strong on 'up-to-the-minute' production of images, and certainly shared a sense of close comradeship with his embedding unit, the Charlie Company of the 1st Battalion, 8th Marine Regiment as it entered Fallujah on 8 November 2004. He describes how he experienced collectively with his unit the fears and frustrations of attack:

> We encountered heavy fire almost immediately. We were pinned down all night at a traffic circle where a six-inch kerb offered the only protection. I hunkered down in the gutter that endless night, praying for daylight, trying hard to make myself small . . . At dawn, the gunfire and explosions subsided. A white phosphorous artillery round burst overhead, showering blazing-hot tendrils. We came across three insurgents lying in the street, two of them dead, their blood mixing with rain. The third, a wiry Arab youth, tried to mouth a few words. All I could think was: 'Buddy, you're already dead'.
>
> (Sinco 2007: 8)

Later, as he travelled around the US with the discharged and traumatized Miller, Sinco describes, in his feature 'Am I to blame for his private war?' a different memory they now shared of Arab youths in gunsights. Fearing that these were not insurgents but civilians trapped in the firefight, Miller, now undergoing PTSD therapy, talked about killing the enemy:

> To try and live with that . . . how do you justify it, regardless of what your causes are or what their causes are? . . . To see somebody in your sights and to

pull that trigger, it's almost like you're with them, seeing their life flash before their eyes as well as taking it. It's an insane connection that you make with that person at that point.

(p. 8)

In memory, Miller believed he had seen through his rifle but never understood – at the moment of blowing young men's heads apart – the reality of 'collateral damage'. Political anthropologist Allen Feldman argues something similar about television and its viewers.

The doublespeak of 'Shock and Awe' and 'Collateral Damage'

For Feldman, US television's visual coverage of Iraq was dichotomized between what we see ('Shock and Awe' fire clouds) and what we don't see (dead civilians beneath the fire, 'collateral damage') (2004a). This is because the US, via its media, was fighting a war of 'cultural imaginaries' for the hearts and minds of people *inside* the US and West, not in Iraq. Feldman argues that US citizens (like the terrorists themselves) were still trapped in the 'memorialization' of those who died on 9/11. The US memorialized their dead people as victims, al-Qaeda their terrorists as martyrs.

But Feldman takes his analysis of public trauma in the West further than the issue of terrorism. He applies it equally to illegal immigration and to new viral scares like HIV/AIDS, BSE, SARS and avian influenza. Feldman argues that national borders today are broken down via the globalized media circulation of images of homeland 'invasion', whether by terrorists or illegal immigrants or frightening new viruses:

> Thus the new wars of public safety target an iconography of demonized border-crossing figures and forces, including drug dealers, terrorists, asylum seekers, undocumented immigrants, and even microbes . . . We are now subjected to a new superstructure of war fantasy in which the targets of warfare, and the enemies of public safety are as malleable and as arbitrary as a dream image.
>
> (Feldman 2004a: 74)

This disappearance of enforceable physical territorial borders was graphically displayed in the 'risk-event' mass visualization of 9/11, and since then, Feldman argues, new 'virtual' boundary sites have been constructed by media coverage of viral, immigrant or further terrorist invasion. The border-crossing transgressors, be they terrorists, asylum-seekers or viruses, may be dream images, but they are located in the real economy of the globalized circulation of images. Feldman describes here a new kind of 'virtual' surveillance of the public via government campaigns against 'pandemics'. This surveillance is based on dichotomizing proper and improper circulation across borders. On one hand, there are the 'orderly spaces' of financial circulation in the globalized 'free market'. On the other, there is the 'police concept of history', which monitors new icons of border transgression and pollution:

This form of policing . . . compensates for the loss of tangible borders by creating new boundary systems that are virtual, mediatized such as electronic, biometric and digital surveillance nets. The virtual border is matched by the virtual or ghostly transgressor; in the last two years we have accumulated a growing number of such ghosts, so one can locate the ever-missing Bin Laden . . . within the same spectrum as the covert carrier of infection, genetically altered comestibles, demented livestock, and undocumented immigrants.

(pp. 74–5)

For Feldman US citizens are subject to a new 'Treatment State', where militaries in political emergency zones increasingly function as *both* surveillance and 'peacekeeping' forces. 'Humanitarian interventions' are controlled by the military and exploit global human rights discourse for citizens back home.

The terrorist and the refugee are both the objects and the consequence of military interventions. The juridical personalities of the terrorist as an 'unlawful combatant' and the refugee and asylum-seeker as an unlawful resident and worker are mutually marked by the denial of their citizenship rights in an existing nation state structure.

(p. 76)

In Feldman's world of the iconic representation of risk-events, the Bush regime sought new 'terrorist' states to survey and invade when politically necessary. Ironically, though, it was not only Baghdad which was being attacked, but US citizens as well in the name of a 'besieged American nationhood' (p. 79). Feldman sees this 'visual culture of war' as an ideology that suppresses any potential agency in the public sphere, which otherwise could transform the structure of the 'Treatment State' into something more democratic and humanitarian.

The iconic but still 'memorialized' images of 9/11 thus generated, via this 'visual culture of war', the iconic images of 'Shock and Awe'. And 'Shock and Awe' images share ground with all those other images of border invasion, from microbes to bin Laden. No wonder, Feldman suggests, we never see images of 'collateral damage'.

Cloning terror

Feldman's thoughts about mediatized viral invasions are extended by W.J.T Mitchell in his important book, *Cloning Terror: The war of images from 9/11 to the present* (2011). Mirroring Feldman's description, Mitchell says:

If human bodies carrying microbes circumnavigate the globe more rapidly than ever in the age of air travel, leading to periodic outbreaks such as SARS and swine flu, the global circulation of digital images on the Internet is even more virulent and rapid. It is no wonder that the circulation of images . . . is often compared to an infectious disease in which the invasive life forms are growing and mutating more rapidly than our defences can evolve to fight them off.

(Mitchell 2011: 74)

But crucially in his argument bringing together cloning and terrorism, Mitchell adds to the Feldman-style metaphor of infectious diseases Derrida's notion of an autoimmune disorder, which in its medical usage refers to the condition where an immune system attacks and destroys its own healthy tissues. Mitchell says, 'Derrida turned to a biological metaphor, but one focused on the defence mechanisms of the organism itself, rather than on the usual picture of terrorism as a foreign invasion by alien microbes' (p. 45). Mitchell compares 'foreign invasion' and 'autoimmune' metaphors via his key belief in a contemporary age of cloning, which is marked by 'the irruption of twins, doubles, and multiples in the sphere of public, mass consumed imagery' (p. 99). So, in a complex argument about cloning and invasion, Mitchell can conclude that the Abu Ghraib hooded prisoner standing on a box attached to electric cables 'is transformed by still photography into an indelible icon of what a Christian nation accomplished in its crusade to liberate the Middle East' (p. 136).

Mitchell asks: 'why did this image become the icon for the entire Abu Ghraib scandal?' He notes the instant recognition by the public (and even by one of the US Army soldiers who took some of the photographs) of a 'double' in this image and other Abu Ghraib photographs. Mitchell says, 'the image of a faceless hooded duplicate, the clone or "uncanny double" of the central icon of Christianity will continue to haunt all attempts to understand this period' (p. 118). In particular he argues that the iconic power of this Abu Ghraib image draws centrally on its 'cloned' ambivalent mix of state and religious power within the iconography of Christ.

> The Hooded Man heightens the contradictions embedded in the theme of state by staging it as an icon that does not remain securely on the positive side of the sacred-secular confusion (e.g. Christian democracy and enlightenment vs. Muslim tyranny and idolatory), but forces an *enjambment* of good and evil, god and the devil, Islam and the Judeo-Christian alliance. That is why the image has 'two bodies', shuttling between sovereignty and abjection, terror suspect and torture victim, criminal and martyr.
>
> (pp. 158–9)

Mitchell's analysis goes beyond Feldman's in claiming an underpinning theoretical merger between the 'much longer durée' of the 'Cloning Wars' (p. 163) and the more recent history of the 'War on Terror' which was 'inaugurated and defined by a date: September 11, 2001' (p. 162). Unlike Feldman he also seeks the 'operational reality' (p. xviii) of images in order to find new and better ways forward.

> It would mean, not just a renunciation of the war metaphor, but an embracing of a positive alternative, a strengthening of the immune system, a refinement of tactics for determining the difference between friends and enemies,

hosts and parasites, natives and immigrants, and a strengthening of the other central biopolitical component of the body politic, a 'healthy constitution'. It would mean strong doses of *preventive* medicine in the form of a world system that has strong institutions of international justice, both politically and economically.

(p. 53)

Given that he argues that biocybernetics, the age of cloning, is the contemporary successor to what Walter Benjamin called 'the age of mechanical reproduction' (p. 20), and that the 'biopicture' is a fusion of the older life of images, fused with the new infinitely reproduced image 'epitomized by the contemporary phenomenon of cloning and the development of digital imaging and animation', it is clear not only why Mitchell sees the Abu Ghraib icon of a hooded man as representing a particular scandal but also the wider Christian-imperialistic system which produced it.

It seems that Mitchell is one major theorist discussed in this book who does believe in a 'before and after, erecting a wall in time between "pre-9/11" thinking and "post-9/11" thinking' (p. 162). He argues for a paradigmatic shift after 9/11 into the era of 'cloning terror'. But we are more convinced by Andrew Hoskins and Ben O'Loughlin who construct a continuity-within-change history of the same period of new media transition.

Mediatized war

In their book *War and Media: The emergence of diffused war* (2010; see also Hoskins 2004), Hoskins and O'Loughlin distinguish between 'mediation', which they see as a relatively linear process of images of war within a specific social context, and 'mediatization', where 'the planning, waging and consequences of warfare do not reside outside the media' (2010: 5). In the latter, the media, as displayed in the embedded relationship between military and media in Iraq, are integral to military practices. Yet, they argue, 'rather than mediation and mediatization being processes exclusive to *different* eras [our emphasis], the two modulate together' (p. 5).

They adopt the same continuity/change approach to their second distinction: between a first and second stage of mediatization. In the first stage, 'Television . . . pivotal to the propaganda in the wars over Kosovo and the Gulf, became the pre-eminent medium over this period in "information" war' (pp. 15–16). It was characterized by 'Big Media' such as the BBC, CNN or national newspapers, not only representing a top-down hierarchy of organization and management, but also by reflexivity about their role:

What defined this stage as mediatized was that the very knowledge of the phenomenon developed into a self-reflexive enterprise: media knew and advertised the fact that they offered a 'front row seat' as they 'brought us history' as it unfolded.

(Hoskins and O'Loughlin 2010: 16)

The second stage of mediatization, for Hoskins and O'Loughlin, is marked by a 'new media ecology' where 'media have entered into the production of events to such an unprecedented extent that those events are *mediatized*' (pp. 17–18). As an example, they offer a convincing case study of television coverage of Saddam Hussein's execution. In this case the first news footage which was based on official Iraqi government film of the hanging presented the event as 'dignified and non-sectarian' (p. 33). But within three days of the initial broadcast, an illicit mobile phone video emerged. 'The calm and relatively contained silent official video was transformed into a PR disaster by the counter-modalities of the shaky and grainy footage and the mob-like jeering of the co-present witnesses to the hanging' (p. 33). This, together with the leakage of the Abu Ghraib images, were examples 'of the emergent power of mobile media to quickly challenge and to subvert narratives facilitated through the astonishing connectivity of the web and other electronic and digital media' (p. 33).

Two terms are particularly central to Hoskins and O'Loughlin's analysis here: 'emergence' of different, sometimes 'amateur' image-interpretations (as in the Neda example) which were then enfolded within 'professional' news broadcasts; and the 'connectivity' of multiple media modalities.

> [I]t is the very existence of a glut of recordings of images and video, amateur and professional, incidental and intended, and their *potential* to emerge and to transform all-that-is-established about an event, that fundamentally unsettle the second phase of mediatisation.
>
> (p. 29)

By theorizing the 'entirely unpredictable emergence of visual and audiovisual media fragments' at Abu Ghraib and the Saddam Hussein execution (p. 30), Hoskins and O'Loughlin extend Best's observations about 'proximity-distance' (Chapter 8) within a sophisticated media theory (p. 168). At the same time they cover Feldman's ground in observing that 'Transnational security threats such as terrorism, pandemics and environmental catastrophe, alongside patterns of global migration, have triggered new paradigms of governance' (p. 11). But they also embed this in a concept of more 'diffused war' where 'mediatization, nonlinear causality and uncertain decision-making' add 'new layers, forms and dilemmas' (p. 147) to the media/terrorism relationship than are captured by Mitchell's 'cloning terror' concept.

In this and an earlier book by Hoskins (2004) they are ambiguous about icons. On one hand, the iconic image seems to stand out as a touchstone of reality. Speaking of the 1991 Gulf War, Hoskins says, that television conveyed:

> an unreal (and highly sanitized) war and in this way the more tangible connections of warfare reside in those images that . . . are captured (and re-mediated) in the photographic . . . The still image captures more of the past, of history, as it appears removed from the essential movement and therefore presentness of television . . . In terms of communicating news and forging history . . . visual images provide us with our 'subliminal points of reference.
>
> (2004: 28, 43, 115)

Yet, on the other hand, the iconic image is itself suspect *via* remediation. Hoskins speaks of 'dynamic and living human memory . . . *reduced* to iconic images' (pp. 29–30, our emphasis), and of the 'iconic fixations of the media' (p. 108) with old and generally historically undated images of Saddam Hussein from the Gulf to the Iraq War.

Despite this ambiguity, Hoskins and O'Loughlin do offer a strong theory which is careful not to emphasize either complete continuity or a clear break pre- and post-9/11 (or between 'old' and 'new' media). The second stage of mediatization, they argue, represents a trend which is 'partial and uneven' (2010: 18). 'Between the stereotype terms "new" and "old" media, we find *renewed* media: mainstream news organizations harnessing citizen or participatory journalism to enhance their news provision' (p. 84).Thus, rather than 9/11 representing a sudden break, it marked 'a crystallization of slow, long-term processes, such as the emergence of networked terrorist groups and the need for an organizing principle for Western security policy after the Cold War' (p. 174). Hoskins and O'Loughlin 'observe the persistence and maintenance of discourses over decades' (p. 167) and argue that both the 'hypersecurity' obsessed West and terrorist organisations like Al-Qaeda 'fit any new events and media content into their longer term narrative' (p. 157).

We turn next to one of the West's most powerful longer term narratives: the discourse of neoliberalism.

Extending the 'New Insecurity' paradigm

As a political anthropologist, Feldman is concerned with nation states, geographical borders and the 'new insecurity' paradigm. He does not include financial globalization in his analysis, except as 'orderly spaces of economic circulation'. Mitchell does include neoliberalism along with the 'evolutionary implications of biopolitics' in his history (2011: 166), though he doesn't explain his 'wall in time' before/after view of 9/11 in the context of his own description of the longue-durée 'framework of neoliberal economics from the eighteenth century to Milton Friedman and the Chicago School' (p. 165).

Yet there could be no better example of new cross-border 'invasions' of national security by 'border-crossing figures and forces' that are virtual and mediatized (Feldman 2004a: 74) than neoliberal economics. As David Harvey says in *A Brief History of Neoliberalism*, 'information technology is the privileged technology of neoliberalism. It is far more useful for speculative activity and for maximizing the number of short-term market contracts than for improving production' (2005: 139).

Neither Feldman talking about public safety wars, nor Hariman and Lucaites' account of the 'ongoing dialectic' in the US between liberal individual and democratic ideals, explain why new kinds of public insecurity occurred. This is because neither offers a political economy of the periods they analyze. Hariman and Lucaites argue that 'Circulation is the common denominator of the two most distinctive institutions of modern society: markets and publics' (2007: 303), but their book is about publics rather than markets.

Iraq and Neoliberalism: David Harvey

Harvey emphasizes the difference between the theoretical ideal and the pragmatic practice of neo-liberalism (2005). For example, after the apparent success of 'Shock and Awe' in Iraq, the head of the Coalition Provisional Authority, Paul Bremer, promulgated Iraqi business ownership rights to foreign firms and the opening of Iraq's banks to foreign control. On the face of it, Bush's policy in Iraq seemed to contradict the free markets and fair trade ideals of neoliberal theory. The orders were certain to give colossal advantage to US companies in Iraq state industrial and commercial sectors; and this is what occurred, with massive contracts landed by Halliburton, a US company of which Vice-President Dick Cheney was previously president.

Harvey also notes that neoliberalism's distrust of state power does not always fit easily with the need for a strong, militarized and, at times, coercive state (p. 2). But in Iraq, as Bush saw it, the US military was guaranteeing the neoliberal functioning of markets internationally. The Iraqi people were thus being 'liberated' in two ways: politically from the ugly rule of Saddam Hussein, and economically by the imposition of neoliberalism. But the 'freedoms' this US policy embodies 'reflect the interests of private property owners, businesses, multinational corporations, and financial capital' (p. 7).

Comparing this Iraq policy with the US government's earlier intervention in the overthrow of the elected socialist Chilean government in 1973 and its direct mentoring of coup leader General Pinochet's neoliberal reforms, Harvey notes that two such obviously similar restructurings occurring at such different times in quite different parts of the world 'suggests that the grim reach of US imperial power might lie behind the rapid proliferation of neoliberal state forms throughout the world from the mid-1970s onwards' (p. 9). But while Harvey argues that this has happened, he is careful to itemize the complexity and multiplicity of neoliberal development. It is these two parts of neoliberal discourse critique – its 'grim reach of power' and its multiply determined 'construction of consent' in different parts of the world – which provides the power of Harvey's critical explanation of what he calls the 'neoliberal turn' (p. 9).

The 'grim reach' of power

The 'embedded liberalism' of Franklyn Roosevelt's 1930s Keynsian economy had seen the state actively intervene in industrial policy and construct a variety of welfare standards in health care, education and social services. In contrast, the move to neoliberalism began in the 1970s, and became fully-fledged state policy, Harvey argues, in the 1980s under US President Ronald Reagan and British Prime Minister Margaret Thatcher. Starting as a small and exclusive group around the Austrian political philosopher Friedrich von Hayek in 1947, a neoliberal group, which included the US economist Milton Friedman, had formulated theory to challenge the 'decline of belief in private property and the competitive market; for without the diffused power and initiative associated with these institutions it is difficult to imagine a society in which freedom may be effectively preserved' (cited in Harvey 2005: 20).

Harvey traces the growth of neoliberal ideas to dominance through prolific voices in the media (often supported by neoliberal think-tank funds), via the business press such as the *Wall Street Journal*, and through the growth of prestigious business schools at Stanford and Harvard universities, which, generously funded by corporations and foundations, 'became centres of neoliberal orthodoxy from the moment they opened' (2005.: 54), becoming 'training grounds' for neoliberal changes in South America as well as at the IMF, the World Bank and the UN. Harvey notes that as early as 1982 Keynsian economics 'had been purged from the corridors of the IMF and the World Bank' (p. 93). He indicates also the opportunities that emerged in media and the new information industries.

> Rupert Murdoch . . . is not above or outside particular state powers, but by the same token he wields considerable influence via his media interests in politics in Britain, the US, and Australia. All 247 of the supposedly independent editors of his newspapers worldwide supported the US invasion of Iraq.
>
> (Harvey 2005: 34–5)

Given this assemblage of educational, economic, political and media institutions behind neoliberal policy, Harvey argues that more than 30 years of 'neoliberal freedoms' have produced immense concentrations of corporate power:

> With disproportionate influence over the media and the political process this class (with Rupert Murdoch and *Fox News* in the lead) has both the incentive and the power to persuade us that we are all better off under a neoliberal regime of freedoms.
>
> (p. 38)

The 'construction of consent'

Harvey's neoliberal critique does not rely on conspiracy theories around individuals. For him it is the embedding of key power-holding individuals in *systemic* change that occurs at crisis moments in the structural economy – in this case the economic breakdown into stagflation of international capitalist economies during the 1960s and 1970s.

Like Stuart Hall and John Berger, Harvey draws on Italian political theorist Antonio Gramsci for his notion of 'constructing consent', particularly Gramsci's distinction between 'common sense' and 'good sense':

> Common sense is constructed out of long-standing practices of cultural socialization often rooted deep in regional or national traditions. It is not the same as the 'good sense' that can be constructed out of critical engagement with the issues of the day. Common sense can, therefore, be profoundly misleading, obfuscating or disguising real problems under cultural prejudices . . . The

word 'freedom' resonates within the common-sense understanding of Americans so widely that Bush could retrospectively justify the Iraq war. Gramsci therefore concluded that political questions become 'insoluble' when 'disguised as cultural ones'.

(p. 39)

Co-constructing images of consent: 'Miss Shock and Awe'

Harvey's analysis, as a critical realist, is about the deep historical structures of neoliberalism and says little of images. But two key features of Harvey's account deserve further examination in relation to the images of 'Shock and Awe'. The first feature is Harvey's linking of neoliberal ideology empirically and strategically to an enormous widening of the gap between wealth and poverty within the US and internationally. The share of the national income among the top one per cent in the US and the UK soared. '[T]he evidence strongly suggests that the neoliberal turn is in some way and to some degree associated with the restoration or reconstruction of the power of the economic elites' (p. 19).

If we follow Harvey's critique of neoliberalism, we would see the militarized images of 'Shock and Awe' as just one part of the 'shock therapy' delivered to the world on behalf of economic and political elites, 'with Rupert Murdoch and *Fox News* in the lead' (p. 38). Paul Rutherford's book *Weapons of Mass Destruction: Marketing the War Against Iraq* examines this further in the media context, arguing that Fox News ratings success, with 'its brand of war coverage, full of bombast and vigour and patriotism', was 'a marketing triumph' (Rutherford 2004: 106), but one with undemocratic implications. All US TV networks, Rutherford argues, 'were infected with a bad dose of patriotism', but Fox News was even more 'pronounced' and 'supportive' of the 'America First Position' (p. 97). Fox emphatically followed what Rutherford describes as the White House technique of 'viral marketing', where Pentagon-mandated terms like 'collateral damage', 'war of liberation', 'Shock and Awe' and 'coalition forces' became automatic television language. Thus Pentagon terminology circulated as 'common sense' through television, 'not just because of the official briefings, but because it was used by anchors, analysts, and reporters . . . The Pentagon had left its mark on the vocabulary of journalism' (p. 64).

This 'natural' convergence of the interests of economic, political and military elites is a key part of Harvey's emphasis on the construction of consent in the US, as it is of Rutherford's who says of the Iraq war: 'Now the state and the various elites, bureaucratic as well as political, business as well as moral, employ the images and the rhetoric of advocacy and public relations to secure the success of their public goods' (p. 112).

In Rutherford's analysis, while Iraq's supposed weapons of mass destruction were bogus, weapons of mass persuasion were used by the US; and democracy was hit by 'a torrent of lies, half-truths, infotainment and marketing' (p. 193). For Rutherford, TV's 'global torrent' and 'flood of images' was coupled with the 'viral marketing' of military language (pp. 10–11). The result was the construction of a brand; 'the good war, that was produced and sold by only one supplier, the United States' (p. 53).

Synergistically, Rutherford argues, the images of the Iraq War were promoted by US TV networks in what he terms as 'the elite collaboration of a "propaganda state"'. For Rutherford, this 'propaganda state' is the counter to democracy. It is 'grounded in the manipulation of symbols, images and words . . . rely[ing] more on spectacle and assertion than on argument' (p. 184). Like John Berger, he contrasts words (that engage the mind) and images (that stun the mind) (p. 115) and cites Baudrillard: 'Gaze at these images long enough and you enter a semi-rational state. Your mind might find it offensive but your senses sit back and enjoy *The Shock and Awe Show*' (p. 86).

The TV broadcasts of 21 March 2003, covering the opening of the 'Shock and Awe' attack on Baghdad, were 'spectacular . . . The tyranny of the visual' (p. 87).

> Now you could make out buildings, clusters of lights, fires and even smoke . . . Like a real place, yes, but a city afflicted by red boils . . . a skyscape full of smoke and destruction . . . akin to the apocalyptic paintings of Hieronymous Bosch, full of dark smudges and flashes of light. Except, unlike a Bosch painting, we did not see any bodies.
>
> (Rutherford 2004: 88–9)

Rutherford argues in his analysis of 'real-time' TV coverage of 'Shock and Awe' that the commodity brand 'good war' was written and imaged in line with the Pentagon script of high-tech war, 'sanitized, cleansed, the dead bodies and the devastation kept at the margins of the story' (p. 135). 'What the networks decided to define as news, the "reality" they manufactured, confirmed the Pentagon's ideal of a clean war. The news downplayed the issue of civilian casualties' (p. 100).

'Shock and Awe' attack on Baghdad, March 2003 © AAP

This is apparent if we examine a powerful 'Shock and Awe' (2003) image easily found on the internet – an image created by fans of Fox News reporter Jennifer Eccleston.

In terms of Hariman and Lucaites' emphasis on visual rhetoric, we notice that this image contains two different vectors of sight and movement. The fire clouds, even in the static image, are boiling and roiling. We can assume that in the actual Fox News footage from which this background was taken they swirled and burst out of frame on all sides. But the main vector of sight in the image is of direct address between the anchor reporter and the viewer. She looks straight at us, slightly smiling. In Hariman and Lucaites' Althuserian sense she is hailing the audience, interpellating them into the image via face-to-face interaction (2007). Rutherford emphasizes that about 80 per cent of 'Shock and Awe' reports focused on the correspondents alone like this, not interviewing anyone.

But there are two other figural resources used in this image to tie down the boiling clouds. First, the reporter's classical, Renaissance-style triangular figuration stabilizes an image otherwise out-of-control, occupying nearly half of it and confining the explosive background to two, also triangular, segments at the margins of the picture. Second, there are the institutional signifiers as to who owns and transmits the 'Shock and Awe' image. At the top left is the big title, FOX; and to the left of the reporter is a rotating logo, Fox News Channel. Most emphatically, beneath the reporter's image are the titles: WAR ON TERROR. JENNIFER ECCLESTON. MISS SHOCK AND AWE.

'War on Terror' is the justificatory Pentagon 'viral' anchorage, the synthesizing device for the image's apparent disparity between beautiful woman and violent attack on a foreign city. No matter that there was no link between Saddam Hussein and 9/11; the association of Iraq's leader, violence and terrorism was a regular explanation on Murdoch's Fox News for the invasion of Iraq. This social knowledge generated by months of government and media rhetoric was embedded here, anchoring the image. 'War on Terror' was on behalf of US homeland security and – with 'branded' humanitarian motives – for democracy in 'other' places.

'Jennifer Eccleston' is the face of that democracy, young, vigorous, intelligent, impeccably manicured, sensual, 'free' in her speech, representing the 'good war' things that the US military must protect, and which can also, benevolently, be exported to Iraq. Symptomatic of continuing emails on the Jennifer Eccleston fan website is the conjuncture of comments like 'What a pretty lady!', 'such a doll', 'just so damn sexy and cute' with others about her 'real', 'down-to-earth' physical mannerisms and intelligence. So, 'Frank on cape cod' says 'Jennifer Eccleston is an independent journalist and chooses to go to the hot spots and makes them hotter'. The common theme is of Fox sending her to 'hot spots'; while the repeated fan anxiety is for her to be safe and out of harm's way.

In addition, Scott (a fan) writes:

> I'm a lawyer from Cleveland, Ohio and I am ready to join the Marines for the chance to be near Jennifer Eccleston. A small price to pay. Jennifer possesses

all of the qualities that would give the word 'beautiful' a home if it jumped off the page of the dictionary and came to life.

(Eccleston 2010)

Our referencing of fans' emails, however, alerts us to the second key aspect of Harvey's analysis. This is Gramsci's emphasis that hegemonic relationships of 'consent' are constructed from below as well as above. This 'Shock and Awe' image was not 'just' from Fox. Rather, it is a photo-montage combination of elite and popular 'common sense'. It is in fact an Eccleston fan website photo-manipulation of two images. One is a standard Fox TV 'Shock and Awe' image of the Baghdad presidential compound under attack. The other is of Eccleston herself as news reporter, transferred to this image from another international Fox location.

In this manipulated combination the term 'Miss Shock and Awe' creates its own fan synthesis of the two propositions above it, 'War on Terror' and 'Jennifer Eccleston'. In the US culture that is being protected from the terrorists, 'Miss' is familiarly found in combination as 'Miss America' or 'Miss World'. Here this beautiful woman is indeed being offered as a fans' articulation of 'Miss America': 'Miss Shock and Awe'.

'Shock and Awe' had already become the media term for US retribution. It would rend with fire those who (allegedly) had struck New York with fire from the air on 9/11. It would purge monstrous dictators through flames and give birth to the phoenix of democracy. The Pentagon perspective of James Blake Miller, the 'Marlboro Marine' whom his commanding officer Major-General Richard F. Natonski described as 'one hell of a young man' (Sinco, 2007: 6), has here been augmented by some Eccleston male fans to include the female 'independence' and 'beauty' that the US military is supposedly protecting. 'Common sense', in Gramsci's usage, is renewed as Murdoch's television elite and these Eccleston fans co-construct a Fox employee as 'Miss Shock and Awe' to 'give the word "beautiful" a home'. We are reminded of Canadian academic Judy Rebick's comment on watching 'Shock and Awe' images: 'The thing I find most troubling is this kind of . . . sexual excitement . . . this thrill over the technology with no comprehension that people are dying' (cited in Rutherford 2004: 176).

We should emphasize that this positioning of Jennifer Eccleston is not her own, either personally or as a professional journalist working for CNN and NBC as well as Fox, and recently a Niemann Fellow in Journalism at Harvard University. Indeed, in what appears to be an interactive comment with the fan site, Eccleston – if the posting is authentic – comments 'I hope this is more about the accuracy and fairness of my reporting than about my hairstyle'. What we are suggesting is that the co-construction of 'hot-spot' journalism and the mobilization of female beauty as television news reporting style by both Fox and 'interactive' fans indicates how Gramscian notions of hegemony operate from 'above' and 'below'.

'Shock Doctrine' and 'Shock and Awe': Naomi's Klein's *Disaster Capitalism*

'Shock and Awe' in Iraq and the 'shock doctrine' of neoliberalism are integrally related in the work of public intellectual, Naomi Klein. Extracts from her book *The Shock Doctrine: The Rise of Disaster Capitalism* (2007a) were widely published, such as three sequential issues of the British *Guardian* in 10–12 September 2007. The second issue on Iraq appeared symbolically on the anniversary of 9/11, which is at the core of Klein's analysis because it was then, she argues, that Friedman's neo-liberal ideology gained entirely new ground. Reacting to the claim that September 11 changed everything by long-time friend of Freidman, Ed Feulner, president of the conservative think-tank, the Heritage Fund, Klein writes: 'Many naturally assumed that part of that change would be a re-evaluation of the radical anti-state agenda that Feulner and his ideological allies had been pushing for three decades, at home and around the world' (p. 295).

Klein argues that this 're-evaluation' should have looked at the 9/11 security failures resulting from neoliberal outsourcing of government-controlled services. Like Harvey, she notes that Reagan's attack on the air-traffic controllers union and his deregulation of the airlines in the 1980s was the 'first major victory of the Friedmanite counter-revolution in the United States' (p. 296). By 2001, the vast majority of the air travel procedures had been deregulated and downsized and the inspector-general of the transport department acknowledged after 9/11 that flight security had been skimped to keep costs down. This was followed by the 'terrorist anthrax' scare soon after 9/11 and by the revelation that the public could not be protected *en masse* because one private laboratory had been given exclusive rights to produce the vaccine against anthrax. Such bad publicity for the neoliberal move into privatization and deregulation seemed, Klein says, to presage a reaction. Furthermore, she adds:

> While CEOs were falling from their pedestals, unionised public sector workers – the villains of Friedman's counter-revolution – were rapidly ascending in the public's estimation . . . The uncontested heroes of September 11 were the blue-collar first responders – the New York firefighters, police and rescue workers, 403 of whom lost their lives.
>
> (Klein 2007a: 297)

Yet, far from being rolled back, neoliberal economics got a massive new 'economic shock therapy' from the White House when hundreds of billions of public money was channelled into contracts (some secret and some without normal scrutiny) for technology, media, communication, incarceration, engineering, education and health (p. 298; see also Urry 2010 on neoliberalism, climate change and the 'planet of excess').

The 'September 11 changed everything' mantra, Klein argues, disguised the ease with which private corporations could pursue their economic interests (p. 9). Whereas in the 1990s technology companies had trumpeted the wonders of a borderless world and the powers of IT to topple authoritarian governments, now post 9/11 the US itself was caught in a series of Feldman's 'risk-events'. So, Klein notes, the great promise of globalization – of dismantled borders – was replaced with increasing border surveillance produced by hi-tech corporations.

Outsourcing of state functions to private enterprise crossed all aspects of the 'war on terror'. As one example Klein notes the outsourcing of intelligence gathering by the CIA to private contractors given responsibility for interrogating war prisoners:

> If these freelance interrogators are to keep landing lucrative contracts, they must extract from prisoners the kind of 'actionable intelligence' their employers in Washington are looking for. It's a dynamic ripe for abuse: just as prisoners under torture will usually say anything to make the pain stop, contractors have a powerful economic incentive to use whatever techniques are necessary to produce the sought-after information, regardless of its reliability.
>
> (p. 305)

Klein's key theme about 'Disaster Capitalism' is that the 'war on terror' 'is limited by neither time nor space nor target' (p. 301). Although the sprawling nature of war on terror may make it militarily unwinnable, from an economic perspective it is 'not a flash-in-the-pan war that could potentially be won but a new and permanent fixture in the global economic architecture' (p.301). Yet, Klein argues, the 'fear and sense of peril' in the US, and the 'disaster capitalism' that has created it, have scarcely been analyzed. Debate has been restricted to individual cases of war profiteering, corruption and the failure of government adequately to oversee private contractors. Only rarely has debate been 'about the much broader and deeper phenomenon of what it means to be engaged in a fully privatised war built to have no end' (p. 306).

To Harvey's data about the colossal increase in wealth of CEOs under the neo-liberal regime, Klein adds her own eye-opening observations:

> While the CEOs of the top 34 defence contractors saw their income go up an average of 108 per cent between 2001 and 2005, chief executives at other large American companies averaged only 6 per cent over the same period.
>
> (p. 307)

Back to Iraq – and 'Shock and Awe'

Klein takes us from one colossal national trauma, 9/11, to another, the Iraq invasion. Entitled 'The erasing of Iraq', her 9/11 *Guardian* extract (2007b: 10–15) begins with 'Shock and Awe' and the conscription by the Pentagon of US news organizations:

> 'They're calling it A-Day,' began a report on CBS News that aired two months before the war began. 'A as in airstrike that is so devastating they would leave Saddam's soldiers unable or unwilling to fight.' . . . The anchor,

Dan Rather, ended the telecast with the disclaimer, 'We assure you this report contains no information that the Defence Department thinks could help the Iraqi military.' He could have gone further: the report, like so many others in this period, was an integral part of the Department of Defence's strategy – fear up. Iraqis, who picked up the terrifying reports on contraband satellites or in phone calls from relatives abroad, spent months imagining the horrors of Shock and Awe. The phrase itself became a potent psychological weapon.

(Klein 2007a: 333–4)

Then war came to Baghdad. On the night of 28 March 2003, as US troops got close to the city, the communication ministry was hit by 'precision' bombs, while four Baghdad telephone exchanges were destroyed by bunker buster bombs. These targeted attacks continued, so that by 2 April there was barely a telephone still working in Baghdad. Klein says that many Iraqis viewed the destruction of the phone system as most 'psychologically wrenching' because they could not contact loved ones or reassure relatives living abroad (p. 335). She quotes *The Guardian's* April 4 report:

'There was no audible explosion . . . but in an instant, an entire city of 5 million people was plunged into an awful, endless night' . . . Baghdad residents could not speak to each other, hear each other or see outside . . . [T]he entire city was shackled and hooded.

(p. 335)

Next came the erasure of Iraqi culture when the National Museum in Baghdad was pillaged, as US soldiers stood by. Hundreds of looters smashed or stole ancient ceramics and other antiquities. But, in Klein's analysis, US officials saw things differently. Peter McPherson was quoted as saying that he was unworried by seeing Iraqis taking state property. McPherson, a former bureaucrat in the Reagan administration, whose job was to privatize state assets and reduce the size of government, termed 'pillage a form of public sector "shrinkage"' (p. 337).

Similarly, John Agresto, director of higher education reconstruction for the occupation in Iraq said the stripping of universities and the education ministry was 'the opportunity for a clean start' (p. 338). As a bizarrely potent example of US-style cultural 'clean start', Klein refers us to 'the love shack' where detainees at Guantanamo Bay were taken when it was finally decided to release them. In 'the love shack', as one bewildered detainee reported to Klein, 'We would get to watch DVDs, eat McDonald's, eat Pizza Hut and basically chill out' (p. 338). Klein comments:

It's hard to believe – but . . . that was pretty much Washington's game plan for Iraq: shock and terrorise the entire country, deliberately ruin its infrastructure, do nothing while its culture and history are ransacked, then make it all OK with an unlimited supply of cheap household appliances and imported junk food . . . all of Iraq was going to be bought off with . . . pop culture – that, at least, was the Bush administration's idea of a postwar plan.

(p. 339)

But, Klein adds, the Bush policy did not work. 'Countries, like people, don't reboot to zero with a good shock; they just break and keep on breaking' (p. 372). So now, Klein argues, the occupiers showed the darker side of disaster capitalism. The Iraqi occupation had begun with claims for a new 'clean war': the initially imaged 'Shock and Awe'.

> It didn't take long, however, for the quest for cleanliness to slip into talk about 'pulling Islamism up from the root' in Sadr City or Najaf and removing 'the cancer of radical Islam' from Fallujah and Ramadi – what was not clean would be scrubbed out by force. That is what happens with projects to build model societies in other people's countries . . . It is only when the people who live on the land refuse to abandon their past that the dream of a clean slate morphs into its doppelganger, the scorched earth – only then that the dream of total creation morphs into a campaign of total destruction.
>
> (p. 373–4)

Thus, Klein's account of Fallujah's '*Marlboro Marine*' image is militarily continuous with her understanding of 'Shock and Awe': as its doppelganger. Indeed, it is a 'double' also in Mitchell's sense of state/Christian ambivalence, 'shuttling between sovereignty and abjection . . . criminal and martyr' (Mitchell 2011: 159).

8 Abu Ghraib, regimes of looking and risk

Icon, index and symbol

Hooded man on box at Abu Ghraib, April 2004 © Press Association

A hooded man is dressed in a black robe, arms outstretched in a pose that many commentators have compared to a crucifixion. His hands are attached to wires plugged into an electric socket, and he is standing on a box. He covers the entire front page of the *Daily Mail* on 30 April 2004 with the accompanying headline, 'Tortured, abused and humiliated . . . The barbaric images that shame

America'. He also appears on the cover of numerous international magazines, including *Der Spiegel* on 19 April with the headline 'The folly of Baghdad'; *The Economist* on 8 May 2004, 'Resign, Rumsfeld' and the *Guardian Weekend* on 18 December 2004 summarizing the 'year in words and pictures'. We call him the 'crucifix man', and on our count he is the most regularly reproduced iconic image to have emerged from Abu Ghraib prison in Iraq. For W.J.T. Mitchell, 'The Hooded Man of Abu Ghraib, accused terrorist, torture victim, anonymous clone, faceless Son of Man, will remain the icon of our time for the foreseeable future' (2011: 167).

Another image from Abu Ghraib, appearing at the same time (April/May 2004) is of US Army Specialist, Lynndie England, grinning to camera, cigarette jauntily erect in her mouth, as she poses, the thumbs of both her hands 'cocked', as she points an imaginary gun at the (pixillated) genitals of a hooded naked Iraqi detainee. He has been forced to masturbate while standing with other naked prisoners in front of her.

Again from Abu Ghraib are three more images that readers will remember. One is of a pyramid of naked Iraqis piled up for the 'trophy shot' poses of US Army 'specials' Graner and Harman. They, like England, grin straight at us from behind the abject pyramid. Another photograph is of England again, standing in her military fatigues, and looking nonchalantly not at us but at a naked Iraqi prisoner lying on the prison floor. She is holding a dog leash. The other end is around his neck. A third image is of a totally naked prisoner, his body cowering into the bars of his prison cell as US soldiers threaten him with savage dogs.

Each of these images became instantly recognisable so quickly and so powerfully that each generated its own sub-genre of political cartoons in the media. For example, in the British press alone during the 'Abu Ghraib month' of May 2004, the following cartoons drew on the crucifix man:

- Dave Brown's 'After Botticeli's Birth of Venus' showing the hooded but otherwise naked man emerging from the sea like Venus, his arms in the same position as hers, but his body wired and standing on a box (*Independent*, 1 May 2004: 38).
- Trog's cartoon of Blair standing electrically-wired to the Capitol building flying the Stars and Stripes (*Sunday Telegraph*, 2 May 2004: 22).
- Dave Brown's cartoon of Rumsfeld, sitting on a naked, bound and hooded Iraqi prisoner while watching Bush's 'apology' on Al-Jazeera TV and waving his hand to the crucifix man who is holding a small internal aerial behind the TV set as the Secretary of State says 'Up a bit . . . Up a bit . . .' (*Independent*, 6 May 2004: 23).
- Nicola's cartoon of the crucifix man standing on his box, wired to a plug labelled 'CIA', accompanying an article by Vikram Dodd, 'Torture by the book: the pattern of abuse of Iraqi prisoners follows established CIA interrogation techniques' (*Guardian*, 8 May 2004: 23).
- S's transcoding of the crucifix man as the Statue of Liberty holding her flame with wired arms, to accompany an article by Ariel Dorfman which says

'torture . . . craves the abrogation of our capacity to imagine someone else's suffering' (*Guardian*, 8 May 2004: 20).

• Peter Brooks' cartoon of the crucifix man replacing the statue on top of the US Capitol dome, his hood, cape and wires illuminated by a full moon behind him in the black night of 'The Haunting' (*The Times*, 13 May 2004: 24).

Each of the other Abu Ghraib images generated cartoon sub-genres, and these iconic photographs frequently illustrated major pieces by public intellectuals in the British press. For example, Susan Sontag's article 'The photos are US' uses the crucifix man and the Lynndie England dog leash images to support her conclusion that

As Mr Rumsfeld acknowledged, it's hard to censor soldiers overseas who don't write letters home, as in the old days, that can be opened by military censors who ink out unacceptable lines, but, instead, function like tourists . . . The administration's efforts to withhold pictures will continue.

(Sontag 2004a)

It seemed evident to many people that images from Abu Ghraib became iconic in the particular sense of powerfully deconstructing US moral authority in Iraq. For example, a Steve Bell *Guardian* cartoon has a US officer in court breaking a camera and shredding its film while another soldier stands to attention. In the cartoon the 'trophy shot' image of the abject, piled naked Abu Ghraib bodies is being smashed over his head, as the judge pronounces, 'For Crimes Against Photography You Are Hereby Sentenced . . .' (*Guardian*, 20 May 2004: 26).

Following on from Mitchell's 'cloning' analysis of the crucifix man in Chapter 7, this chapter investigates contrasting academic theories about the shocking images of Abu Ghraib. Here we draw particularly on recent feminist theory (including differing positions for analyzing these images) and on contemporary risk theory.

Regimes of looking: Feminist theory and Abu Ghraib

In her co-edited book *War and Terror: Feminist Perspectives* (Alexander and Hawkesworth 2008), Mary Hawkesworth argues that traditional academic analyses of war, women and indigenous people tend to situate war atrocities in a discourse of 'failed states', a definition which justifies Western military intervention on ostensibly universal humanitarian grounds. Further, in the social sciences as in the popular imagination 'Race and sex are typically construed as individual attributes or demographic characteristics . . . understood as biological traits rather than as political constructs' (Hawkesworth 2008: 2). Hawkesworth says that their book 'differs from all these theorizations by focussing on practices of racialization and gendering in armed conflict, demonstrating how wars and various modes of terrorism produce, naturalize, and maintain racial, ethnic, and gender hierarchies' (p. 2).

It is a key part of her book's argument that the production of racialized policies and gendered hierarchies is systemic, not only in war and terror, but as part of 'the routine practices of liberal democratic, neoliberal, and Islamic orders' (p. 30); and it is part of Hawkesworth's conceptual aim as editor is to explain and promote the local agency by women in the face of Islamist or neoliberal practices.

> Highlighting women's agency even under conditions of dire constraint, the articles challenge traditional stereotypes of women as perennial victims, perpetual peacemakers, or embodiments of nation that men seek to protect and defend. Contributors demonstrate how women negotiate their survival, enact resistance to oppressive and supposedly liberating forces, mobilize to protest war and counter its effects, participate in redefining war, and appropriate war discourses to advance their own political agenda.
>
> (Hawkesworth 2008: 5)

A second part of the book's conceptual project is to show, however, how hegemonic patriarchal and racist discourses *appropriate* this agency. This tension between 'agency' and 'control' theories in the book is apparent when we read Dorit Naaman on Palestinian women suicide bombers. For Naaman, while these women may politicize their actions in new ways by emphasizing the Israeli occupation of their territories, 'Western accounts construct these political agents as deluded, manipulated, disgraced or depressed' (Hawkesworth 2008: 20). Similarly Arab media and politicians 'frame the actions of women suicide bombers in ways that minimize or subvert the overt confrontation of gender politics present in the women's own narratives and actions' (Naaman 2008: 131). Ethnicity and gender operate together in this tension between local/global control and agency.

In her chapter 'The politics of pain and the uses of torture', Liz Philipose emphasizes even more than Naaman the 'control' rather than 'agency' side of the book's conceptual dilemma. She focuses on state terror tactics in US military detention centres like Abu Ghraib and on the circulation of torture photographs. 'The global circulation of the Abu Ghraib photographs depicting detainees being tortured by US soldiers played a critical role in the cultivation of a new regime of looking' (Philipose 2008: 391).

Philipose draws on Foucault to challenge the dominantly racialized 'regimes of looking' which, she says, equate surface difference (as in dark skin colour) with the moral judgment of victims as 'suspects' at Abu Ghraib and Guantanamo Bay. In the case of Abu Ghraib detainees:

> Rather than a desperate human being in desperate circumstances, the terrorist is constructed as cunning, violent and operating by stealth . . . Medicojuridical discourses routinely dispense with the complexities of specific histories of struggle that might explain particular instances of violence. Instead they posit hidden truths – violent propensities, dispositions, inclinations lodged deep within the subject – that account for observable behaviour.
>
> (Philipose 2008: 397–8)

Thus whereas Barthes' emphasis is on mythical images suppressing the histories of individual struggle, Foucault, in Philipose's usage, explores the 'scientific' tendency of modern professions like medicine, psychology and law to suppress specific histories of struggle by finding 'deep' psychological and biological truths within the individual human subject. The main theoretical thrust of Philipose's analysis is a combination of feminism, Foucault and post-colonial understanding of the 'Other' (see Chapter 10), whereby surface appearances, whether of the black man or the terrorist, are seen to reveal deeper, violent propensities.

Her central methodological approach is inter-textual. Philipose draws attention to the interpretations by Susan Sontag (2004b) and Dora Apel (2005) who note similarities in content and effect between the photographs of lynching circulated widely through the US in the early twentieth century and those of Abu Ghraib. In each case 'the photographs document the extra-judicial infliction of violence'.

> In each situation, whiteness is affirmed and blackness is abjectified. In each case, masculinity and sexuality are targeted in ways that privilege the white, hypermasculine racial order of the United States . . . There is rarely a photo of a lynching that does not include a group of onlookers, who typically look directly into the camera . . . Traces of lynching iconography appear in the Abu Ghraib photos, which display detainees as . . . naked and sexualized. The photos include triumphant poses of the torturers . . . The use of dogs by lynch mobs to capture African American men is recalled in the Abu Ghraib photos, where dogs were used to intimidate shackled detainees.
>
> (Philipose 2008: 400–2)

In exploring the sexual humiliation of both lynch-mob victims and the tortured detainees at Abu Ghraib, Philipose brings together feminist gendering analysis with the concept of racialized 'regimes of looking'.

> Lynching iconography is apparent in the photos of detainees who are meta-phorically castrated and emasculated through sexual humiliation. Several of the Abu Ghraib photos depict men who are forced to wear women's under-wear on their heads, to touch one another, to simulate fellatio and masturba-tion, and to be unclothed. Sexualized violence feminizes male detainees by forcing them to act homosexual sex scenes of simulated fellatio.
>
> (p. 403)

In contrast to this racialized representation of abject and dehumanized sexuality among the detainees, Philipose argues that other circulated photographs of Lyn-ndie England and Charles Graner having sex with each other 'reassert the heter-onormativity' (p. 404) of the patriotic white US soldiers.

The iconic Abu Ghraib photographs – of the dominant, heterosexual white woman, Lynndie England pointing to the masturbating, 'deviant', Arab men; of the abject pyramid of detainees' dark, naked bodies piled high and emasculated as trophies before the heteronormative power of Graner; of the masculinized Eng-land as 'dominatrix' holding her prostrate, naked male prisoner on a dog leash; of the cowering Iraqi detainee before dogs (which have always hunted black slaves)

– represent in Philipose's analysis white, heterosexual power and moral superiority over the 'black/terrorist' enemy of the US nation.

> The complex interpellations proffered by orientalism, terrorism, lynchings, and whiteness mingle in the Abu Ghraib photos to produce a new regime of visibility . . . Standing powerfully beside, behind, and sometimes on top of prisoners, holding leashes and directing the scene, the men and women of the US military are masculinized.
>
> (p. 408)

One of the crucifix man photographs released from Abu Ghraib includes Graner supervising the torture, with camera. These iconic images, Philipose suggests, represent masculinized US soldiers as

> agents of a legitimate state empowered to use the law to serve national interests and military necessity. By contrast, the victims are arrested under conditions of lawlessness – albeit lawlessness created by the US invasion . . . Circulating globally, the photos of their abjection contain [a] new racial grammar [that] erases any possible empathy for the tortured body.
>
> (p. 409)

In Chapter 7 we examined theories of media and economic surveillance, via Feldman, Mitchell, Harvey and Klein, which tended to leave the viewer passive in the face of the power of ideology and visual rhetoric. This tendency has been extended in this chapter where, despite some feminists' focus on human agency in specific historical situations, Liz Philipose's article about the images from Abu Ghraib puts almost all its emphasis on the interpellation of the viewer within racialized and sexualized regimes of visuality (as does Feldman (2004b) in his own analysis of the Abu Ghraib images).

This emphasis on the total dominance of the visual regimes of looking is made even stronger by Philipose's reliance on feminist appropriation of Lacan's psychoanalytical theories, leaving little space for resistant agency. Hence her conclusion is that the viewer can have no 'possible empathy for that tortured body' (2008: 409). In contrast, in the same book Denov and Gervais analyze the agency of sexually exploited women in the civil war in Sierra Leone (2008). But Philipose explores no such military agency in the case of Lynndie England. Nor does she consider England's 'trailer park' background which helped propel her into the army. England's interviews where she described herself as a sex-toy of the brutally masculinist Graner, are not mentioned. In Philipose's analysis England is simply 'masculinized'. She is a 'White' image of heteronormativity, an unwitting function of a racialized regime of looking.

In the remainder of this chapter we turn to academic theories that begin to challenge this emphasis on 'interpellation' that dominated Chapter 7 and this chapter thus far.

The 'indexical quality of the images': The 'near-distant' and Abu Ghraib

Kirsty Best points to the power of the Abu Ghraib images to *disrupt* surveillance ideologies. She argues that the potent Abu Ghraib images taken by US soldiers on digital cameras created a 'problematic excess' for other, more governmentally controlled images of the Iraq War (2004: 12):

> [T]he indexical quality of the images coupled with their inexplicability . . . worked positively to disrupt more flattering and heroic images of warfare. The very fact that they were taken and distributed by soldiers themselves, the perpetrators of the acts, leaves a trace on the images which may serve to affect viewers more deeply than journalistic depictions of civilian damage and bloodshed.
>
> (ibid.)

Best is aware that experience itself is already mediated and framed by particular discourses. But she is challenging the pessimistic view of other academics about the supposed 'refusal to know' of contemporary US publics. Our own examples here are Feldman's notion of 'risk-event' wars that create 'spectatorship ideologies of inattention and distraction for the televisual witness' (2004a: 78) and Philipose's US public without 'any possible empathy for that tortured body' (2008: 409). Best argues instead for a determined and desperate 'drive to meaning' among spectators of these media risk-events that can take the path of alternative ways of knowing: via identity, affect, or visceral ethics.

Clearly, the analyses of Philipose and Best, both feminist theorists, are incompatible in terms of interpreting the degree of public empathy with the torture images from Abu Ghraib. Philipose applies her analysis to the entire (white) nation. 'These racialized anxieties are national anxieties, and if we take the nation as the embodiment of masculine values of virility and potency . . . these are also anxieties about the state of masculinity in the twenty-first-century United States' (p. 409). In contrast, Best argues that the Abu Ghraib images, drawing on a new media form, established an *indexical* 'near-distant', soldier/photographer-to-audience relationship of the prison images, which allowed viewers of the images to 'readily relate to the pain, suffering and confusion permeating the images of a tortured body' (2004: 10).

Yet Best does not explore her central concept of indexicality. Two who do are Judith Butler in her book *Frames of War*, and British MA Photography graduate William Sadowski who took this issue further in his 2009 exhibition *Surface Tension*.

Framing Abu Ghraib: Icons of 'others whose loss is no loss'

Whereas Best focuses on the indexical content of the Abu Ghraib images, Butler's *Frames of War: When is life grievable?* is more interested in the photographic forms which present indexical content. She says 'I want to understand how the *frames* that allocate the recognizability of certain figures of the human are themselves linked with broader *norms* that determine what will and will not be a grievable life' (2010: 63–4). Although she notes that her view is not new about 'how we respond to the suffering of others . . . [which] depends upon a certain field of perceptible reality having already been established' by photographs (p. 64), her use of the words 'grievable life' takes the observation into Butler's own sophisticated sense of affect and ethics.

In her introductory chapter 'Precarious Life, Grievable Life', Butler says she is

> seeking to draw attention to the epistemological problem raised by this issue of framing: the frames through which we apprehend or, indeed, fail to apprehend the lives of others as lost or injured (lose-able or injurable) are politically saturated. They are themselves operations of power. They do not unilaterally decide the conditions of appearance but their aim is nevertheless to delimit the sphere of appearance itself,
>
> (Butler 2010: 1)

When, she argues in her book, the Israeli military kill children by shelling their schools and justify this by claiming they were used as a 'human shield' by Hamas; or when many people in the US feel enormous emotional affect for the death of some 3000 of its citizens in the 9/11 attacks, but little or nothing at all about the hundreds of thousands of citizens killed after the US invasion and occupation of Iraq, the issue of 'grievability' is focussed. Not to grieve at the precariousness and death of innocent others, Butler argues, is not to 'know' about them, an epistemological deficit. But the problem is also ontological:

> since the question at issue is: *What is a life?* The 'being' of life is constituted through selective means; as a result, we cannot refer to this 'being' outside of the operations of power, and we must make more precise and specific the mechanisms of power through which life is produced.
>
> (ibid.)

Images are, for Butler, one of those key mechanisms of power. In her chapter, 'Torture and the Ethics of Photography' she takes issue with Susan Sontag's claim

> made repeatedly throughout her writings, that the photograph cannot by itself offer an interpretation, that we need captions and written analysis to supplement the discrete and punctual image. In her view, the image can only affect us, not provide us with an understanding of what we see
>
> (p. 67)

Yet, Butler says:

> Recent war photography departs significantly from the conventions of war photojournalism that were at work thirty or forty years ago, where the

photographer or camera person would attempt to enter the action through angles and modes of access that sought to expose the war in ways that no government had planned. Now, the state works on the field of perception and, more generally, the field of representability, in order to control affect – in anticipation of the way affect is not only structured by interpretation but structures interpretation as well.

(p. 72)

The embedding of journalists in the military units during the Iraq War was an operation of power over the visual where the 'mandating of what can be seen – a concern with regulating content – was supplemented by control' over the *formal* perspective through which destructive war could be seen. 'By regulating perspective as well as content the state authorities were clearly interested in regulating the visual modes of participation in the war' (p. 65). Embedded reporting, Butler says:

> implies that reporters working under such conditions agree not to make the mandating of perspective *itself* a topic to be reported and discussed; hence these reporters were offered access to the war only on the condition that their gaze remain restricted to the established parameters of designated action.
>
> (p. 64)

Even when soldiers themselves took the photographs, as at Abu Ghraib, Butler argues it was an implicitly embedded view. 'The camera angle, the frame, the posed subjects, all suggest that those who took the photographs were actively involved in the perspective of the war, crafting, commending and validating a point of view' (p. 65).

Via this framing, the 'photograph itself becomes a structuring scene of interpretation . . . The photograph is not merely a visual image awaiting interpretation; it is itself actively interpreting, sometimes forcibly so' (pp. 67, 71). Inhumane force was being used, yet there was apparent consensus among the US soldiers before and behind the camera.

> There are photos of bodies bound together, of individuals killed, of forced fellatio, of dehumanizing degradation, and they were taken unobstructed. The field of vision is clear. No one is seen lunging in front of the camera to intercept the view. No one is shackling the photographer and throwing him or her in jail for participating in a crime. This is torture in plain view, in front of the camera, even for the camera. It is centred action, with the torturers regularly turning towards the camera to make sure their own faces are shown, even as the faces of the tortured are mainly shrouded.
>
> (p. 84)

Furthermore, Butler argues, it

> seems clear that these images were circulated, enjoyed, consumed, and communicated without there being any accompanying sense of moral outrage. How this particular banalization of evil took place, and why the photos failed to cause alarm, or did so only too late . . . are [questions] doubtless crucial to ask.
>
> (p. 91)

Butler's answer includes a crucial notion of homophobic *collusion* between aspects of Islam and US military culture.

> Paradoxically, this may be a situation in which the Islamic taboo against homosexual acts works in perfect concert with the homophobia within the US military. The scene of torture that includes coerced homosexual acts, and seeks to decimate personhood through that coercion, presumes that for both tortured and tortured, homosexuality represents the destruction of one's being.
>
> (p. 90)

Sexualized images were, then, freely circulated within this military culture, and both those soldiers photographed and photographing knew it would be so. As Butler says, the 'soldiers and security personnel photographed are clearly at ease with the camera, indeed playing to it' (p. 88). The problem here, she adds, is not 'the practice of eroticized seeing . . . but the moral indifference of the photograph coupled with its investment in the continuation and reiteration of the scene as a visual icon' (p.91). The astonishing number of these photographs – some seen but most still unseen by publics – suggests their repetitively iconic status within US military culture; as ubiquitous and as emblematic of dominant meanings, perhaps, as icons of deities and saints in a medieval European town.

Dominant norms and the image-frames that convey them are, Butler says, the 'first two hinges' of this culture. But her third hinge 'is suffering itself' (p. 75).

> There are ways of framing that will bring the human into view in its frailty and precariousness, that will allow us to stand for the value and dignity of human life, to react with outrage when lives are degraded or eviscerated without regard for their value as lives. And then there are frames that foreclose responsiveness, where this activity of foreclosure is effectively and repeatedly performed by the frame itself – its own negative action, as it were, toward what will not be explicitly represented. For alternative frames to exist and permit another kind of content would perhaps communicate a kind of suffering that might lead to an alteration of our political assessment of the current wars. For photographs to communicate in this way, they must have a transitive function, making us susceptible to ethical responsiveness.
>
> (p. 77)

This quest for 'alternative frames' is similar to John Berger's description of a few 'alternative' photographs that he admires. For Butler, clearly the 'iconic' circulation of the Abu Ghraib images within the US military operate as frames of 'foreclosure . . . repeatedly performed'. But – and this is where Butler moves beyond the description of dominant visual regimes of looking we discussed earlier in the chapter – the Abu Ghraib images leaked out of the total institution of military life.

> The photos have clearly travelled outside the original scene, left the hands of the photographer, or turned against the photographer him or herself, even perhaps vanquished his or her pleasure. It gave rise to a different gaze than the one that would ask for a repetition of the scene.
>
> (p. 92)

As Butler says, the photographs, circulated first within the prison, then by the world's media, have functioned in a variety of ways:

> as an incitement to brutality within the prison itself, as a threat of shame for the prisoners, as a chronicle of a war crime, as a testimony to the radical unacceptability of torture, and as archival and documentary work made available on the internet or displayed in museums in the US, including galleries and public spaces in a host of venues.
>
> (p. 92)

In different venues the images were engaged by different discourses, and changed 'their meaning depending on the context in which they are shown, and the purpose for which they are invoked' (p. 80).

In military courts 'the photo is considered evidence from within a frame of potential or actual legal proceedings and is already framed within the discourse of law and of truth' (p. 81). In parts of the world's media, the photographs have 'become iconic for the way that the US government, in alliance with Britain, spurned the Geneva Conventions . . . governing the fair treatment of prisoners of war' (p. 79). The venue where Sontag, in Butler's estimation, condensed and elaborated her feeling of outrage over the images and her frustration that they failed 'to show her how to transform that affect into effective political action', was at the curated Abu Ghraib photograph exhibition at the International Center for Photography, New York.

For Butler, too, of course, there is another venue for making meanings about Abu Ghraib: in her book which questions 'When is life grievable?' Rarely, she says, does the

> operation of mandatory and dramaturgical framing that is embedded in state and military regulatory regimes become part of what is seen . . . But when it does, we are led to interpret the interpretation that has been imposed upon us, developing our analysis into a social critique of regulatory and censorious power.
>
> (p. 72)

She draws on Barthes' notion of the photographic image having the capacity to work in the tense of the future anterior. When we look, after the event, at a photograph of a prisoner waiting to be hanged, or perhaps of a loved parent active before death, or of Abu Ghraib prisoners humiliated by soldiers in prison recognising they will be named and shamed after release, we are in that future anterior situation, Butler says (quoting Barthes), where the

> photograph relays less the present moment than the perspective, the pathos, of a time at which 'this will have been' . . . [E]very photographic portrait speaks in at least two temporal modes, both as a chronicle of what has been and protentive certainty about what will have been
>
> (p. 97)

This is a central way in which a photograph conveys grievability over the precariousness of the human life we share with all others.

This, Butler argues, is a condition of 'co-constitution that implies the need for a reconceptualization of the ontology of life itself' (p. 76), which can offer us the chance to see the precariousness of ourselves symbiotically amidst the precariousness of others. In contrast, war photographs determined by what she calls the 'forcible dramaturgy of the state' (p. 73) encourage us to 'not see' the precariousness of the 'other'.

> This 'not seeing' . . . that is the condition of seeing, became the visual norm, . . . a national norm, one conducted by the photographic frame in the scene of torture. In this case [of Abu Ghraib], the circulation of the image outside the scene of its production has broken up the mechanism of disavowal, scattering grief and outrage in its wake.
>
> (p. 100)

In particular, what is specific to the Abu Ghraib photographs – the potentially radicalizing perceptual content which could be liberated by their multiple venues of public disclosure – was the fact that while the torturers were full-face to camera, the tortured faces were hooded or glazed. Drawing on Sontag's point that the dead are profoundly disinterested in us, Butler concludes: 'This rebuff to visual consumerism that comes from the shrouded head, the averted glance, the glazed eyes, this indifference to us performs an auto-critique of the role of the photograph within media consumption' (p. 100). Extending Hariman and Lucaites' point about iconic images that 'just won't go away' (2007: 202), Butler argues that these are photographs that 'haunt' us (she adopts here Sontag's word about her own emotion) 'because the photograph acts on us in part through outliving the life it documents; it establishes in advance the time in which the loss will be acknowledged as a loss' (2010: 98). It contains the potential power – a resistant power to the 'forcible dramaturgy of the state' – to convert, in Butler's terms, racist icons of the 'ungrievable' into icons of human grief (p. 24). As Butler says, 'others whose loss is no loss, and who remain ungrievable' (p. 24) here enter shared frames 'that bring the human into view in its frailty and precariousness' (p. 77).

Index and icon: Lynndie England as holograph

William Sadowski's exhibition exploring the trauma of Abu Ghraib images on wider social consciousness does this in a different way. It was held in a disused building in Park Crescent Place, Brighton in 2009. To reach his Abu Ghraib holographs, including one of England, thumbs and cigarette cocked, the viewer had to push through the stable door entrance, then through a vestibule to a very small curtained, windowless room. In the dark the viewer was invited to find the Lynndie holograph with a torch, the image moving, dissolving and escaping resolution until a high torch position revealed the familiar icon of England, signified by those thumbs, cigarette, body posture and military fatigues.

Sadowski comments on this process of leading the viewer to the icon and yet breaking up this image:

> Using holograms, I reduced the images to their basic component, an ephemeral outline that hovers on the edge of consciousness. Following this work I went to the US in February to interview Lynndie England . . . The interview material has been compiled into book form alongside other imagery of the American landscape.
>
> (Sadowski 2009)

In the vestibule Sadowski displayed a naturalistic colour photograph of 'the American landscape'. It is of a dead deer, which he describes as US road kill photographed a few yards from where he interviewed England. The viewer watches this image while listening on headphones to extracts from the England taped interview. The image/sound juxtaposition suggests that England herself is 'road kill', like the deer Sadowski found dumped unceremoniously and disregarded after being hit by the 'civilization' of cars just out of frame in his photograph. This 'machine-like' civilization (on the road in the US, in the prison in Iraq) is one intended meaning of this image.

But there are also the 'everyday' meanings conveyed by England's audio-taped voice: about the control Graner had over her; about her experiential sense that 'It was cold' when the photographs were taken; about the awful prison location where 'you had the sewage smell and you had the smoke smell, fires going on around, stuff got blown up'; about her unhappy web interaction with Lynndie England hate sites. Sadowski says that he is trying, visually via the viewer's interaction with the holograph and audibly via these multiple identities that England's interview voice conveys, to draw away from the settled meanings conveyed by the iconic image of her at Abu Ghraib.

Sadowski's exhibition originated in his MA Photography course at Brighton University. Course leader Joanna Lowry positioned the work of all her photography students via ontological theories of index and icon generated by French film scholar André Bazin.

> Bazin, mediating upon the particular ontology of the photographic image, described it as being poised 'between the hallucinatory and the real'. And in

that coining of a phrase he identified quite precisely that inter-space occupied by the photograph, in the narrowest of spaces between the mute objectivity of the world transcribed by a machine and the return of that world to us in the form of an image, invested with imagination and desire.

(Lowry 2009: 4)

Lowry argues that traditional approaches to this ambivalence of the photographic image between 'the iconic and the indexical, the allegorical and the documentary, the simulacrum and the referential' (p. 4) tend to push us towards one or other pole of this ontological binary of 'hallucinatory and real'.

Bazin's designation, however, of the space 'between' suggests a more subtle and open-ended destination for the photographic, in a space that, though it may be literally paper-thin, is nevertheless, in its lack of certainty, available to be negotiated, investigated and explored. His evocation of the hallucinatory reminds us of the complex ways in which the image is tethered to the workings of the imagination, to the deep swell of the currents of the unconscious mind, and the powerful compulsion of desire. His conjuring of the real, on the other hand, reminds us that the origins of the photograph are always in some sense 'elsewhere': in the secret, impenetrable dialogue between the world and the camera itself, impervious to meaning, beyond artistic control.

(pp. 4–5)

It is the 'hallucinatory' edge of this inter-space which allows artistic and social agency, whether that of the photographer-interviewer, Sadowski, or of the trailer-park 'torturer', England. And, Lowry says, it is the 'machine-real' camera that records the image, allowing the 'meditative' space between icon and index. She argues that this space 'between' ontologies of imagination and objectivity, this preoccupation with icon (the social compulsion of 'desire') and index (the 'real') is what marks the work of all her graduating students. In Sadowski's work, the viewer relationship in his 'ghostlike' holographic simulacrum of Lynndie England is a space 'between' in two senses: visually as the viewer's changing torch position shifts the image between the iconic image of England's 'desire' and the spectral break-up of that image; and generically as the exhibition viewer shifts physically from the holograph room to the 'road kill' photograph. This photograph itself both informs and is dissipated by the taped voices of England.

The agency of the photographer as holograph artist lies here in disinvesting the iconic image of its settled meaning: of the soldier-torturer-fantasist with cocked thumbs. The agency of the viewer lies in finding and deconstructing England's iconic posture in light and in then re-finding a structural meaning in 'the American landscape' (Lynndie England as road-kill) before deconstructing this, too, across the audio traces of her different everyday identities.

Lowry's photographic course, including Sadowski's work, extends Best's emphasis on the indexical power of the Abu Ghraib images. It offers agency to both photographers and their audiences, and creatively destabilizes the iconic conventionality of the Lynddie England image *both* by unframing *and*, in Butler's sense, by 'framing the frame' (Butler 2010: 74).

Risk theory, communicative culture and transgressive images

Sadowski's hologram work is one way of restoring individual agency to the iconic fixity of Abu Ghraib icons. Another approach, at a broader public level, is offered by current risk theory. One year before the Abu Ghraib story broke, debate over imminent US pre-emptive strikes in Iraq without UN authorization had generated the largest display ever of public opposition in the London march of February 15, 2003. Risk theorist Piet Strydom (2002) analyzes public demonstrations of this kind as part of a new era of 'risk society' consciousness, which began with a changed, more reflexive public awareness in the late twentieth century.

Risk theory has analyzed an historical shift in western societies (Beck 1992): from a medieval religious culture carried by the church, through a modern scientific culture carried by the state, to a new communicative culture carried by the public sphere. Thus Strydom argues that

> Whereas the scientific movement, in conjunction with the state, originally played a crucial role in relegating religion both institutionally and culturally to the background, it is the new social movements of the late twentieth century that led the way in putting science in its place.
>
> (Strydom 2002: 104)

In this latest phase, risk discourse is regarded as a public process of communication around a succession of science/technology-generated uncertainties such as nuclear power dangers, global warming and biotechnological issues like GM food. Crises of this order, generating pressure groups and large social movements 'outside the core of formal decision-making institutions' (p. 113), have shifted mainstream media attention from core to periphery areas of the public sphere. Thus Strydom takes a new approach to Hall's and Shotter's contrast of 'centre' and 'margins'. He argues that within our increasingly complex, differentiated and multi-perspectival culture a reflexive 'public discourse about risk which the civil society and the social movements were . . . able to generate became the medium for opening up, exposing and reflecting upon the cultural models and cognitive structures informing the risk politics of our time' (p. 162). As a result, 'civil society obtains the chance to exert power over the political system' (p. 113).

Strydom follows Habermas in noting the influence of 'journalists, publicists and press agents commanding both communicative and social power' in this new condition of 'crisis consciousness'. Journalists and others in the communicative professions now regulate 'access to the public sphere through the mass media' (p. 113). But like Beck, Strydom emphasizes also the plurality of 'argumentation craftsmen' involved in this process (Beck 1992: 32). Thus, in any risk communication diverse stakeholders (scientific/technical experts, government, politicians, public relations practitioners, lobbyists, journalists etc.) promote differing and often competing risk definitions in an attempt to win public support (Styrdom 2002: 61).

Unlike Feldman and Philipose with their social control notions of the popular media, Strydom includes the media in the long-term preoccupation of reflexive risk theory with conflicting rationality claims among socially legitimated 'experts'. But, on the other hand, Feldman, Philipose and Strydom share similarities in not engaging seriously with differences within media systems, especially within individual newspapers in terms of conflicting rationality claims.

The same is true of the risk analysis of media images by the Swedish research team of Ferreira, Boholm and Löfstedt (2001); but their approach can still be used valuably in relation to images from Abu Ghraib. Focussing, like most other risk theorists on technological aspects of risk, they explore images associated with the poisoning of a Swedish farming area by the injection of acrylamide sealant into the Hallandsas railway tunnel nearby. The Swedish researchers draw centrally on anthropologist Mary Douglas' theories of cultural boundaries, transgression and uncertainty in arguing that whereas newspaper readers were accustomed to the conventional image-assemblage of the 'rural' as composed of 'the dairy farm as an integrated whole including people (the farmers), animals (the cows), the landscape (pasture) and product (the milk)', in the case of the prolonged media coverage of the Hallandsas tunnel crisis, 'they were now facing something that looked very different' (Ferreira, Boholm and Löfstedt 2001: 290). An assemblage of newspaper images showed a close-up of a deformed dead cow, a man squatting and pointing to a stream of polluted water, a farmer dumping milk into a urine reservoir and a family posing next to their poisoned drinking well. Seen together, these images reflected something 'Other', a new 'testimony of disorder . . . Like the mixing of water and poison, the mixing of milk and urine . . . plays upon one of the strongest "taboos" in every society' (p. 291).

On one hand, this unexpected 'taboo' cluster of images broke with long-established pictorial conventions of the 'rural' and created uncertainty. On the other, a newspaper double page image-spread of the Hallendsas crisis conjured up and contrasted 'the Swedish cultural imagery of "open landscapes" and "stone terraces" with the darkness, fear, and mystery of underground [harshly lit tunnel] imagery' (p. 293). This explicitly evoked the contrast of order/disorder by juxtaposing two long-term visual metaphors that were not normally associated: the deeply resonant cultural memory of healthy Swedish landscape and the metaphoric image of the tunnel.

Importantly, the Swedish researchers' analysis challenges here the rationalistic approach of technico-scientific theories of risk by arguing that 'the potential of visual images to communicate emotive and intuitive knowledge . . . makes them an effective medium for social constructions of messages about risks' (Boholm 1998: 126–7). For these risk theorists:

> The theory of rational choice . . . overlooks the fact that choices are made according to available alternatives that are themselves symbolic constructs. . . . The argument forwarded here is that stigma (its mark and visibility) . . . is *implicated* from already existing ideas about how the world is socially constructed.
>
> (Ferreira, Boholm and Löfstedt 2001: 297–8)

This concurs with the conventionalized symbolism attached to rural and tunnel images. Thus as water (or milk) breaks its familiar contextual boundaries (of farms, farmers, rough stone walls and healthy cows grazing in fields) in cultural representation and transgresses into other visual contexts (dead cows, milk poured into urine pits, farm families squatting beside toxic water, hellish train tunnels beneath the fields). A major uncertainty is created for viewers of these new 'risk images' and a hazard 'flow' from one image-assemblage to another becomes 'a main feature of risk events' (p. 297).

To explore the extent to which these rather different risk theories are useful in illustrating 'periphery' power in the media, and/or the operation of transgressive symbolism, we researched the reporting of Abu Ghraib in the British press, exploring separate newspapers as assemblages of verbal and visual rhetorics.

Newspaper assemblages at the periphery

The Independent is probably Britain's most left-leaning national newspaper; and the only one to oppose the Iraq War editorially. Here we will look at how different aspects of the newspaper assemblage cohere around this 'peripheral' position.

The front page

The entire front page of *The Independent* on 22 May 2004 was constructed schematically: by way of boxes, linked by directional arrows, and by images supporting the headline: 'Abuse and torture in Iraq: Where does the buck stop?' This amounted to a mapped summary of *The Independent*'s dominant discourses constructing 'Iraq' after the invasion as a place of *systemic* abuse. This interpretive map points to a globally constituted 'post-conflict' place, where the war was illegal and the militaristic 'reconstruction' from the top was far from humanitarian.

Arrows point down from this Abu Ghraib section of *The Independent* front page to a row of small photographs of the people accused of committing torture: Ambuhl, Davis, England, Frederick, Graner, Harman, Sivits, with the words: 'This week Specialist Jeremy Sivits was convicted of mistreating detainees. He was jailed for a year and discharged from service'.

Next down the front page, an arrow takes us to larger photographs of:

- 'The Interrogator. The Commander of Guantanamo, Major General Geoffrey Miller [who] went to Baghdad last August. Used forms of interrogation that included hooding, sleep-deprivation and exposure to extremes of cold and heat. Under orders from Stephen Cambone these methods were reportedly expanded to include abuse and sexual humiliation.
- Special Ops. Stephen Cambone . . . Rumsfeld's intelligence advisor set up ultrasecret operation of several hundred spies in the Pentagon. Unit encouraged physical coercion and sexual humiliation of Iraqi prisoners in an effort to generate more intelligence. Helped by General William Boykin, a born-again Christian who delivered a church sermon equating the Muslim world with Satan.

- Donald Rumsfeld. The key to the torture scandal lies in the decision of the Defence Secretary, Donald Rumsfeld, to expand a highly secret operation aimed at breaking al Qa'ida suspects to include the interrogation of Iraqi detainees.'

Cambone and Miller are linked to Rumsfeld by directional arrows, and to their right are two other images, themselves linked to Cambone by arrows.

- '*The Arab Mind*: Torturer's Bible. At the centre of the torture controversy, this book by Raphael Patai is the "bible" of the "neo-conservative" lobby. It includes a 25-page chapter on Arabs and sex, stating that the biggest weakness of Arabs is shame and humiliation.
- School of the Americas. US Army centre at Fort Benning, Georgia, linked with controversial interrogation techniques. Its training manuals advocated torture, blackmail and other forms of coercion.'

At the bottom of *The Independent*'s front page, linked to the Miller/Cambone/Rumsfeld loop by directional arrow, is the largest photograph: of George W. Bush:

- 'President Bush knew of the secret programme, according to the *New Yorker*. But in the time-honoured tradition of secret US operations, there was no paper trail and no budgets or congressional oversight. When a military policeman first reported the abuses and handed over a CD full of images and videos, on 13 January, it was reported to President Bush within days. Mr Rumsfeld reportedly tried to reassure the President that the scandal would die down. Once the photographs of abuse were leaked, the scandal exploded around the world. The Pentagon's attempts to persuade the world that it was the fault of several "rotten apples" was also disbelieved.'

The words 'no paper trail and no budgets or congressional oversight' justified *The Independent*'s use of a one-directional arrow, from Rumsfeld to Bush. The protocols of responsible journalism could allow no more than this accusation (via a story in the *New Yorker*). Nevertheless, the newspaper picked away consistently at that hidden relationship: how much did the politicians at the very top know, advise and order?

Editorials

In its editorial of May 8, *The Independent* turned its systemic focus on British government practices. The editorial argued that the photographs of British soldiers supposedly torturing Iraqi prisoners published in the *Daily Mirror*, and already believed to be fakes, illustrated nevertheless a different truth about systematic abuse to detainees in Iraq by British and US forces. Both International Red Cross and Amnesty International reports, delivered months before to the respective governments but only now shown to the press, had revealed widespread systematic abuse.

The consequence was, the editorial said, that Ministers had been challenged with these facts from prominent NGOs, and *The Independent* asked why they were not made public before. It concluded that the British government had tried to cover up other allegations against British troops.

The growing controversy about Abu Ghraib was itself launched by television in the USA, and this stance of *The Independent* was a clear case where a British newspaper made it part of a very broad risk discourse, where, as Strydom would predict, the discursive interrelation of the antagonistic frames of the different actors – parliamentary and NGO in *The Independent* reports – led to a sustained sequence of competitive risk politics in May 2004.

Cartoons

The Independent's cartoons during the Abu Ghraib period (from the story first breaking on 30 April 2004, through most of the May issues) were consistently supportive of the editorial stance. On 1 May 2004, the cartoon by Dave Brown (*Independent*, 1 May 2004: 38) played on the Saddam-like role being taken by the US in Iraq, not only in the torture within Saddam's most notorious prison, but also via harshly imposed 'democratization' and 'reconstruction'. It is captioned 'The rebirth', and is a framed image of Botticelli's *Birth of Venus*. But Venus is replaced by the hooded crucifix man, wired to Bush on the left. A voice balloon says, 'For the last time . . . how does it feel to be free of a brutal dictator?' The cartoon supported the newspaper's editorial that day, which questioned the 'bad apple' approach to the Abu Ghraib abuses suggested by Blair and Bush, preferring to see a systemic problem within the US military, with clear and established links between Abu Ghraib, Guantanamo Bay, the holding of prisoners without charge in Iraq and finally the employment of private security firms in order to get around the Geneva Convention.

Schrank's cartoon on 2 May has Blair himself as the crucifix man, staring at us without a hood, the stars and stripes on his gown, his body wired to electric cables, with the caption 'Isolated, humiliated, abused' (*Independent* 2 May 2004: 22). The newspaper here fuses its pre-war emphasis on Blair's isolation from other European leaders with the humiliation and abuse of Iraqi civilians. Blair stands on an upturned box, with an arrow pointing 'This Way Down'.

On 7 May, the cartoon by Dave Brown parodied the Lynndie England image where she holds a prostrate, naked Iraqi detainee on a leash (*Independent* 7 May 2004: 30). But in the cartoon it is Bush (bow-legged as a cowboy and wearing military fatigues) who holds the leash, and it is Blair, tongue lolling, who is prostrate, naked, with the leash around his neck. Bush is saying, 'Treatin' Eyerrackees like dogs is abhorrent . . . Hell, it's a priv'lege they gotta earn!' The cartoon is overtly pointing to several positions held by *The Independent*: that Bush has been arrogant and ignorant in his dealings with Iraq and with the whole Middle East 'problem'; that 'democratization' and 'reconstruction' is based on Iraqi subordination to US power and values ('they gotta earn!'); that Blair, once potentially a leader within a strong European Union, has instead become an isolated lickspittle (the long, lolling tongue); and that the two leaders of the 'coalition of the willing' are now in a prison of their own making.

Every newspaper can mobilize images (photographs, book covers, cartoons) and words (editorials, features, op-eds, letters). *The Independent*'s particular assemblages of words and images during May 2004 constructed a powerful journalistic discourse, representing a wide range of arguments from 'non-core' social movements, thus subverting the core 'new wars' rhetoric of 'militaristic humanism' and 'democratization'.

Were there space in this chapter, we could demonstrate that newspapers in Britain on the right of the political perspective such as the *Daily Telegraph* and *The Times* were suggesting at the time of Abu Ghraib that the 'core' system was working well overall. It had delivered the Iraqi people to the democratic process, but had made mistakes which, when recognized, had been acknowledged and apologized for, with 'repair' (like demolishing Abu Ghraib prison) on the way. The overall consensus of these newspapers was that at the end of proper legal process, the 'bad apples' of Abu Ghraib would be duly tried, found guilty and punished.

Transgressing symbols

Our account so far suggests that 'Left' and 'Right' newspapers aligned wholly with either 'periphery' or 'core' affiliations, giving support to Strydom's broad dichotomy. But analysis of editorial-page assemblages within individual newspapers can suggest a different story. For example, the 9 May *Telegraph* cartoon, which shows Bush kicking Rumsfeld – in a parody of the fake *Mirror* photograph of a British soldier kicking a detainee – with the caption, 'Is this photograph a fake?' seems to be asking whether Bush's reprimand of Rumsfeld is as fake as the *Mirror* photographs.

Sometimes the editorial stance could also be challenged on the cartoon page by strongly reasoned opinion pieces, as for example on 5 May by Simon Jenkins in *The Times* (2004: 16). Here he argued that far from the Abu Ghraib scandals being the work of a few 'bad apples' in the military, the pressure on prison guards by incoming military or private contractors to 'soften up' prisoners was more systemic, and had a long history. He reminded his readers of what happened, during the Vietnam War at My Lai and the earlier British torture and execution of Mau Mau suspects at Hola Camp, when soldiers under military duress were ordered to 'show aggression'.

But occasional 'alternative' polemics in the British press also have a long history and may be more easily rejected by readers than the cartoons. Following the arguments of Boholm *et al.* about the more intuitive, tacit or affective power of visual symbolic transgression, it is arguable that critical and 'alternative' cartoons are more powerful. On 8 May 2004, *The Times* printed a cartoon entitled 'Abu Ghraib' on its editorial page which translated the 'Three Studies for Figures at the Base of a Crucifixion' (1944) by British artist, Francis Bacon from its original World War II context into an image of the crucifix man. For Bacon, the merging of flayed carcass, crucified pose and silently screaming alien creatures represented inhumanity among humans and between humans and animals. But in the US democratic project of the Iraq invasion, the crucifixion of Christ was seen, especially by Christian fundamentalists close to Bush, as redemptive and as a basis for Western civilization.

In his own discussion of the crucifix man image, W.J.T. Mitchell comments:

> On the one hand, the image is a kind of ideological X-ray, exposing that mission as a Christian crusade that aims to 'convert' the Muslims into Christian martyrs. On the other hand, it provides . . . a kind of mirror reversal of its intended purpose. Instead of eliciting useful intelligence about the Iraqi resistance, it had the effect of intensifying that resistance, serving as a recruiting poster for jihadists through the world.
>
> (Mitchell 2008: 202)

He adds:

> If ever an image has been 'cloned' in the circuits of the mass media, this one was, both in the sense of indefinite duplication, and in the further sense of taking on a 'life of its own' that eludes and even reverses the intentions of its producers.
>
> (pp. 202–4)

Mitchell points to a mural in Baghdad which couples the black-hooded prisoner with the white-hooded image of the Statue of Liberty 'portrayed as a knight of the Ku Klux Klan' (p. 204).

Variations of this 'twinning' of the crucifix man and the Statue of Liberty occurred often in cartoons in the Western media at the time of the Abu Ghraib scandal. But, whereas Mitchell refers to this imagistic overlay as 'cloning', we prefer risk theorists Boholm et al.'s notion of symbolic border transgression. The crucifix-man of *The Times* cartoon 'Abu Ghraib', we suggest, is an image which confounds symbolic borders (e.g. Christ/terrorist), disordering these established visual metaphors, potentially generating what Ferreira, Boholm and Löfstedt call new inflections of emotive and intuitive knowledge (2001: 291–6). It also presents the agency of its cartoonist in using Francis Bacon to raise issues of 'Christian' institutional negligence in denying human agency to the 'Other'. There is a strong parodying edge to this cartoon that at the very least creates an unsettling ambiguity on the editorial page. Paul Rutherford comments, in the context of his own analysis of editorial cartoons during the Iraq War, 'The serious business of politics is invaded by the spirit of carnival' (2004: 5). This was certainly true of cartoons in some 'core' British newspapers during May 2004, as we have also seen in the *Times* and *Telegraph* cartoons of Blair as crucifix man linked to the Capitol.

In Beck's term, different 'argumentation craftsmen' operate within the pages of any one newspaper, especially when social movements are as strong and constitutive a part of a newspaper's potential readership as they were during the Iraq war and its 'reconstruction' period. So concerned about this readership was the *Daily*

Telegraph in February 2003 at the time of the massive anti-War march in London, that the newspaper's editorial recognized that many *Telegraph* readers probably were part of it. Then it patiently spelled out its reasons for supporting the war. It is in this situation that, in both *The Times* and *The Telegraph*, 'we witness a multiplicity of antagonistic definitions advanced on the basis of the competing and conflicting rationality claims of the different actors struggling for more general acceptance by the public'(Styrdom 2002: 61). Political cartoons as well as op-ed articles in both *The Times* and *The Telegraph* supported the editorial line on some occasions, and potentially subverted it on others, as the newspapers tried to refurbish the political 'core' on one hand and yet satisfy the 'periphery' section of their market on the other.

Conclusion: cloning or mediality

We have focussed on iconic images from Abu Ghraib prison in Iraq in this chapter to explore tensions between (or hybrids of) 'social control' and 'agency' theories which seek to explain the power of their iconicity. In particular, we have looked at different kinds of feminist and risk theory, as well as some current photographic practice in developing notions of index, icon and symbol. There has been a growing emphasis on the hybridity of 'emotive' and cognitive knowledge, 'core' and 'periphery' knowledge, and the space between 'hallucinatory' and 'real' ontologies.

Our preference has been for theories establishing continuity (and hybridity) rather than rupture between iconic usages pre- and post-9/11. Here we agree with feminist Griselda Pollock who has critiqued Mitchell's 'cloning terror' concept from within a 'continuity' framework, arguing that 'cloning terror' is too simplistic and 'organic' as 'a means of analysis of highly charged and politically complex historical events that themselves replay but also revise the historical legacies that determine them'. Pollock adopts a 'replay/revise' approach to continuing historical legacies:

> Cloning is, I suggest, an inadequate metaphor for the proliferation of socio-historical factors that might increase the number of jihadists prepared to fight against the allies in Iraq or elsewhere. The political is not only midwifed by longer plaits of history, but the complex product of 'many determinations' (Marx).

> (Pollock 2008: 210, 211)

Instead, Pollock prefers Freud's theory of the 'uncanniness of the double and Aby Warburg's theory of "the iconology of the interval" that hinges emotion and thought, time and system. I wanted to allow psychic ambivalence rather than biological replication into play' (p. 212).

Pollock's emphasis on uncertainty and the 'interval' between emotion and thought parallels the emphasis of this chapter, relating for example to Lowry's space 'between', and also to Ferreira *et al.*'s notion of 'emotive knowledge'. For us, one of the most interesting new approaches taking this 'replay/revise' sense of continuity-within-hybridity forward is Richard Grusin's theory of affect and 'mediality'. Grusin relies on two main conceptual claims for his analysis: first, that the governance of images is, in Foucault's sense, 'the way in which biopolitical power controls and manages (but also makes possible particular forms of) people, bodies, cultural and economic practices, and so forth', where 'mediality necessarily participates in this project through all forms of media today' (2011: 7); second, that affect is distinguishable from and precedes emotion, 'felt first by the body, and only afterwards recognized as a particular emotional state' (p. 9).

Like Mitchell, Grusin points to the differences between traditional and new media forms, in so far as digital cameras make possible an increase in the magnitude and instantaneity of circulation of photographs, with a significant effect on the private/public balance of distribution 'as photos that once would have been mainly shown to friends or family can now be distributed across the globe to strangers in different countries or cultures, or perhaps to a neighbour next door' (p. 3). But despite the similarities, this is more Pollock's 'replay/revise' sense of continuation of the media (and governmentality) by other means than Mitchell's sense of historical rupture.

For Grusin there are several kinds of continuity-within-change evident in the circulation of the images taken at Abu Ghraib. First, they were initially distributed to a world public through the traditional media of television and newspapers, but 'were made available through the pervasiveness of digital cameras and networked digital media' (p. 3). Second, like Pollock, Grusin draws on theorists whose concepts long preceded 9/11 (in his case, Benjamin, Bataille, Bergson, William James and Spinoza). In particular, whereas Mitchell's sees a rupture between Walter Benjamin's age of mechanical production and the era of 'cloning terror', Grusin draws on Benjamin's theory of the cinematic body (as read through Deleuze and Guattari) in a 'replay/revise' mode to think about 'what it feels like to live in a networked culture' (p. 8). Third, Grusin sees continuity within the new usages of the internet generation (which, of course, began before 9/11). Here he quotes Susan Sontag's argument that the Abu Ghraib photograph of a young woman leading a naked man around on a leash, a classic dominatrix image, was perhaps inspired by the huge store of pornographic images available on the internet.

But, fourth, Grusin goes beyond Sontag's focus on the horrific content of the images, to argue for 'an affective continuity between our looking at the Abu Ghraib photos and our seeing photos of friends, family, or co-workers, or our everyday practice of seeing photographs in the news' (p. 5). Here again Grusin's theory blends new and traditional forms of media, while emphasizing the new opportunities for everyday-life communication facilitated by the internet (and see here, also, Grusin's important discussion of the continuity between 'remediation' and 'premediation' after 9/11, despite the greater emphasis after that event on media premediation: i.e. 'trying to imagine or map out as many possible futures as could plausibly be imagined' (2004: 28)). His most important point is in highlighting 'the continuity between our ordinary digital photographic practices, including posting them on the internet and emailing them to friends, and the media practices engaged in at Abu Ghraib' (2011: 5). Crucially for Grusin this continuity is what generated the affective shock when people saw the photographs.

> [I]f our everyday practices of digital photography or photo sharing also involve an affective relationship with our media, and these practices are continuous with the media practices at Abu Ghraib, then looking at the Abu Ghraib photographs would be experienced affectively as well as cognitively, would somehow impact on or alter our prior affective relationship with our everyday media practices . . . In the case of the photos from Abu Ghraib we are outraged because we are shocked, rather than being shocked because we are outraged.
>
> (Grusin 2011: 9)

Like Hariman and Lucaites, Grusin is seeking to move beyond the 'totalizing narratives' interested either in the subversion or 'hegemony of global capital, or patriarchy, or ideology' (p. 8). But unlike them (despite their emphasis on iconic images and trauma), he turns in conclusion to consider how the medial function of the Abu Ghraib photographs works in relation to wartime post-traumatic stress disorder (PTSD). He discusses a US Army investigation of the NFTU website which initially was created for men to exchange pornographic images of wives and girlfriends, but after military censorship became a site where soldiers in Iraq posted images of mutilated dead bodies and body-parts of Iraqi civilians and insurgents. Grusin compares the more traditional Vietnam War with the Iraq insurgency where 'gunmen so often disappear into crowds that many [soldiers] have the feeling that they are fighting ghosts' (p. 11).

> So if Benjamin is right that the formal and technical properties of cinemas and other forms of mechanical reproduction provide a way to cushion people from the shocks of modernity, then it makes sense to think about how taking digital photos of Iraqi dead might become a way to cushion and even to distribute the shock or traumatic affect of fighting in Iraq across media artefacts . . . If the adrenaline surge produced by an enemy attack [as in traditional warfare] . . . can't be released by attacking the enemy, it can perhaps be released, at least in part, by taking digital photos or videos of a suicide bomber's decapitated head, or an insurgent with his limbs blown off, or even some Iraqi civilians who have been wounded, maimed, or violently murdered . . . [T]he digital images, captured, downloaded to one's computer, and circulated among friends on the front, friends and family back home, and then with sites like NFTU to strangers on the web, can serve to distribute the affect of anger and perhaps in some small way work to dissipate or release it.
>
> (pp. 11–12)

Thus Grusin offers both a PTSD-based theory for the affect among US soldiers leading to the images from Abu Ghraib (or to photographs of bodies posted on the NFTU website) and a mediatization theory for the continuity between this very specific military affect and the shock of such images on international publics: 'part of the horror of these images . . . is the bodily feeling both of the affect distributed across these images and of the affinity between our practices of distributing affect across our media as well' (p. 12).

Grusin's theory leads us to consider the agency of soldiers in Iraq in circulating images, to the everyday agency of wider publics in circulating intimate images of their own, and also to our focus on PTSD theories of war and terror in the next chapter.

9 Witnessing terrorism in New York and London
Trauma icons

A person falls from the north tower, World Trade Center, September 11, 2001: the 'Falling Man'. Photograph taken by Richard Drew © Press Association

In the picture, he departs from this earth like an arrow. Although he has not chosen his fate, he appears to have, in his last instants of life, embraced it . . . He appears relaxed. Hurtling through the air. He appears comfortable in the grip of unimaginable motion. He does not appear intimidated by gravity.

(Junod 2003: 1–2)

The graphic Richard Drew photograph, 'Falling Man', one of the estimated two hundred 'jumpers' from the Twin Towers on 9/11, is the initial focus of this chapter, along with another vivid image from the terrorist attack on London in 2005, now labelled as '7/7'.

Journalist Tom Junod continues his vivid description of the 'Falling Man':

> In all the other pictures, the people . . . who jumped . . . appear to be struggling against horrific discrepancies of scale. They are made puny by the backdrop of the towers . . . Some of them are shirtless; their shoes fly off as they flail and fall; they look confused . . . The man in the picture, by contrast, is perfectly vertical, and so is in accord with the lines of the buildings behind him. He bisects them: everything to the left of him in the picture is the North Tower; everything to the right, the South. Though oblivious to the geometric balance he has achieved, he is the essential element in the creation of a new flag, a banner composed entirely of steel bars shining in the sun. Some people who look at the picture see stoicism, willpower, a portrait of resignation; others see something else . . . : freedom. There is something almost rebellious in the man's posture, as though once faced with the inevitability of death, he decided to get on with it; as though he were a missile, a spear, bent on attaining his own end.

(pp. 1–2)

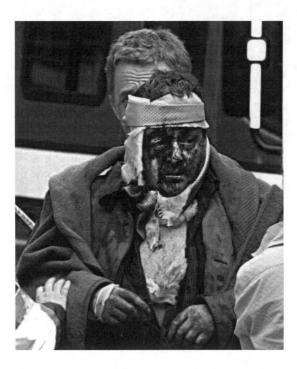

John Tulloch after 7/7. Photograph taken by Abbie Trayler-Smith © Eyevine

Our second image is a close-up of a survivor of the 7 July 2005 terrorist bomb attacks in London. He was a metre or so from the suicide bomber Mohammad Sidique Khan in the Circle line underground train when the terrorist detonated his bomb.

This image shows the man seriously wounded about the head. Blood is encrusted all over his face: his own blood, perhaps the terrorist's blood and probably other people's blood because passengers died very close to him. The photograph was taken about one hour after the explosion. His head is roughly bandaged. A bystander's blue silk tie holds the bandage in place, signifying the pressure on London emergency services in response to this unexpected disaster. The man's hair, grey with dust, sticks out above the bandage. Wearing his ragged, bomb-damaged coat he looks to his left, his eyes unfocussed and bloodshot. *The Sun* newspaper carried this image above its banner front-page headline the day after the terrorist attack.

Then it appeared again on 8 November 2005; this time covering the front page of *The Sun*. 'Terror Laws: Tell Tony He's Right' shouted *The Sun* newspaper's front page headline. Below the full-page image of the wounded man is a small photograph of an alert-looking Tony Blair. The words 'Tell Tony He's Right' are ascribed to the injured man, inserted on the front page next to his mouth. There is no doubt about the interpellated message here. The subsidiary headline, '*The Sun* Says' heads the image of Blair with the words:

> *The Sun* today calls on its army of readers to back Prime Minister Tony Blair and DEMAND 90-day detention for terror suspects. Phone our special hotline NOW to make your voice heard. The people's will can force MPs to bring safety to Britain's streets.

The main image on *The Sun*'s front page was one of three which the British media pronounced 'iconic' in representing the London horror of 7/7. It is the image of the first author of this book and was considered more relevant to *The Sun*'s front-page purposes than other iconic 7/7 images (the exploded red London bus and the woman whose face is covered with a surgical mask) because this bloodied image had the mouth and the blood-saturated victim-credibility to 'Tell Tony He's Right'.

In Chapter 2 we considered Hariman and Lucaites' (2007) rhetorical analysis of trauma images. They spoke of the icon of the 'napalmed girl' as an image that continues to reappear, 'ghost-like'. It will just not go away.

In this chapter we examine quite different theoretical approaches to icons from two of the most traumatic public events of our time: the terrorist attacks of 9/11 and 7/7. The first of these images, the 'Falling Man', looked as though it would become an iconic image of the event. But it only circulated for one day, unlike Hariman and Lucaites' icons. Tom Junod notes that there were immediate public outcries against media that showed this image, on the grounds that it stripped the dying man of his dignity and represented a voyeuristic pornography of the image which would bring terrible hurt to those still living who recognized and loved the

'Falling Man'. So, fearing readers' and advertisers' reactions, the US media coast-to-coast withdrew the image from circulation. If it was an icon, it initially lasted only a day in public circulation. Moreover, no-one came forward to own the subject of this image, so that 'even as Drew's photograph became at once iconic and impermissible, its subject remained unnamed' (2003: 2).

Later, though, the 'Falling Man' reappeared; for example in TV documentary coverage during the tenth anniversary of 9/11 and also, as Andrew Hoskins notes, on numerous book covers. As Hoskins argues, this had led to a 'diminishing sanitization over time as the image is seen (in terms of assumptions about the audiences made by producers, editors, broadcasters, etc) as moving from the trajectory of the event into a more historical mode of circulation, remediation, reception' (private communication). The strong passions (and fears) among advertisers and media companies about their audience were reworked years later; and the 'Falling Man' was re-circulated and mediated in new ways.

The second image was iconic much more continuously. In the years since 7/7 it has regularly appeared to mark anniversaries of the event. But unlike the moral-universal quality of Hariman and Lucaites' understanding of icons, this image has reappeared for overtly political reasons. Because the first author is both an academic analyst of risk and also someone who experienced first-hand one of the more traumatic risk-events in British public life this century, his 7/7 image provides an unusual opportunity to explore the *agency* of trauma. Indeed, that will be the focus of our exploration of both images of trauma in this chapter.

The 'Falling Man': A criminologist's analysis

As a journalist, Tom Junod traces different family responses to 'the jumpers' who leapt to their deaths from high in the Twin Towers. His main focus was on a Catholic Puerto Rican family who rejected their identification with the 'Falling Man' because of their shame that a husband and father had deserted them, and, because, as a Catholic, to commit suicide was mortal sin. But Junod also speaks of another grieving woman who saw her two sons together on a window ledge in the burning towers, and was comforted seeing them, at the last, together. She, unlike the Catholic family, chose to live with her sons' final loss of hope

> as an absence that we, the living, now have to live with. She chooses to live with it by looking, by seeing, by trying to know – by making an act of private witness. She could have chosen to keep her eyes closed.
>
> (Junod 2003: 3)

Junod's comparison raises issues of personal subjectivity, trauma and witnessing which are taken further by professor of criminology, Alison Young, who has explored the 9/11 terrorist attack in terms of subjective trauma and ethics. Young adopts a personally subjective approach in response to the 9/11 images of 'the jumpers' while focusing on the USA's national sense of trauma (especially among

New Yorkers who witnessed the event). She is particularly interested in the relationship between Post Traumatic Stress Disorder (PTSD) and visual trauma, where PTSD as a therapeutic technique deals with

> representations produced not in the immediate pain of loss but in the difficult interim space of the succeeding years – a time of 'present pasts' . . . whose imagery is a product of a struggle between memory and amnesia, between trauma and its resolution
>
> (Young 2007: 31)

Griselda Pollock has raised the question about an image of a German soldier executing a Ukrainian women and her baby during the Second World War: 'Is it traumatic or is it iconic and hence a fetishizing displacement of what its existence indexes?' (2008: 219–20). She compares this image with the 'Falling Man' and asks: 'is Drew's gaze as deadly as the photographer in the Ukraine?' (p. 227). Is the 'Falling Man' protected from what Pollock calls the Orhpic gaze backwards (depriving the victim of humanity) in so far as the image of the vertical towers in the background is a 'formal index of the verticality that both confirms the fall and holds it forever above the earth where an already happening dying will be unimaginably horribly affirmed' (p. 227). It is clear that Pollock's answer to her question about the 'Falling Man' is 'no'; and she instead, quoting the artist Bracha Ettinger, argues for a 'transport-station of trauma', where the artist seeks a 'borderspace' in a 'relation or openness to the other' (Ettinger 2000: 9, cited in Pollock 2008: 231ff). Here, from her feminist viewpoint, Pollock is arguing similarly to Judith Butler, for

> an ethical move of co- and trans-subjectivity, the sharing of the humanity of others or the dehumanising pain of others which can be invoked in us by the creation of a threshold, a border space that never collapses, never closes.
>
> (Pollock 2008: 235)

Arguably Young's analysis of a film by Mexican Alejandro González Iñárritu does this by pointing to the film-makers' blending of 'verticality' images of 'the Jumpers' with the sound effects of their impact on the pavement where death is 'unimaginably horribly affirmed'. Iñárritu had initially prepared a series of photographs taken on 9/11, called 'Blinded By the Light', but this was refused publication for being 'out of step with the spirit of the times' and, in Iñárritu's words, 'politically incorrect' (Young 2007: 40). He then drew on the experience of those photographs to make a short film for French producer Alain Brigand. In 2002, Brigand commissioned eleven internationally respected filmmakers from different countries to each direct a nine-minute film in response to the events of 9/11. The film was never given public release in the USA on the grounds that it was anti-American. In analyzing this film Young is operating in terms of several identities. As both academic criminologist and film theorist, she says the question is not one of censorship:

Iñárritu's vanished photographs constitute an image of absence underlying the ways in which relations between sound, image and editing (which usually work seamlessly together as the *kinesis* of cinema) will foreground the possibility of an ethical response to the demands of witnessing catastrophe.

(Young 2007: 40)

But Young also works from a subjective identity in her methodology for this textual analysis. This consists of going to see the film in a cinema and describing her developing personal emotional responses. In this way, she attempts to understand and represent the trauma of a larger imagined audience by combining academic analysis with subjective experience of trauma through the mediated images of 9/11.

She begins by describing her experience of the film's opening, which displayed an unsettling black screen, accompanied by muttered voices of Mexican Chamulas Indians and faint musical sounds. This, she feels, is almost a 'failure of cinema', because she sees nothing (p. 41). Then, after a prolonged 'atmosphere of anxiety' caused by the 'jittering' sounds and the black screen, there is a sudden interruption. It is the briefest flash of an image, hurting the eyes, before the screen reverts to black. The brief flashes are repeated, and are lengthier on each appearance until the images are discernible: 'they are images of people falling or jumping from the towers of the World Trade Center' (p. 41). Accompanying the flashes, matching their duration, she hears 'found sound' from segments of broadcasts on September 11 from many countries: Vietnam, South Africa, Poland, Portugal, Italy, France, Germany, Canada. This 'soundtrack jostles with the exclamations of shock and utter dismay, as screams compete with journalists' attempts to describe the sight of the World Trade Center'(p. 41).

The images of the falling bodies are shown for increasing duration, until the announcement of the towers falling is told over a black screen, followed 'by five different consecutive shots of the falling . . . shown in great deliberation' as the sound increases in volume – 'chaotic, impenetrable, deafening' (p. 41). Silence interrupts this terrible noise, punctuated by two visual sequences, as first one, then the other tower falls. 'The bright sunlit daylight seems almost shocking after the black screen. The towers' descent seems both astonishingly fast, yet at the same time in slow motion, in contrast to the preceding flashes' (p. 42). The Native Americans' chanting voices return over a black screen, which dissolves to pale green, then to white as orchestral string music merges with the Mexicans' voices. Out of the white screen a written text emerges, in Arabic, then English, asking, 'Does God's light guide or blind us?', a reference to Iñárritu's banned photographs, but also to the 'God' both of the terrorists and President Bush's aggressive Christianity. Two 'dazzling white lines of light eclipse the screen, and leave only the voices in prayer, which are cut as the screen returns to black with the end of the film' (p. 42). As Young narrates this sequence of filmic events, she emphasizes the trauma.

For the audience, this soundscape repeats and accelerates the experience of those at the time who watched, looked, witnessed. Such accelerated repetitions [of the bodies falling] have the character of trauma, dwelling on and in memory without resolution or respite.

(p. 41)

Whereas Tom Junod's focus as a journalist was on personal images of trauma, as acts of private witnessing or of keeping one's own eyes closed, Young as a criminologist extended this act of witnessing to include issues of law and judgment, but still retained a focus on personal emotions. She emphasizes her physical and emotional state.

> My experience of watching the film in a cinema is as memorable to me as the film itself; I can well recall the sensations of physical stress that I felt while watching it . . . And the film's alternating blackness of screen and shocking images of the moments just before death heightened the film's sounds. To the extent that cinematic spectatorship involves an entire phenomenological raft of effects, for me, Iñárritu's film is a sensorium of sonic and visual trauma.
>
> (p. 42)

But this personal view is quickly inter-cut by her academic voice. The impact of the film, she says, comes from the tension between the film's compression and acceleration of 9/11, and the effects of dislocating the familiar cinematic signature of unified sound and image (p. 42). When she views the film a second time she says: 'I realized that I had made myself forget the film's sounds, and their overwhelming affective impact. And the images of the falling bodies were *still* dreadful to me' (p. 42).

Like Junod, Young calls these the 'repressed images' of a national trauma. But the images of the jumpers that Iñárritu uses in his film were very different from the iconic 'Falling Man'. Junod says of this latter image:

> Photographs lie . . . Especially great photographs . . . The photograph functioned as a study of doomed verticality, a fantasia of straight lines, with a human being slivered at the centre, like a spike. In truth, however, the Falling Man fell with neither the precision of an arrow nor the grace of an Olympic diver. He fell like everyone else, like all the other jumpers – trying to hold on to the life he was leaving, which is to say he fell inelegantly.
>
> (Junod 2003: 3)

It was the photojournalist Richard Drew who chose the arrow-like, aetheticized image of this falling, flailing, tumbling human being. Drew did so, in Junod's view, because of his photojournalistic professional eye (Drew, cited in Junod 2003: 2). Similarly, 'the jumpers' images in Iñárritu's film are selected professionally and inserted into the aesthetics of image and sound by a leading film-maker. Iñárritu chose long, indistinct shots of bodies falling and, disturbingly for an audience, he added to the soundtrack the intermittent noise of them hitting the ground. In Junod's account, 'Those tumbling through the air remained, by all accounts, eerily silent; those on the ground screamed' (p. 2). Iñárritu's film includes the screaming onlookers and the shouting journalists. But in addition he added the sound made by the falling bodies as they hit the pavement.

Young notes that the falling images appear in the film before the planes hit the towers and that we hear the roar of the towers falling before we see the images of that event. 'The viewer is located at the moment of the disaster and experiences it as trauma' (2007: 43).

In her analysis, Young is drawing on a number of professional identities. One is that of a PTSD therapist, fully aware of therapy's play between images 'now' (the film) and images 'then' (on 9/11). Another is that of a subjective individual who feels traumatized by watching the film. Thirdly, Young is drawing on two academic identities; one as a criminologist, the other as a psycho-analytically oriented screen theorist of film spectatorship. In her summary to this, she quotes Žižek who commented:

> this is what the captivating effect of the collapse of the WTC was: an image, a semblance, an 'effect', which, at the same time, delivered 'the thing itself' (Žižek 2002: 19). This notion should not be understood as an endorsement of the oft-repeated claim that September 11 saw the intrusion of reality into the culturally sheltered lives of Americans. Such a claim appears in statements such as 'last Tuesday's monstrous dose of reality' (Sontag 2001: 32). Rather, the imaginary burst through the screen of reality.
>
> (Žižek 2002, cited in Young 2007: 44)

Young is now operating at the level of epistemology via the opposed positions of Sontag and Žižek in relation to the real. She quotes Žižek again to drive her point home.

> We should therefore invert the standard reading according to which the WTC explosions were the intrusion of the Real which shattered our illusory Sphere: quite the reverse – it was before the WTC collapse that we lived in our reality, perceiving Third World horrors as something which was not actually part of our social reality, as something which existed (for us) as a spectral apparition on the (TV) screen – and what happened on September 11 was that this fantasmatic screen apparition entered our reality.
>
> (Žižek 2002, cited in Young 2007: 44)

The Lacanian psycho-analytical sharing of ground between Young and Žižek allows a melding of her screen theory with his analysis of the Imaginary/Real – although it is not clear how far they agree epistemologically, given Žižek's basically Marxist-psychoanalytical epistemology. For Žižek, the falling walls of the Twin Towers penetrated the combination of imaginary/reality of spectators in New York; but they also represented the return of another imaginary/reality conjunction from behind those Other walls of tragedy and oppression which Žižek, Stuart Hall and John Berger all speak about.

Those other walls, at any rate, are not Young's concern in this piece. Rather she is seeking to relate 'visual trauma' in New York to legal-ethical discourse.

> There is, of course, a sense of ethical demand involved in witnessing – the demand that the witness interpret what she sees. Such an interpretation makes history, faces up to the question of what sense history will make of what has been seen and of what actions have been taken by the witness, the one who sees.
>
> (Young 2007: 44)

Going beyond the acts of private witness which Junod describes, Young's criminological analysis explores two texts, Iñárritu's film and the final report of the National Commission into Terrorist Attacks Upon the United States, or *9/11 Commission Report* (2004). Despite the fact that the terrorists had clearly imagined a ground-breaking change in the conventional patterns of terrorist attack by committing suicide via passenger aircraft, the *Report* repeatedly carried the implication that this 'Al-Qaeda plot is . . . resistant to any analysis, unable to have been predicted or prevented: *unprecedented*' (Young 2007: 36). The dominant motif of the entire *Report* was that this attack was 'unimaginable'. Young argues that the *Report* offered a narrative of daily events 'unimaginably' disrupted instead of a consistent weighing up of evidence and judgment. The genre of the *Report*, she observes, is a thriller or mystery where the names of passengers, flight crew and relatives are identified.

> It deploys the convention well known in the establishment of a cinematic narrative – that of showing key protagonists going about their usual activities or locations in a state of equilibrium or tranquility (with such normality or tranquility poised on the verge of disruption).
>
> (p. 36)

Thus conventional narrative design, from everyday tranquility to 'lack', operated as an alibi in the *Report*, replacing systemic judgment. Key moments of potentially alternative outcomes were listed: terrorist pilot Mohhamad Atta being selected for extra screening by a computer programme and the fact that the national security was on 'blinking red' alert throughout the summer of 2001. But they were consigned to a failure 'in imagination' (National Commission into Terrorist Attacks Upon the United States 2004: 339, cited in Young 2007: 38). Young argues that 'consistent with the Commission's refusal to assign blame, it withholds any agentic subject from the listed failures . . . they are failures *which simply exist*; they are not failures *by* any particular individual, agency or government' (p. 38).

> For the *Report*, trauma subsists in the awful realization that national security has become insecure, and that a plot exceeding the imagination of the American government had spiraled out of control. Such a trauma focuses on the loss of control; the *Report* seizes the opportunity to assert retrospective

representational control over the event by constructing an integrated narrative, a recounting which allocates place, time and consequence to all its component elements.

(p. 44)

In analyzing the *Report,* Young is drawing together psychoanalytical with PTSD theory to establish her criminological 'ethic' in a complex argument where, finally, 'the text is driven to live on in the event, so that its present tense occupies the space of both the past and the future' (p. 45). In contrast, she argues that the Iñárritu film 'responds to the trauma of the event by remembering the pain of witnessing it and creating a film which embodies the suffering such witnessing entails' (p. 45). She insists that the entire film 'embodies the experience of trauma: through its insistent jolting images, its discordant sounds, its disintegrated narrative, and its dislocation of the catastrophe from an explanatory frame' (p. 45). The film ran into trouble in the USA, Young implies, because it 'does not seek to efface the politics which led to the attack, to sooth anxieties about America's international relations, or to bolster our conceptions of community, as the *9/11 Report* does' (p. 45).

To drive home her comparison of the discursive differences between report and film, she takes one key event that appears in both of them: phone calls from people in the planes and towers that were never answered.

In the *Report* the unanswered calls are signified as mistakes in 'an otherwise perfectible system: communication has failed due to a circuit overload or to mechanical problems' (p. 45). But in contrast, Iñárritu's film text 'moves away from communicative failure and towards a moment whereby the film simply witnesses the *possibility* of communication' (p. 45). Young, watching this film again, suddenly realizes that one key telephone call in the film, when a man about to die simply says 'Michelle?' twice over, is an unanswered call – a call that will be received when he is already dead. For Young, 'his speaking of those words cannot be undone . . . Iñárritu's film places us in the position of coming too late to answer but not too late to *witness* his voice' (p. 46). Thus, she says, the film moves from the trauma of the event to the pains and restorative potential of response (p. 46).

Young concludes by emphasizing that her focus is not on the disaster itself, but on the interim months and years after it, because this is when PTSD manifests itself. The two texts she has analyzed have, she says, tried *later* to re-imagine the disaster, in substance and effect.

Young's article is a compelling account of images and PTSD, emphasizing PTSD therapy's focus on 'images which rehearse and repeat our fall into the abyss of trauma'. At the same time, it imaginatively blends notions of 'witnessing' from criminology with concepts of 'seeing' (and being positioned to see) from screen theory. In its finale, it celebrates the disjuncture of image and sound, narrative and diagesis, which has been seen as the hallmark of cinematic reflexivity in film theory for thirty years. But here it is given the restorative power of 'unlocking' traumatic images, which is the goal of PTSD therapy.

While Young's is a convincing argument, working well within its particular theoretical frames of reference, we do have some questions about it. As one of us was the actual PTSD victim of a terrorist attack, we ask to what extent is the blending of 'witnessing' and 'spectating' from different academic discourses (criminology and psycho-analytical screen theory) anything more than Young's construction of a metaphorical representation of trauma? To what extent is it an analytical category of 'visual trauma' which is separate from the trauma itself in so far that, in her analysis, it seems to be available to *both* the close-up population of New York who experienced the event viscerally via all their senses *and* the author of the article who presumably saw the event on television thousands of miles away? Psychoanalytically describing visual trauma as the 'primal scene' of 9/11, Young imposes an academic-Freudian image of analysis. In contrast, the 'unlocking' of the image by PTSD cognitive behaviour therapy (CBT) takes place through a new combination of images by the traumatized survivor her/himself. It is not provided by the 'expert' therapist, or, as in Young's case, the 'expert' filmmaker.

Secondly, as film scholars ourselves, we can suggest alternative reasons for Iñárritu's film not gaining a release in the US. First, there was the censorship of 'the jumpers' images right across the US commercial media industry. Second, there was the fact that Iñárritu's film was only one segment of eleven in Brigand's composite film and it is possible that other segments were more instrumental in attracting its condemnation as 'stridently anti-American' (*Variety* magazine, cited in Young 2007: 41). For example, Ken Loach's segment systematically linked September 11, 2001 with September 11, 1973, when General Pinochet's US-backed military coup in Chile overthrew and killed the democratically elected President, Salvador Allende. This 'other 9/11' – or, for Loach, the 'first 9/11' in his narrative critiquing US neoliberal foreign policy – was far more likely to have led to the charge of 'strident anti-Americanism' in the US, and to have stood in the way of its distribution there than Iñárritu's film. To put it another way, in Young's terms, giving voice to a dead man's words is indeed 'the prior question' for Loach; and Allende's 'voice' was a key part of the composite film which many in the USA did not want to hear, especially so soon after 9/11. This is not an either/or prioritization of dead men's voices. Rather, it indicates, again, that the theoretical questions we ask will lead to different analytical emphases in what Young calls the 'struggle of politics and interpretation'.

7/7 Icon: A risk-sociologist's analysis

In Chapter 8 we introduced risk theory as a way of positioning our analysis of Abu Ghraib images in the context of the Iraq War. In this chapter we take another risk perspective. Here we will explore the relevance to understanding iconic images of two different risk theory approaches: emphasis on 'lay knowledge' and 'governmentality' theory.

The 'lay knowledge' approach argues that the power of experiential knowledge that people's everyday lives gives them is usually denied, and the outcome of risk can often only be determined by others. Thus, in a special 2008 issue of the journal *Health, Risk and Society* on living with risk and uncertainty, the editors Alaszewski and Coxon note that in the 'risk society' individuals have become responsible for managing an increasing range of risks, many of which are generated by global processes and can only be identified by specialist expertise. Yet,

> While experts with their specialist knowledge are a possible resource for making sense of and managing uncertainty . . . the evidence tends to indicate . . . when expert predictions based on cognitive rationality are compared to non-expert predictions grounded in lay heuristics there is little evidence that experts are better at predicting the future.
>
> (Alaszewski and Coxon 2008: 419)

In Chapter 8 we saw a similar claim with Boholm challenging technico-scientific theories of risk because they ignore intuitive and emotive knowledge (1998: 126–7). As Beck's (1992) 'risk society' theory was adapted through the 1990s and into the twenty-first century of terrorism, there developed within it different epistemological positions (Lupton 1999; Tulloch 1999, 2008a, 2008b). In particular a greater emphasis emerged on 'lay knowledge' and individual-subjective experience (Wynne 1996) to counter Beck's continuing emphasis on 'expert knowledge'; and, in contrast, there developed a Foucauldian emphasis on different kinds of 'governmental rationality' exploring the power of professional expert discourse (O'Malley 2008; Tulloch 2008a: 452).

An example of the former emphasis is Iain Wilkinson's analysis of the importance of emotions and cultural representation, and the need to focus on everyday lived experience in relation to risk subjectivity. 'A major concern here is that the genuine voice of suffering people is effectively silenced by the translation of their experience into the language of science and technical expertise' (Wilkinson 2006: 3).

The latter emphasis in risk sociology includes Mitchell Dean's criticism of Ulrich Beck's assumption that risk can be understood within a single cultural narrative of the modernization process, i.e. risk modernity. In contrast, Dean argues that 'it is easy to show the virtue of focusing on the concrete and empirical and to analyze specific types of risk rationalities and practices' (1999: 136).

Dean, for example, describes the different discourses of (i) *insurance risk* (depending on specific quantitative and calculative techniques such as statistical tables and probability analysis); (ii) *epidemiological risk* (quantifying rates of mortality and morbidity within a population); (iii) *case-management risk* (mainly qualitative assessment via face-to-face case analysis of 'at risk' individuals in areas such as alcoholism, sexual diseases, trauma from violence, or welfare dependency); and (iv) *comprehensive risk management* (or what Dean calls 'worst case scenario' government risk strategies at sites where disaster could get completely out of hand, as in nuclear reactor accidents like Chernobyl).

On 7 July 2005, this book's first author, John Tulloch, having written about risk subjectivities with Deborah Lupton (2003), suddenly found himself the victim of a terrorist attack. Going through slow physical, psychological and intellectual recovery from his injuries, he had the rare opportunity to explore what Wilkinson calls the 'voice of suffering people' even as he went through the translation of his trauma via the media and PTSD therapy's 'language of science and technical expertise' (Wilkinson 2006: 3).

Exploring his own 'lay knowledge' as the 'client' of PTSD therapy, Tulloch drew at the same time on the other strand of current risk sociology, mobilizing Dean's calculative techniques to explore his own agency during recovery. Thus he argues that in terms of the insurance risk discourse of 7/7 he avoided media contact in this area of 'compensation', adopting the simplistic identity of one of the 'lucky' people recovering from the attack (Tulloch 2008). In the area of epidemiological risk discourse (in his case, medical specialists' contradictory quantifying of his percentage chances of recovering his hearing, since both his eardrums had been damaged by the blast), his response was primarily private, communicating in personal emails about medical advice and ear surgery with other Australian survivors. In terms of case-management risk technologies (in his case, therapeutic advice to him by PTSD psychologists, social workers, occupational therapists and physiotherapists, who all employed a version of cognitive behaviour therapy in their contact with him), he found himself subjected to its logic of targets linked to identification of, and living with, physical and psychological imagistic triggers to systemic breakdown.

In reconsidering this process, Tulloch recognized that whereas in some areas of risk discourse he had avoided agency (insurance risk discourse), had privatized agency (epidemiological risk discourse), or had found his agency subjected to 'expert' medical case-management risk targets as in his PTSD therapy, it was in the area of comprehensive risk management discourse and media engagement that he was most agentive.

The media representation of 7/7 and terrorist risk-surveillance was a specific kind of comprehensive risk and disaster management, which worked closely in harmony with government, even when particular newspapers resisted politically the counter-terrorism policies of the party in power. *The Sun*'s November 2005 front-page use of Tulloch's iconic image was an example of this harmonizing, vociferously supporting the Prime Minister's proposed anti-terror legislation 'to bring safety to Britain's streets'. As a political identity, Tulloch had strongly opposed the Iraq War. As an academic identity, he had engaged with risk subjectivity theory. As a physical entity, he had been severely injured by suicide bomber Mohhamad Sidique Khan. Tulloch discusses how in his contact with the media he tried, via using media images of himself and Khan, to emphasize both his and Khan's multiple identities (2008).

In a BBC2 *Newsnight* interview, for example, which challenged *The Sun*'s use of his iconic image to support counter-terror legislation that he opposed, Tulloch offered both visual and verbal cues emphasising his own and Khan's multiple identities, beyond that of simple 'victim' and 'killer'. This met varying degrees of success in terms of what was finally broadcast. In an ITN national news broadcast on 7 July 2006, he secured conceptual, voice-over and editing control of his item on the identities of Mohammad Sidique Khan (Tulloch 2006; 2008a).

Like Alison Young, Tulloch was particularly interested in the relationship between PTSD and visual trauma, in so far that PTSD as a therapeutic technique dealt, in Young's words, with 'representations produced not in the immediate pain of loss but in the difficult interim space of the succeeding years – a time of "present pasts"' (Young 2007: 31). But whereas Young approached PTSD therapy's 'unlocking' of trauma images in psychoanalytical terms, Tulloch drew on PTSD within its own discourse rationality, and positioned this in the context of the recent thrust within sociological risk theory on behalf of subjective approaches to living with risk and uncertainty.

Tulloch describes how, within his PTSD therapy, there was a 'dual' Eye Movement Desensitization and Reprocessing (EMDR) technique, designed to allow the client to access empowering ways of reframing the original trauma (2008). The idea here was to release the body's 'trapped' emotional changes, and so enable current, adaptive recall of the traumatic event without the 'locked-in' anxiety. This technique was thus based on the traumatized patient's *self*-construction of images to challenge the 'locked-in' images of trauma. Images were not produced by expert knowledge, as in Young's example. Tulloch discusses both his problems and the therapeutic value of his encounter with PTSD therapy techniques. In particular he had some emotional and cognitive difficulties with EMDR.

First, despite EMDR's claims for rapidity of effect and not forcing the client back into distressing details of past events, the very nature of its three-part (target, negative belief, positive belief) structure is likely to bring the patient back again and again to 'seeing' in minute detail images of the painful events. Indeed, in face-to-face therapy one is actually encouraged to seek new images of the event which might 'unlock' the negative memory. This can work very well, as it seems to have done with another 7/7 victim in Tulloch's underground train carriage. This man found he had PTSD flashbacks every time he heard something funny in conversation or on TV, until he recalled (during a PTSD therapy session) the image of himself reading a humorous novel at the moment of the explosion. This 'positive belief' recovery helped resolve his flashback problem. But where the technique is not working quickly it can and, in Tulloch's case, did draw the patient through many hours of painful recall and image searching.

Second, the therapist's request to her 'client' to quantify his emotions and feelings on a ten-point scale can, subjectively, seem very arbitrary (especially to an academic qualitative social researcher like Tulloch). To him it seemed an artefact of the therapy experience itself. As Tulloch sat in his chair, visualizing 'new images' and recounting their context in detail week after week as the therapist tapped on his knees and shoulders using a modified EMDR technique, this sense of arbitrary scoring seemed to him sometimes more about the communication between a professionally sensitive psychologist and an exhausted client (who, she said, was 'thinking too much' as an academic) than about getting rid of his body spasms. So he felt a failure in that role of therapy 'client'.

Third, after focussing for many weeks on the 'double trauma' of an earlier mugging Tulloch had encountered in Spain, all these various emotions then impacted when the therapist came back to using EMDR in relation to his 'locked' memories of 7/7. As a media academic, Tulloch was only too aware that what 'trapped' him most (consciously, at least) in these therapy recall sessions was the realization that his memories of 7/7 had been constructed in part via his process of talking about the event to the media. By the time he reached the final session with his PTSD therapist, he was so aware of this imagistic media narrative obstructing his therapy that he was ever more urgently searching for 'new images' of the 7/7 event. This time in the 'negative belief' stage, perhaps half-consciously, he adopted a film director's crane-shot view, looking down on himself on 7/7 from a height, seeing in the cut-away image of the carriage the explosion throwing him violently back against the seat, then forwards into the pole that caused such damage to his head, then back again, leaving him lying in the rubble. This invented (and probably inaccurate) image, together with other 'received' TV images which he recalled from his memory during his image search in that final PTSD session, made him aware of the link between his multiple subjective responses (as 'victim', 'client' and 'academic') and *both* media *and* PTSD 'risk technologies'. These included his own 'academic media specialist' cues in seeing 'new images'.

By focussing empirically on the ways in which he engaged with two of Dean's institutional risk rationalities – case-management risk in relation to PTSD therapy and comprehensive risk-management in relation to his mass media engagement – Tulloch, like Dean, sought to move beyond the notion of risk as a single cultural narrative of modernization, while also responding to Wilkinson's call for a focus on lived experience in relation to trauma and risk subjectivity. Yet, telling these tales of subjective anxiety and suffering in the context of Dean's emphasis on Foucault and the variability of discourse technologies, revealed, Tulloch argues, that there was too much of a dichotomy in Wilkinson's formulation between subjective understandings of 'lived experience' and 'the language of science and technical expertise' on risk.

In the case of his PTSD therapy, it seemed clear that his own everyday emotional risk traumas led him not only to many PTSD sessions, despite the anxiety they caused, but also to scanning the new media for further 'science and technical expertise' (such as using the internet to find out more about CBT and EMDR) because he found that was empowering, both cognitively and emotionally. And in the case of his engagement with the mass media usage of his own iconic image, it was also clear that intellectual expertise about subjectivity and multiple identities from within the social and human sciences informed not only his performance in television, radio, newspaper and magazine interviews, but also framed the politics of his representation of the suicide bomber, Mohammad Sidique Khan. In media interview after interview, and in his book *One Day in July: Experiencing 7/7* (Tulloch 2006), the multiple identity of Khan, as 'bomber-Khan' and 'citizen-Khan', reappeared in his talk and in his images. His preparation strategy for these interviews was to try to think of ways (again calling on his media experience) of ensuring that at least some of this political/academic discourse survived the programme edit. At the same time, Tulloch believed, his long-term injuries from 7/7 had given him a particular subjective intensity going well beyond 'the language of science and technical expertise'. The attempt to 'go on' when unable to walk, read, hear, control his body spasms, or to give lectures had led him to a range of subjective strategies in relation to both the media use of his iconic image and the PTSD therapist's prompting of new images 'between trauma and its resolution' (Young 2007: 31).

Conclusion

This chapter has considered terrorism images and public trauma in terms of the professional discourses of criminology and risk sociology. In each case the professional discourses were themselves composite: as in Young's theoretical amalgam of criminological, film and PTSD theories with subjective responses; and in Tulloch's blending of different developments in risk theory with PTSD rationality. Central to the arguments here is the notion of witnessing the reality of the terrorist attacks of 9/11 and 7/7, witnessing their images, and the ways in which both actual and iconic images of terror are selected, circulated, and modified or repressed by agentive individuals.

10 Culture warriors

Icons of the colonial, then and now

Julie Dowling, *Walyer*, 2006, synthetic polymer paint and red ochre on canvas, National Gallery of Australia © DACS 2011

A female warrior, an Indigenous Australian, stands in the foreground of a recent painting, *Walyer*, by Julie Dowling (2006). This was a painting at the *Culture Warriors* exhibition in Canberra, 2007/8, by a Badimya/Yamatji/Widi artist. It is of Walyer, a Tasmanian Aboriginal resistance fighter, a woman of the Tomeginee people who died from the colonists' imported disease of influenza shortly after her capture in 1831.

As Assmann and Conrad have written, post Cold-War

> the colonial past and the long history of imperialist interventions, repression and genocide have emerged as privileged issues in a politics of global account-ability . . . The colonial experience implied foreign rule, economic exploita-tion and cultural dispossession, and its varying legacies guarantees its lasting status as a crucial site for understanding not only the past but also the present, and to derive values for a globalizing age.
>
> (2010: 7, 9)

In this chapter we begin with *Walyer* and other works at the Canberra *Culture Warriors* exhibition to set the scene for a discussion of a foundational text of post-colonial studies, *Orientalism* by Edward Saïd. Saïd's position is then critiqued via Bhabha's postmodern epistemology as we return to *Culture Warriors* to offer insights into icon-breaking and icon-making.

Walyer: Aboriginal resistance fighter

Julie Dowling says of her painting:

> I painted Walyer gesturing towards a group of colonial houses in the distant right. The moon shows light behind the clouds, outlining her cloaked body as she holds two guns. She is gesturing to the viewer, as if they were one of the fighters she has assembled to battle the colonial encroachments on their land and hers . . . Walyer stands in action, holding a fowler's rifle with a small flintlock pistol held in the belt around her skirt. She wears a *bookah* (kangaroo cloak), a shell necklace and clay ornamentation covers her hair.
>
> (J. Dowling, cited in Croft 2007: 95)

Carol Dowling asks viewers to look through Aboriginal eyes as oppressed peoples:

> My *nurrumba* (sister) Julie Dowling confronts complex issues about native title, social/spiritual/cultural degradation and the devastating destruction of our natural heritage. She also constructs the far-reaching legacy of the brutal oppression of Aboriginal people in Australia, which continues in the Stolen Generation who were wrenched from their families and society . . . Julie has always been a culture warrior for us all. She lures onlookers, both Aboriginal and *Wudjula* (non-Aboriginal person) into her world.
>
> (C. Dowling, cited in Croft 2007: 96)

Julie Dowling's representation of the warrior figure Walyer via direct address to the viewer reminds us of Hariman and Lucaites' discussion of the Kent State University photograph of a weeping woman (Chapter 2):

> The iconic picture must rely on the viewer's recognition of typical settings . . . Any text will hail an audience, but one source of a photograph's power is that its lines of interpellation can be a direct imitation of face-to-face interaction . . . She addresses the state: 'How could you do this?'
>
> (Hariman and Lucaites 2007: 143)

In *Walyer* the woman at front-centre, as in the Kent State photograph, again has an arm outstretched, and again is using it to hail an audience, encouraging us to re-think the image's relationship to state-colonial oppression. The tree-obscured road behind Walyer to which she gestures is, in a symbolic sense, like the road behind the naked 'napalmed girl' Kim Phuc in Vietnam, since it is in military control. The houses in the Dowling picture are emitting smoke, a small, domesticated sign of white, state-military presence, as Walyer's holding of two guns herself is clearly meant to signify. The billowing napalm clouds in Nick Ut's Vietnam photograph and the discrete, trailing smoke in Dowling's painting collectively represent colonial power, brutality and ownership in the midst of natural environment and luscious vegetation. The full-frontal, close-up portrayal of a female figure is common to both Nick Ut's 'napalmed girl' and Julie Dowling's *Walyer*. Walyer, naked above the waist beneath her *bookah*, and with bare legs and feet, is clothed ethnically and functionally, both as an Aboriginal and as a warrior. And, as with the 'napalmed girl' and Kent State images, there is a direct rhetorical relationship between the image subject and the viewer.

But there are also significant differences between Dowling's painting and these Vietnam icons. Wayler's eyes are not 'on the state' (as in Hariman and Lucaites' Kent State example), but directly on us, as viewers. Her outstretched arm gesture is not part of a cry of helpless anguish, as it is in the Vietnam photographs, but a firm, indexical statement of direction and an invitation for us to look back at her with Aboriginal and not state-centric eyes.

Indigenous artist and curator of the exhibition Brenda Croft says that *Walyer* 'is a rallying cry of opposition. Dowling's protagonist, standing like an Antipodean Boudicca, is a culture warrior, overturning the myth of passive submission' (2007: xv). Croft's analogy with Boudicca is carefully chosen: identifying Walyer not only with another prodigious female warrior, but with one who, in the islands later to become Britain, felt the power, cruelty and brutality of an earlier imperial master, Rome. The painting includes an appeal to a white audience to see with the eyes of the oppressed. Walyer's image becomes part of the politics of apology and reparation in a contemporary world.

As curator of the inaugural National Indigenous Art Triennial exhibition, Croft comments in her catalogue that the social activism in the gallery's chosen *Culture Warriors* title reflects the ongoing issues of culture, history and nationalism:

Of the thirty Indigenous artists represented in *Culture Warriors*, twenty-one were not considered citizens of Australia, nor counted in the national census until 1967 . . . In the 179 years preceding the 1967 referendum, Indigenous Australians – the First People of this continent – have endured the ongoing effects of colonization: loss of access to traditional lands, dislocation from customary practices, including language, and forcible removal of children from families and communities.

(Croft 2007: xi).

Croft's invocation of culture warriors – fighters then and artists now – is focussed on describing systematic *state* terror against an Indigenous people that sought to eliminate their sociality and their culture, and reveals an equally systematic cultural imperialism that imported to the 'empty land' its own imagistic and iconic forms. Against that, she posits a painting of an active freedom fighter, *Walyer*, and supports Indigenous artists who challenge the icons of imperial colonialism. In the *Walyer* painting, social knowledge in Hariman and Lucaites' terms is fused with the paradigmatic scene of war, collective memory is being reshaped with respect to the historical past, and citizenship is being modelled in terms of its recent absence for the Indigenous people of Australia. *Walyer*, and the other images by Indigenous Australians we describe here, are part of what Assmann and Conrad describe as a new 'engagement with symbolic representation and the emergence of global icons that can be understood as a characteristic feature of memory in a global age' (2010: 10).

Indeed, the entire exhibition speaks directly to this material, social, and cultural relationship of terror and exploitation. But the Indigenous artists represented in the exhibition address this historical past and collective memory iconically in different ways. For example, Kudjla/Gangalu artist, Daniel Boyd, emphasized generic and iconic remediation in repainting well-known portraits of the English late-eighteenth century elite, as he questioned the romantic notions that surround Australia's birth. Boyd writes, 'With our history being dominated by Eurocentric views it's very important that Aboriginal and Torres Strait Islander people continue to create dialogue from their own perspective to challenge the subjective history that has been created' (Boyd, cited in Croft 2007: 71).

Two of Boyd's reworked, Romantic-style portraits caught our attention. One was of a King (*King No Beard*), the other of an Admiral (*Governor No Beard*). They represented respectively the British heads of the colonizing and the colonized state. Each has a parrot on his shoulder, and each state leader has an eye-patch. We can approach the parrot and eye-patch references via a third Boyd painting displayed at the exhibition, which is simply a map of Australia. But it is also complex as a map, showing the many Indigenous groups in the country. Across the middle is the prominent title, 'Treasure Island'. This inter-textual reference to Robert Louis Stevenson's novel, with its pirate-engaged, eye-patched, and parrot-carrying protagonist Long John Silver, draws an iconic image in English popular culture. The 'Treasure Island' of Australia was, as British economic thinking of the 1930s proclaimed (when the Hollywood films of *Treasure Island* were first circulating), all about white 'Men, Money, Markets' (Tulloch 1982: chapter 5).

There is another historical reference to piracy in Boyd's work, as Tina Baum, Curator of Indigenous Art at the National Gallery of Australia, notes. The map, she writes, seems innocuous at first glance and unconnected to other works. But it is a replica of a 1994 Australian Institute of Aboriginal and Torres Strait Islander Studies map showing more than 300 Indigenous language groups in the country.

> For an Indigenous person, this map represents sadness and loss as well as strength of culture. It reminds us just how many of our people since 1788 have been dispossessed and denied access to our language, lands and basic human rights; yet it's also a beacon of hope as Australia's Indigenous people have shown great resilience and strength in surviving as the world's oldest living culture.
>
> (Baum, cited in Croft 2007: 72)

It is this mix of a formally bland but emotionally powerful map that energizes our perception of Boyd's portraits of King George III (the British monarch at the time of colonization), Captain Cook (who 'discovered' Australia) and Governor Arthur Phillip. As Baum explains:

> Key figures in Australia's discovery and growth into nationhood are altered with here an eyepatch, there a macaw parrot, and, now and then, a jolly Jack. The historical figures of King George III, Cook and Phillip have been extensively discussed and portrayed in terms of their impact on Indigenous peoples throughout the new worlds. Today, hundreds of years later and several continents apart, Boyd's work encourages the idea of parallel dialogues between different cultures through a kind of visual mimicry.
>
> (Baum, cited in Croft 2007: 72)

Speaking of his portrait *Captain No Beard* (2005), Boyd says that he based it on the posthumous portrait of Cook painted by John Webber, hanging at the National Portrait Gallery in London. Before seeing that painting, he had come across documents where King George gave power to Cook to seize land without the consent of the 'natives':

> I immediately drew parallels between a common practice of the time, the act [of] Piracy. Nationalistic rivalry with Spain and others drove the practice of employing privateers to engage in combat with other countries, resulting in the British indirectly participating in piracy.
>
> (Baum, cited in Croft 2007: 72)

Baum explains that the expression 'no beard' inscribed on each of these paintings refers to when Cook first landed in Australia and it was said Aboriginal people thought he was a woman because he had no facial hair. She adds:

> While this is funny enough, as a *name* No Beard is also a reference to the well-known pirate Black Beard, with whom the clean-shaven King George III,

Cook and Phillip have much in common, as in Boyd's terms they all performed acts of piracy':

(Baum, cited in Croft 2007: 72)

Political, peripatetic people: simulacra and reality

The Australian *Culture Warriors* exhibition fused two major conceptual dimensions.
One is the emphasis on re-describing through art forms a history of repression.
Brenda Croft clearly indicates this 'venal and brutal' state oppression to Indigenous people in quoting Australian Labor Prime Minister Paul Keating's speech at
the launch of the International Year for the World's Indigenous People in December 1992.

> Didn't Australia provide opportunity and care for the dispossessed Irish? The
> poor of Britain? The refugees from war and famine in the countries of Europe
> and Asia? Isn't it reasonable to say that if we can build a prosperous and
> remarkably harmonious society in Australia, surely we can find just solutions
> to the problems which beset the first Australians – the people to whom the
> most injustice has been done . . . With some noble exceptions, we failed to
> make the most basic response and enter into their hearts and minds. We failed
> to ask – how would it feel if this were done to me?
>
> (Keating, cited in Croft 2007: xviii)

Croft adds, 'However, as the Tasmanian Aboriginal woman resistance fighter
Walyer indicates, Indigenous people did not simply abdicate their rights, their lands,
their customs and their lives to the colonisers' (p. xviii). We should understand that
Walyer's eye-to-eye contact with her audiences, and her gesture to them, explores
Paul Keating's realist question: 'how would it feel if this were done to me?'

The second conceptual dimension of the exhibition is formal and philosophical.
It draws on current postcolonial debate to challenge colonial icons and images,
and it seeks to make alternative icons in their turn. When Julie Dowling, Danie
Mellor, Daniel Boyd, Christian Bumbarra Thompson and many other Indigenous
Australian artists work through the genres of Western art forms to demystify icons
that have emerged out of the stereotypes of power, they are also seeking to define
a new iconicity in current, often urban Aboriginal art.

All of the Aboriginal artists described here play across their own multiple identities, as tribal people, colonized people, Indigenous people, urban people, people
of mixed colour, professional artistic people, peripatetic people, political people.
All of them are reflexively aware through their everyday lives as well as their art
of this tension between identities, as simulacra and reality at the same time. Some
are clearly aware, via their art college training, of current postmodernist theories of cultural hybridity, simulation and orientalism. Danie Mellor, a teacher at
the Canberra School of Art, for example, speaks of the 'spectacle' of his art, the
'simulation of reality', and the 'fables that depict the exotic and the fantastic, the
Oriental and the Other in faraway places' (Croft 2007: 125). Christian Bumbarra

Thompson speaks of 'Notions of cultural hybridity' being dominant in his art practice (p. 125).

On one hand, Carol Dowling refers to the precise historicity which links 200 years of Indigenous struggle with colonization in Australia, and she undoubtedly spoke for most of the exhibitors and curators at the *Culture Warriors* exhibition when she wrote:

> We struggle to maintain our languages, our customary law and our oral tradition. With the ratification of the Universal Declaration of the Rights of Indigenous Peoples, we dream that the world will hear our call for justice and freedom as the oldest living culture on the planet.
>
> (C. Dowling, cited in Croft 2007: 96)

On the other hand, many were also aware, via both cultural theory and daily, multi-identity practice, of the global nature of both (post)colonialism and Indigenous struggles. They were thoroughly aware of the concept of 'state terror' and 'orientalism'.

Edward Saïd: *Orientalism*

When Danie Mellor speaks of colonial discourse concerning 'the Oriental and the Other in faraway places' (Croft 2007: 125) he is referring in particular to the concept of Orientalism. Edward Saïd's book *Orientalism* (1978) has been a foundational text of post-colonial studies. In his survey of Saïd's work shortly after his death in 2003, John Higgins speaks of Saïd as 'an academic iconoclast, revered by some and never forgiven by others' (Higgins 2003: 2):

> He broke two of the main taboos of institutionalized academic study. The first of these was the unspoken rule that forbade the making of direct connections between the ideals of culture and the reality of past and present political life ... The second was the refusal of disciplinarity and specialization, which he believed tended to weaken and depoliticize the intellectual strengths of academic writing.
>
> (ibid.)

The first of these principles helps explain Saïd's enormous influence on post-colonial literary theory, and also in the art world via a succession of international exhibitions, such as *Culture Warriors* (2007/8). This is the principle underlying the first of the conceptual dimensions of the *Culture Warriors* exhibition.

Saïd's second principle underpins the exhibition's other conceptual dimension – engaging philosophy with form. Just as Indigenous artists like Danie Mellor and Christian Bumbarra Thompson spoke clearly about their cultural hybridity, so, too, did Saïd. He described in many interviews how, after seeing the images of the 1967 Arab–Israeli seven day war, he shifted from being a US professor of comparative literature to the professor who was 'completely immersed in politics and the Palestinian resistance movement'.

Theory

Saïd's first theoretical principle is his challenge, like John Berger, to 'The distinction between pure and political knowledge' (Saïd 1978: 9). He says of Orientalism in the nineteenth century:

> it is, above all, a discourse that is by no means in direct, corresponding relationship with political power in the raw, but rather is produced and exists in an uneven exchange with power political (as with a colonial or imperial establishment), power intellectual (as with reigning sciences like comparative linguistics or anatomy, or any of the modern policy sciences), power cultural (as with orthodoxies and canons of taste, texts, values), power moral (as with ideas about what 'we' do and what 'they' cannot do or understand as 'we' do). Indeed, my real argument is that Orientalism is . . . a considerable dimension of modern political-intellectual culture, and as such has less to do with the Orient than it does with 'our' world.
>
> (Saïd 1978: 12)

In Saïd's analysis Orientalism was the distillation into power of stereotyping ideas about the Orient. His particular emphasis here is on Michel Foucault's specification of discourse and power, and Antonio Gramsci's understanding of hegemony.

> My contention is that without examining Orientalism as a discourse one cannot possibly understand the enormously systematic discipline by which European culture was able to manage – and even produce – the Orient politically, sociologically, and imaginatively during the post-Enlightenment period.
>
> (p. 3)

Regarding Gramsci, Saïd notes:

> the influence of ideas, of institutions, and of other persons works not through domination but by what Gramsci calls consent . . . [T]he form of this cultural leadership is what Gramsci has identified as *hegemony*, an indispensable concept for any understanding of cultural life in the industrial West. It is hegemony . . . that gives Orientalism . . . durability and strength.
>
> (p. 7)

In Saïd's analysis, following Gramsci, a common sense consensus developed among Western populations that 'oriental' rulers were prone to despotism and brutality, 'oriental' women were especially sensual and 'oriental' people generally were backward, unpunctual and inefficient.

This combination of Foucault's discourse-as-power and Gramsci's concept of hegemony are clear in recent art exhibitions on Orientalism, which have been strongly influenced by Saïd. Thus, in the catalogue to the Art Gallery of New South Wales' exhibition, *Orientalism: Delacroix to Klee* (Benjamin and Khemir 1997), curator Roger Benjamin writes:

> Delacroix gave currency to violence in an exotic frame that remained one of the mainstays of Orientalist art . . . One such prejudice – that the natural political order of the East is despotism – is given powerful expression in Delacroix's *The death of Sardanapulus*, 1827. Inspired by a play by Byron, this riot of bloodletting is premised on the eastern . . . ruler's brutal control over the destiny of his people, beasts and treasures of the household, which he destroys rather than have them fall into enemy hands.
>
> (Benjamin and Khemir 1997: 8–9)

Although Saïd concentrated on writers rather than painters in *Orientalism*, French artist Jean-Leon Gerome's *The Snake Charmer* was reproduced on his book cover, and the curators of the 1997 *Orientalism* exhibition drew on this painting to extend Saïd's analysis of heterosexual Orientalist sensuality. As Caroline Jordon describes it:

> *The snake charmer* has been held up as an exemplar of Orientalism by Edward Saïd . . . and by the art historian Linda Nochlin. For Nochlin, *The snake charmer* is a fantasy concoction based on cultural misrecognition dressed up as documentary realism. The magic-weaving spell of the charmer or the storyteller is the quintessential stuff of an *Arabian Nights* fantasy. There is a touch of taboo, too, as well as mystery, in the anticipatory atmosphere of this all-male scene, hinted at by the phallic snake coiled around the naked, muscled body of the young boy-performer. This sublimated homoeroticism creates a more subtle sexual display than that found in Gerome's comparable scenes of exotic entertainments featuring women, where the body is in full-frontal view.
>
> (Jordon, cited in Benjamin and Khemir 1997: 99)

Methodology

Saïd emphasizes that writing a text involves delimitation by which some things are cut from a mass of material, and he draws on Althusser's idea of the problematic: a concept or word cannot be considered in isolation from its theoretical framework (1978: 16).

Althusser's notion of the problematic was not simply a matter of theoretically designating a point of departure, but of defining what is chosen textually in terms of what is *not* chosen. Hence Saïd's methodological rejection of 'an encyclopedic narrative history of Orientalism' (p. 16).

Saïd delimits his 'problematic' methodologically in four ways. First, he admits that, although *Orientalism* covers wide historical ground, it focuses particularly on one period, the nineteenth century, and one major area, the Middle East and

North Africa. This is for precise historical reasons relating to his problematic: 'Orientalism in the West'. It was then that the combination of colonialism, militarism and linguistic/cultural discourses established, especially in France and Britain, a greater range, yet also tighter consensus, of Orientalist language and imaging.

Second, while engaging with current postmodernist and constructivist theory in terms of images, rhythms and discursive motifs, his emphasis is fundamentally on the 'material' institutions of Orientalism. Here Saïd parts company with conventionalist postmodernism. So, although he does argue that 'strong' ideas are produced through discourse – hence his adherence to Foucault's notion of the development of scientific disciplinary regimes of thought in this period as constituting technical-rational discourses of surveillance – he also argues, following Gramsci, that these discourses and regimes are embedded in specific material-historical circumstances:

> Without those emphases and that material effectiveness Orientalism would be just another idea, whereas it . . . was much more than that . . . [M]y hybrid perspective is broadly historical and 'anthropological' given that I believe all texts to be worldly and circumstantial in (of course) ways that vary from genre to genre, and from historical period to historical period.
>
> (Saïd 1978: 23)

It is his critical realist emphasis on the agency of 'willed human work' in real 'worldly' contexts that leads to his main disagreement with Foucault:

> Foucault believes that in general the individual text or author counts for very little; empirically, in the case of Orientalism . . . I find this not to be so. Accordingly my analyses employ close textual readings whose goal is to reveal the dialectic between individual text or writer and the complex collective formation to which his work is a contribution.
>
> (p. 24)

When Saïd said he hoped his book would reach 'readers in the so-called Third World' (p. 25), it is clear that he was speaking about the real power of the western world's discourses embedded in a 'deep structure'. For his 'Third World' readers, 'My hope is to illustrate the formidable structure of cultural domination and, specifically for formerly colonized peoples, the dangers and temptations of employing this structure upon themselves or upon others' (p. 25).

Third, Saïd's focus on a real-structural order of things explains a further delimitation of his work. He (and Linda Nochlin who extended Saïd's work into art criticism) were criticized by the curator of the *Orientalism* exhibition, Roger Benjamin who said their theories' 'continued viability is called into question today by the popularity of Gerome and his disciples with the very people – in particular, art collectors from Saudi Arabia and the Gulf States – his pictures were said to denigrate' (Benjamin and Khemir 1997: 17). But Saïd would have drawn on Roger Benjamin's own carefully reasoned discussion of this issue (under the title *Painting and*

Petrodollars) to argue that today the rich purchasers of Gerome in the contemporary Arab world are facing an historically changed, hybrid experience of Orientalism as a result of globalization. The reality of the situation, Saïd would say, is that the impoverished people in Palestine, for whom he particularly sought justice, will never be buying paintings by Gerome.

A further criticism of Saïd by Benjamin reveals a fourth methodological delimitation: around Indigenous artists in the Arab world in the late nineteenth century. Benjamin says 'It is at such a point that the dichotomous, oppositional model of Orientalism as defined by the early Saïd falters again' (p. 28). He draws attention to the work of Mohammad Racim as

> a new, hybrid art form that combined the virtues of several traditions, eastern and western . . . It is appropriate that the exhibition close with an artist who transcends the [Saïd] stereotype, who offers an affirmation of the value of art forged *between* cultures, and yet simultaneously looks back to a time before colonial subjection, and forward to the renewal of Algerian sovereignty.
>
> (p. 29)

Benjamin's comments open up the question of artistic *alternatives* to Orientalism, which Saïd himself discusses:

> Perhaps the most important task of all would be to undertake studies in contemporary alternatives to Orientalism, to ask how one can study other cultures and peoples from a libertarian, or a nonrepressive and nonmanipulative, perspective. But then one would have to rethink the whole complex problem of knowledge and power. These are . . . tasks left embarrassingly incomplete in the present study.
>
> (p. 24)

The point is that Saïd's focus is mainly on one specific period of Orientalism, located in the particular subjectivities of specific western countries expressed in different ways in different professional discourses and different genres of art. That is the *problematic* he is concerned with in the book *Orientalism*. To explore alternatives to Orientalism is to engage with a different, more hybrid problematic. Different problematics relating to 'art forged *between* cultures' require new notions of hybridity and reflexivity.

Critiquing Orientalism

Continuing debate about Saïd in the art exhibition world indicates the productivity of his thesis, even when most criticized. For example, Nicholas Tromans, the curator of *The Lure of the East: British Orientalist Painting* exhibition at Tate Britain emphasizes that: 'From the outset . . . we . . . find ourselves in the hot waters of the Orientalism debate sparked by the book of that name . . . (published in 1978 by the late Edward Saïd)' (2008: 11). The curators of this exhibition featured Saïd, symptomatically, at the centre of their own catalogue's 'hot water' debate.

For example, in 'Cultures Crossed: John Frederick Lewis and the Art of Orientalist Painting', Emily Weeks adopts a feminist-textualist approach highly critical of Saïd. What had initially been seen as 'brilliantly incisive' in Saïd now appeared, she said, 'ahistorical, gender-blind, inductively reasoned and ambiguous. Issues of class were ignored, as were specific political economies and local social circumstances' (2008: 24). Criticizing Saïd for neglect of individual artists, and focusing on *The Reception* by British Orientalist painter John Frederick Lewis, Weeks argues that Lewis was highly aware of the signs, symbols and icons of harem life as social practice in Egypt, where *The Reception* is set, and also displayed intimate knowledge of Edward William Lane's book *An Account of the Manners and Customs of the Modern Egyptians*. Hence when Lewis in *The Reception* apparently confuses the *mandarah* (the only room in the private Cairo house where male visitors are received) with the *qa'a* (the private space women can enjoy alone), Weeks insists that Lewis knew what he was doing. By 'Adopting the lifestyle of a well-to-do Turkish "bey"' Lewis, was 'Not quite the average Egyptian, and no longer overtly British' (p. 29). This hybridity, she says, explains Lewis's 'stubbornly ambiguous position' (p. 30), and his reversal in *The Reception* of the 'gendered geography of Islamic homes' (p. 27) which 'explodes architectural conventions and patriarchal systems of order, and leaves in their place a disquieting allusion to female power' (p. 30).

Weeks adds that Lewis' picture might also have 'been received with considerable discomfort in Victorian England' (p. 30), where it was being argued that the deplorable condition of women in the Middle East should help British women accept their continuing 'helpmate' role, domestically and politically. Thus Lewis' painting, with its physical transposition of the geographical and masculine centre of the Middle Eastern household, was 'not merely disruptive . . . to Muslim ideologies and social conventions'. It was also 'a threat to accepted rationalizations for British imperial and domestic policies' (p. 31).

Starting with a text used centrally in Saïd's thesis, Lane's *Modern Egyptians*, Weeks challenges him by way of textual, inter-textual and local historical analysis. She criticizes Saïd's 'too simplistic and essentialist' binary of 'East' and 'West' (p. 24). She also criticizes the development of Saïd's thesis by art critics like Linda Nochlin who assert that the 'pseudo-documentary' and meticulously polished, 'scientific' style of Orientalist paintings such as Gerome's disguised a 'sordid imperialist agenda' (p. 24). Instead, Weeks argues, *The Reception*'s 'meticulously painted veil of realism' frustrated male fantasies and accorded women domestic power in both Cairo and London (p. 30).

Weeks' comparison of Egyptian and British women's cultures as 'not so different after all' might be a reasonable comment from a feminist perspective. But it is too simplistic in other areas of cultural difference. Weeks' accuses Saïd of ignoring areas of class and ethnicity, but Rana Kabbani's essay in the exhibition catalogue is in marked contrast to this view. In 'Regarding Orientalist Painting Today', Kabbani argues that her two decades of writing about Orientalist painting 'as an "Oriental" . . . to try to understand how it depicts my world' has left her as convinced as ever she was by the power of Saïd's analysis (2008: 40). 'If anything, the interventions by Britain and America in the Middle East that we are witnessing [in the Iraq War] have made it increasingly difficult to look at these pictures with anything like an indulgent eye' (p. 40).

Kabbani implicitly contests Weeks' argument about the genuine hybridity of Lewis' position. While she sees differences 'of style but not of substance' between French Orientalist painters like Gerome and British artists like Lewis, Kabbani argues, following Saïd, that these painters in France and Britain, whether they dressed 'Turkish' or not, shared similar attitudes 'as far as religious and racial prejudice and colonial ideology was concerned' (p. 43). 'Similar strains of fascination and repulsion convulsed the imagination' (p. 43)

Lewis' class-hierarchical position is, in Kabbani's analysis, what really counts. Whereas Weeks reads current feminist theory and media/cultural studies' preoccupation with 'textual play' and 'resistant readings' (see Introduction) back into Orientalist paintings, Kabbani clearly reads forward between nineteenth and twentieth century imperialist histories. She argues at the beginning of her essay:

> If the British military occupation of Egypt inspired some of the striking paintings in this exhibition, what images might future generations retain of the present-day occupation of Iraq? . . . This time around . . . it would not be the work of professionals . . . Rather, it would be . . . the photographs of prisoners abused at Abu Ghraib prison . . . casually taken by participating American soldiers.
>
> (Kabbani 2008: 40)

Kabbani's focus is on 'emblematic' images of orientalism 'then' (in nineteenth century paintings) and 'now' (in Iraq's Abu Ghraib). By placing side by side on the catalogue page Columbian artist Fernado Botero's painting of piled up naked bodies in his *Abu Ghraib 57* (2005) and Ingres' painting of sensuously entwined bodies in *The Turkish Bath* (1862), Kabbani implies a continuity between current abuses and the meticulous, 'exotic' classical style that Saïd described – especially in so far they permit voyeurism, as at Abu Ghraib, of the naked body of the 'Other'.

Botero, Kabbani argues, reads back to the Ingres painting some of its hidden depths. She suggests that Orientalist painters, like Ingres, Gerome and Lewis were 'content to paint a static world of exquisite surfaces' (p. 41). They painted unchanging landscapes, ruins, harem interiors, daggers, turbans, silk robes and veils, jewels, ostrich fans, lutes, cushions, carpets, elaborately carved wood screens, colourful tiles, fountains, courtyards, arches and domes, 'all with "photographic" exactitude.' (p. 41). Via her Berger-style analysis of these '"goods" of Empire', Kabbani adds that 'in presenting so carefully and minutely this rich panoply of covetable material wares, these paintings signally failed to meet the sterner challenge of uncovering the spirit of the people or the meanings of place' (p. 41).

Kabbani's analysis as a female 'Oriental' is clearly deeply indebted to Saïd's discussion of Western male fantasies when she speaks of the 'Oriental' woman as 'the coveted stereotype of what was sexually permissible in an inhibited and repressive age' (p. 42). It is clear that Kabbani's comment about being reduced to a body to be looked at, to a colourful spectacle, or as part of an implicitly violent sexual drama, applies equally to the images from Abu Ghraib and to Ingres' *The Turkish Bath*, Gerome's *For Sale: Slaves at Cairo*, or to Lewis' fully clothed women of *The Reception*.

But another essay in *The Lure of the East* catalogue, Fatema Mernissi's 'Seduced by "Samar"', sees beyond the binary theoretical impasse between Weeks and Kabbani. Mernissi, draws on a central concept in Islamic values: the universal sense of *umma*. Pointing to the 'Cartesian superman' (2008: 35) of rationalism in the Western post-enlightenment world view, Mernissi says that the

> secular Western State – which anchors its identity in the defense of its geo-graphic frontiers – programmes its citizens to erect the difference between the day (rationality) and the night (unconscious) into a dangerous border. Islam, by contrast, encourages its followers to aim at a universal *umma* (community), which transcends geography and programmes the faithful to dance skillfully between day and night, reality and dreams.
>
> (p. 33)

Like Saïd, a traveler from a Muslim society to a Western university, Mernissi remembers with amusement her first experience of the suspicion of night, sleep and the moon among her new Western neighbours. In contrast, she emphasizes the lunar dimension of Islamic culture, traced to the fact that 'Islam was born in a desert environment, where the sun can easily kill you and where the night is therefore survival itself' (p. 34).

Mernissi invites viewers to the exhibition to look long at the Orientalist paint-ings with *samar* in mind by observing the aspects of this 'darker loom' of harems, courtyards and alleys. She notes that:

> *Samar* is one of the Arabic languages' magic words that weaves together the sense of 'dark colour' with the pleasure you get from opening up to the mys-terious 'Other', all the while being stimulated by the moonlight. The dark night however might also be enchanting during the day, when you manage to create it artificially by retreating to an inner cocoon-like space, of which the archetype is the harem.
>
> (p. 34)

It was, Mernissi adds, 'when I saw that these artists really enjoyed painting *samar* (and some of them even practised it, like John Frederick Lewis, who organized nightly entertainments in his lavish Cairo house) that I suddenly realized they escaped Edward Saïd's theory of an unbridgeable divide between conquerors and conquered' (p. 34). Mernissi quotes Saïd's Foucaultian comment 'As a cul-tural apparatus Orientalism is all aggression, activity, judgment, will-to-truth, and knowledge' (1978: 204) in order to question him.

> Is Orientalism really all judgment and knowledge? . . . Were there not emo-tions that our conquering Westerner could not control as far as he would

rationally have willed? I would like to suggest that enjoying *samar* – the dark in general and harems in particular – enough to want to keep recreating it in their painting, shows that these British artists had a human dimension which transcended their own civilization's programming.

(pp. 34–5)

Lewis intuitively was reaching out, she suggests, to Islam's universal *umma*:

For an artist such as John Frederick Lewis systematically to spread geometric symbols all over his paintings was to escape the realism of the images his culture programmed him to favour, in order to taste the universal by delving into the uncharted territories of the boundless dream world.

(p. 38)

Looking 'for hours' at Lewis paintings in the exhibition sends Mernissi back to question 'Saïd's conception of Orientalism' (p. 38):

Not only can we not condemn the nineteenth century British artists as Middle-Eastern 'aggressors', but we can go further and state that their suppressed dreamy side was nurtured by the conquest. And this means that even when sheer force tilts the balance to one party, the weaker side has still a cultural or a spiritual potential to share.

(p. 39)

The side-by-side juxtaposition of western feminist, class-based and Islamic discourses in the *Lure of the East* catalogue tells us two things: it clearly illustrates the continuing power of Saïd's Orientalism theory in the professional image world; but it also gestures to new hybridities.

Postmodernism and hybridity

Whereas Weeks challenges Saïd in terms of hybridity in colonial (Western) identities, a different, postmodernist problematic among post-colonial academics has addressed both the notion of hybridity and of 'alternatives to Orientalism'. For example, whereas Saïd emphasized the ethnocentrism of western discourses, Homi Bhabha has argued that:

The wider significance of the postmodern condition lies in the awareness that the epistemological 'limits' of those ethnocentric ideas are also the enunciative boundaries of a range of other dissonant, even dissident histories and voices – women, the colonized, minority groups, the bearers of policed sexualities. For the demography of the new internationalism is the history of postcolonial migration, the narratives of political diaspora, the major social displacements of peasant and aboriginal communities, the poetics of exile, the grim prose of political and economic refugees.

(Bhabha 1998: 936)

So whereas Weeks, Kabbani and Mernissi, in their different ways, focus on affluent and professional middle-class writers and artists in relation to cultural hybridity, Bhabha discovers a new set of mobile, transitory, oppressed peoples in his discussion of the 'new internationalism':

> Increasingly 'national cultures' are being produced from the perspective of disenfranchised minorities . . . The great connective narratives of capitalism and class drive the engines of social reproduction, but do not, in themselves, provide a foundational frame for those modes of cultural identification and political affect that form around issues of sexuality, race, feminism, the life-world of refugees or migrants, or the deathly social destiny of AIDS.
>
> (p. 937)

Himself a migrant to the UK, Bhabha argues that the centre of 'national culture' (as perceived by Saïd) no longer holds. 'The Western metropole must confront its postcolonial history, told by its influx of postwar migrants and refugees, as an indigenous or native narrative *internal to its national identity*' (p. 937). In other words Bhabha's is the world of Bangladesh in Brick Lane we discussed in Chapter 3.

But as well as finding new subjects embedded in violence and trauma for Saïd's 'alternatives to Orientalism', Bhabha establishes a different temporality as he draws on postmodernism both as a period in our history and as an epistemology:

> Such cultures of postcolonial *contra-modernity* may be contingent to modernity, discontinuous or in contention with it, resistant to its oppressive, assimilation-ist technologies; but they also deploy the cultural hybridity of their borderline conditions to 'translate' and therefore reinscribe, the social imaginary of both metropolis and modernity.
>
> (p. 937)

Bhabha's postmodern epistemology generates this issue of 'borderline conditions'. There is no homogenous, totalized identity we can recognize, either in the metropolis (London, Paris, New York, etc), or in the countries where the travelling refugees and migrants came from, since these people are no longer seen as 'total' citizens nor identities 'back home'. Indeed, they are the 'unhomely' in each of their places of residence. This is the 'newness' and the 'in-between' space of the socio-cultural 'borderline.'

Artistically the difference between Saïd's and Bhabha's notions of cultural hybridity resides between an art that, in Bhabha's words, recalls 'the past as social cause or aesthetic precedent' and an art that 'renews the past', refiguring it as a contingent 'in-between' space, that innovates and interrupts the performance of the present. This distinction throws light on the differences among the Indigenous artists represented at the 2007/8 *Culture Warriors* exhibition. Some of these artists, like Julie Dowling, certainly draw on memories, histories and mythical narratives as 'social cause.' But others, particularly those whom the exhibition curator calls the 'bowerbirds' of international travel, embody 'in-between' spaces: between countries, but also between the 'newness' discourses of high technology and traditional identities.

These are, in Homi Bhabha's analysis, post-colonial people in 'borderline conditions', peripatetic residents of 'in-between' spaces. When, at the *Cultural Warriors* exhibition, we saw Christopher Pease's *Wrong Side of the Hay* (2005), at first we seemed to observe two white Western farmers engaged in taming the land, carving a British-style 'country' out of the European binary mythology of 'bush' and 'city' which has dominated so much of white Australian 'common sense', popular literature, poetry and cinema (Tulloch 1981). But what at first appeared to us as wheat stacks are abandoned Aboriginal shelters. Anyone caught by the whites within this area would have been shot. Across this superficially peaceful scene is inscribed a ghostly pattern of lines, which in part reflects the disorderly lines of the clouds in the sky above, but to us as westerners resembles the lines of altitude on a topographical map. Yet in the catalogue Bullen speaks of *Wrong Side of the Hay* as a European-style landscape interrupted by the Dreaming motif in those disorderly lines. 'The two men depicted in the work are unaware of the framework of spiritual inheritance embodied within the land, which is the birthright of every Indigenous person, depicted by the artist as unbroken curves over the horizon' (Bullen, cited in Croft 2007: 144). This is Pease's visual signification of Indigenous structure and reality. Bullen continues that Pease's work seeks to extract the natural order of things without imposing 'An Order':

> It is this self-contained world-within-worlds approach that makes Chris' work unique. Like him it seeks a balance between science, logic and the deep underlying mysticism that is part of his cultural heritage. The two are not in conflict but co-exist and feed each other.
>
> (Bullen, cited in Croft 2007: 144)

This is Pease, an artist from the Miang/Wardand/Balardung/Nyoongar people, working in an 'in-between' space, involved, as Bhabha says, in an 'insurgent act of cultural translation'.

When we see Christian Bumbarra Thompson's *Gates of Tambo* photographic series, we are observing what cultural anthropologist Marianne Riphagen describes as an Indigenous contemporary artist involved in the various cosmopolitan modernist and post-modernist art worlds of the twenty-first century. The series includes, for example, a dramatic profile of Thompson posing as Australian Aboriginal photographer Tracey Moffatt with camera and a frontal image of Thompson as Andy Warhol, the white hair contrasting with the darker face as 'Warhol' spews towards camera. But Riphagen also notes that Thompson's photographic series has Indigenous biographical reference, since the 'gates' represent two bottle trees that Thompson's great-uncle planted outside of the town of Tambo, north-west of Brisbane. The artist uses this local, familial reference to signify an Indigenous perspective through which he sees, as he constructs and deconstructs 'the amalgam making up his identity' (Riphagen, cited in Croft 2007: 162). Through his impersonations of Indigenous artists like Moffatt and international white artists like Warhol, Riphagen writes, Thompson sees himself both as a young man with a keen interest in 1980s pop culture *and* as the Indigenous artist in remote Australia. Thompson is another Indigenous Australian, from the Bidjara people, involved in an 'insurgent act of cultural translation' 'in-between' borders. There were many more at the *Culture Warriors* exhibition.

Conclusion

Saïd's hegemonic consensus of colonialism is, for Bhabha, a position of 'dissensus' and of 'cultural displacements', a place out of colonial control. It is also, at the level of theory, an epistemologically postmodernist 'beyond control'. Bhabha says 'Our task remains to show how historical agency is transformed through the signifying process; how the historical event is represented in a discourse that is *something beyond control*' (1998: 941). Hence the role of the critic and the artist are as important as ever they were in Saïd's consensus of Orientalism. But now, among 'First Nation' artists in Australia and elsewhere, they represent hybridity, alterity, dissensus.

Bhabha speaks of key Mexican and Puerto Rican artists working in the USA today as utilizing 'self-conscious manipulation of materials or iconography . . . the combination of found material and satiric wit . . . the manipulation of . . . artefacts, codes and sensibilities from both sides of the border' (Ybarra-Frausto, cited in Bhabha 1998: 938). They are celebrants of 'the migrant act of survival, using . . . mixed media works to make a hybrid cultural space that forms contingently, disjunctively, in the inscription of signs of cultural memory and sites of political agency' (p. 938). He might easily have been describing the work of the bush-to-city Indigenous migrants and the 'bowerbirds' of the *Culture Warriors* exhibition. Bhabha's artists and novelists dwelling 'in the beyond' as a 'space for intervention in the here and now' (p. 938) are responding, in terms of travel, place and time and in terms of epistemology, as they 'do battle for the creation of a human world – that is a world of reciprocal recognitions' (Fanon, cited in Bhabha 1998: 939).

To this degree Bhabha has responded to Saïd's call for new studies which seek 'to ask how one can study other cultures and peoples from a libertarian, or a nonrepressive and nonmanipulative, perspective . . . to rethink the whole complex problem of knowledge and power' (Saïd 1978: 24). This is why we begin and end this chapter with a focus on the icon-breaking and icon-making work of artists at the *Culture Warriors* exhibition. Here young urban and mobile Indigenous artists speak back from their current hybridity to Western icons of war and state terror without abdicating their histories as 'the world's oldest living culture' (Croft 2007: 2).

11 Conclusion

Walls and borders

This book has engaged with a large number of theories in its quest for claims of the iconic. We have preferred to link key concepts and risk-events, chapter by chapter, to important theoretical and epistemological traditions rather than try to cover every piece of literature relating to our substantive field. The latter would be impossible in the space we have and would probably obscure the key debates within it.

Those key debates are, explicitly or implicitly, about the theories of knowledge (epistemologies) that have been used to define and describe images of war and terror from the Vietnam War to the terrorist attack of 7/7. We have tried to make what is sometimes implicit in these accounts explicit in terms of those theories. As a consequence of this approach, our conclusion will not be a descriptive summary of what we have said so far, but a further explication of the supposed 'battle' between critical realist and conventionalist-postmodernist epistemologies as they define the iconic.

Empiricism, critical realism and social constructivism (conventionalism)

One of the earliest, and still among the best, discussions of the three epistemological positions operating within communication, media and cultural studies is Terry Lovell's *Pictures of Reality* (1980). Lovell defines each of these positions structurally in the context of the others, in terms of their similarities and differences. Thus empiricism (or positivism) is one limit position, claiming a relatively unproblematic intellectual access to reality, while conventionalism (or social constructivism) is at the other limit, arguing for a 'reality' constructed by way of language and theory. Critical realism is positioned between the other two epistemologies in her account, since it believes in a reality accessible to inquiry, but one that is also humanly constructed. This structural positioning of the three epistemologies in the context of the others is still current: thus Kate Wright comments that critical realism appeals to her as a former journalist who now teaches and researches in Journalism Studies because 'it represents a middle path between constructivism and positivism: acknowledging the independent existence of objective reality, but asserting the constructedness of human knowledge about the nature of reality' (2011: 159).

For Lovell 'Empiricist ontology posits a real world which is independent of consciousness and theory, and which is accessible through sense experience' (1980: 10). The term 'positivism', first coined by sociologist Auguste Comte, was then an epistemological doctrine of applying an empiricist account of scientific method to the human sciences: viz. 'that the source and foundation of knowledge is in the experience of objects of the external world, through the senses' (p. 10). A classic example in science would be the laboratory experiment where the human senses (the eye) gains access to the real world of microbiological life via the scientific method of the microscope. But, equally, mainstream historians have applied their own meticulous methodologies to the material artifacts 'revealing' the stories of humankind; and Simon Schama (Chapter 1) describes dramatically his own revelation of art history 'through the senses' via Caravaggio's key.

In contrast, Lovell argues, the 'limit position which all conventionalisms more or less approach is one in which the world is in effect constructed in and by theory' (p. 15). Critical realism, as an epistemology, Lovell argues, follows conventionalist critiques of empiricist epistemology in agreeing that knowledge is socially constructed. But the term 'generative deep structures', used by key critical realist theorists Roy Bhaskar and Rom Harré in the 1970s, is central to realism's notion of bringing together empiricist and conventionalist theories of knowledge. Thus, for Lovell, critical realist theories 'develop models of real structures and processes which lie at a "deeper" level of reality than the phenomenon they are used to explain. The theory explains the phenomenon because the phenomenon and the "deep structures" are causally connected' (p. 18). Similarly, Wright, describing the different layers of reality conceived by Bhaskar, speaks of the 'specific generative mechanisms' at the deepest level of 'underlying social, economic, or political structures' (2011: 163). Concerned as a journalist to construct a non-reductive critical realism where individual professionals are constrained but not determined by the 'generative mechanisms' of the capitalist newspaper world, Wright argues in her conclusion that:

> I explored the notion of examining journalists' 'inner conversations' (Archer, 2000, 2003) in a manner which would take their accounts seriously, but which would also pay due attention to the effects of underlying social, political and economic structures in undercutting or constraining their intentionality (Bhaskar, 1979, p. 44; Toynbee, 2008, p. 272).
>
> (Wright 2011: 168)

A new surge in critical realist analysis emerged in the early twenty-first century within Journalism Studies. Raymond Lau notes that 'In recent years, critical realism has risen to prominence' in part because of the pedagogic contradiction between realist and constructivist epistemologies in teaching journalism studies (2004: 693):

> In the existing literature, approaches highlighting extraneous factors are all implicitly realist; the social constructivist school that focuses on the internal factors of routine journalistic practices is explicitly anti-realist; while the

epistemological nature of news values, which constitute internal factors, is left unexamined.

(Lau 2004: 693)

As Wright emphasizes, this teaching inconsistency left journalism students anxious and often angry, as evident from one of her undergraduate surveys, where a student wrote: 'I was told I was naïve for talking about reality without using scare quotes in my essay but I got given marks . . . for checking what really happened in my [practical assignment]. It's as if I'm studying two *totally* different subjects' (2011: 157). Wright takes this point further by arguing that

> *I also* experience frustration, anger, and even a sense of alienation from academia as a result. So I should make it plain that, for me, re-examining the ontological premises of Journalism Studies is not only an intellectual exercise to underpin teaching and research more satisfactorily. It is also part of something far more personal for me as a 'hackademic': a quest to try to bring together my past and present senses of what 'good' journalism can and should be, why it is important, and how best to think about it meaningfully.
>
> (p. 157)

Wright summarizes:

> I have argued that CR [Critical Realism] is ethically and politically suited to Journalism Studies . . . Firstly, it allows us to articulate notions of reality, truth, and knowledge in ways which acknowledge the important contributions constructivist work has brought to journalism research, while also avoiding moral relativism, which would be fundamentally incompatible with existing journalistic norms and working practices. Indeed, CR's re-working of the 'God-terms' of Journalism – fact, truth and reality (Zelizer, 2004) – re-enforce the political and ethical needs for critically alert, thoughtful journalism, as well as the need for researchers to be active in holding media practitioners to account for the adequacy of their representations, and for the practices which produce them. Secondly, I stressed that this critical 'holding to account' involves academics acknowledging the importance of both journalistic agency *and* the real material and social structures which both shape – and are shaped by – journalists' choices. Such lines of critique are only possible because CR offers scholars the theoretical means with which to explore recursive links between structure and agency, subjectivity and reality.
>
> (p. 167)

Wright concludes that a critical realist thrust in Journalism Studies is exciting because it opens up the opportunities for inter-relating of different theoretical traditions and fields of analysis.

But this synthesizing intent is taken up in a different way within another field altogether, risk and environmental sociology. Here Alan Irwin disagrees with both Lovell and the current Journalism Studies critical realists in rejecting the notion that social constructivism is necessarily (or even mainly) relativist; and he also argues that methodologically 'it is very different from the more sweeping and less empirical style of postmodern philosophy' (Irwin 2001: 164). Yet, in his different way, Irwin, too, argues for an integrating theory that moves beyond the conventionalist/critical realist divide. '[I]t may be that this entrenched battle over "realism versus constructivism" has become rather pointless . . . The challenge, instead, is to draw creatively on a broad range of sociological insights – whatever their theoretical provenance' (p. 168).

For Irwin, the future of theory is as an '*actively generated co-construction*. Co-construction . . . captures the dual process of the social and the natural being varyingly constructed within environmentally related practices and particular contexts' (p. 173).

What Irwin is offering here is 'an empirically grounded sociology that does not simply trade in sweeping generalizations but also considers the complexities (and contextual specificities) of environmental understanding' (p. 178). As Irwin says, Environmental Studies constructivist theories focus especially on different actors' *claim-making* about 'reality' and on the contexts, communication and contestations of these different claims. Taking this further, his own call is for a *hybrid* theory which crosses domains and interlinks competing categories of analysis (p. 174): 'In this way, we will avoid both objectification of the natural world and social relativism' (p. 16).

Within Irwin's 'hybrid theory' context, the call of Journalism Studies 'hackademics' – reflexively stretched between 'past and present' claims of what '"good" journalism can and should be' (Wright 2011: 157) – can now be seen as a particular case of epistemological hybridity. It is embedded on one hand in the very particular practicalities of professional journalism's commitment to a 'truth' frame and to a realist set of ethics (pp. 159–61), and on the other the constructivist paradigm of academic journalism theory. For Irwin, these theories need to be assessed not only on the basis of their philosophical strengths, 'but in terms of how they help us interpret, unravel and contextualize social and environmental problems' (p. 186). At the micro-social level of specific groups – like the 'hackademics' with multiple identities, stretched between professional values, socio-economic 'deep structures' and academic constructivist paradigms – Irwin's formulation is empirically realist as well as philosophically 'soft constructivist' (2001). This is why he can conclude that 'there may be more in common between critical realism and social constructivism than is keeping them apart' (p. 186).

While emphasizing that he is writing within the constructivist sociological tradition 'in a self-critical fashion' (p. 16), Irwin also notes that within critical realism 'a limited form of social construction is granted' (p. 19). He also notes that 'soft' constructivists do not deny the reality of environmental problems. 'The position instead is that both real and imaginary problems need to be socially constructed if they are to find a place on the environmental agenda' (p. 21–2). It is this making of claims about 'reality' in order to get on the political or intellectual agenda that is central to Irwin's 'soft' constructivism.

Certain problems are seen to be more pressing than others at particular points. In order to get onto both a personal and an institutional agenda, such problems must be 'constructed'. Someone needs to persuade others that the problem in question deserves particular attention and that something must be done.

(Irwin 2001: 20)

As Irwin notes, the constructivist sociologist John Hannigan has emphasized that 'From a sociological point of view, the chief task here is to understand why certain conditions come to be perceived as problematic and how those who register this "claim" command political attention in their quest to do something' (Hannigan 1995: 2–3).

It is in the 'spirit of renewal' and the 'hybridity' of critical realism and 'soft' constructivism (Irwin 2001: 16) that this book on iconic images has been written. The various academic and public intellectual interpretations of iconic images that have been surveyed here are all registering 'claims' in the face of dreadful human trauma and physical destruction. They are all, in an important sense, a 'quest to do something'. But rather than adopt what Irwin calls the pointless and 'entrenched battle over "realism versus constructivism"' (p. 168), we agree fully with his view that 'we should critically scrutinize the merits of different approaches but then be prepared to move on in both theoretical and empirical terms' (p. 186). That is what we have tried to do here, both empirically and theoretically.

Furthermore, in the 'renewal' spirit of Irwin, we have preferred to do this positively, in three ways. First, we have wanted to scrutinize critically, side by side, not only 'current debate' but also 'historical debate', stretching over a timeframe in parallel to that of the iconic images we survey. Second, we have not wanted to dismiss airily analyses from either side of the critical realist/soft constructivist frame we ourselves have adopted. Thus Baudrillard, whom many constructivists would include in what Irwin calls 'the more sweeping and less empirical style of postmodern philosophy' (p. 164), is important here, not as a celebrity intellectual, but for the power of his claim-making debate, as presented in Chapters 4 and 6, between the different approaches of Baudrillard, Hammond, Kellner and Merrin. Similarly, Schama is not drawn on at the beginning as a token 'empiricist', to be quickly got out of the way before we engage with the 'battle' between critical realists and social constructivists. Quite the contrary: Schama is here because, like Baudrillard, we respect the power of his argument, and because he is so clear in laying out his critical position on the identifying of iconic art. Furthermore, there is a case – which Irwin himself notices (pp. 23–4) – for seeing a constructivist aspect in Schama's work discussing artistic landscapes. Rather than a contradiction – either in Schama's thinking or in our own – we think that this is another example of the 'hybridity' which Irwin valorizes in current theory-making. It is another Schama identity to add to those we discussed in Chapter 1.

Third, rather than dismiss epistemological positions as being 'embattled epistemologies', 'naïve empiricism' or 'sweeping postmodernism', we want to conclude by placing side by side two particularly powerful critical realist and postmodernist/constructivist tropes – walls and borders – which have appeared many times among the theoretical claim-making we have been discussing.

In adopting his 'soft' constructivist approach, Hannigan has laid out six factors required for successful claim-making. They are: scientific authority validating the claims; popularizers acting as a bridge between scientific and broader communities; media framing of the claim as important and novel; dramatization of the problem 'in symbolic and visual terms' (1995: 55); economic incentives for taking action; and the emergence of institutional sponsors supporting the legitimacy and continuity of the claim (see also Irwin, 2001: 21). We end by taking just one of these factors for further discussion in terms of 'walls and borders': the dramatization of the problem in symbolic and visual terms. We will do so by focusing on two public intellectuals who have made a career out of remediating the iconic.

John Berger: Realism's walls

Walls in Berger's analysis are real, visceral, and increasingly visible signs of material separation and injustice:

> UN resolutions and the International Court of Justice in the Hague have condemned the building of Israeli settlements on Palestinian territory (there are now nearly half a million of such 'settlers') and the construction of the 'separation fence', which is an 8-metre high concrete wall, as illegal. The Occupation and the Wall nevertheless continue. Every month the IDF's stranglehold across the territories is tightened. The stranglehold is geographic, economic, civic and military . . . Special highways for settlers, forbidden to Palestinians, transform old roads into dead-ends. The checkpoints and tortuous ID controls have seriously reduced for most Palestinians the possibility of travelling or even planning to travel within what remains of their own territories . . . The Wall enclaves, cuts off corners . . . fragments the countryside and separates Palestinians from Palestinians.
>
> (Berger 2007: 7–8, 10)

The Wall, when it is finished, says Berger, will be 'the 640-kilometre long expressionless face of an inequality' (p. 15). This inequality is between those who have the latest military technology (Apache helicopters, Merkava tanks, F.16 planes) to defend the place they have seized and 'those who have nothing, save their names and a shared belief that justice is axiomatic. The stance of undefeated despair works like this' (p. 15).

'Undefeated despair' is the title of Berger's essay. Yet, as its author, he finds a residually important human quality in this state of undefeated despair. In another essay, 'Ten Dispatches About Endurance in the Face of Walls', Berger probes this sense of agency among the poor:

> The poor have no residences. They have homes because they remember mothers or grandfathers or an aunt who brought them up. A residence is a fortress, not a story; it keeps the wild at bay. A residence needs walls . . . [The poor] are accustomed to living in close proximity with one another,

and this creates its own spatial sense; space is not so much an emptiness as an exchange. When people are living on top of one another, any action taken by one has repercussions on the others . . . Their elaborate sign languages of gestures and hands are an expression of such physical sharing.

(Berger 2007: 91–2, 98)

Communication in these places, for Berger, is not high-tech, but of closely proximate exchange; and clearly for Berger 'dialogue' there can be gestural as well as verbal. In contrast, there are the place configurations of the rich who build walls, because they are not in the majority. 'This is why the essential activity of the rich today is the building of walls – walls of concrete, of electronic surveillance, of missile barrages, minefields, frontier controls, and opaque media screens' (p. 92).

Berger's is a powerful analysis of walls and the 'proximate exchange' of 'a quality which no post-modern or political vocabulary today can find a word for'. Yet postmodernist analysis can present boundary play and pleasures that are powerful too, while still challenging political exploitation.

Yinka Shonibare: Postmodernism's borders

The art work we look at here is an installation by contemporary Nigerian/British artist Yinka Shonibare MBE which reproduces Fragonard's 1767 painting *The Swing*. But, unlike Fragonard's iconic painting, in Shonibare's installation the young French aristocrat on the swing has lost her head; and Shonibare dresses her in Dutch wax ('African') fabrics instead of the silks of Fragonard.

Shonibare says of this installation:

> I am deliberately taking this [eighteenth century] period as a metaphor for the contemporary situation . . . showing very wealthy Europeans in very wealthy clothes, but because I changed their clothes into African textiles, I give an indication that the luxury they enjoy, the labour of making the clothes is supplied by others who are less fortunate . . . The ever-widening gulf between rich and poor and themes of discrimination and exclusion are symptomatic of the post-9/11 world we occupy.

(cited in Kent, Hobbs and Downey 2008: 15)

The reference to power and wealth in Shonibare's *The Swing* is playfully stretched across a number of 'doubles' as a post-modern hybrid. First, there is the issue of money, leisure and exploitation both 'then' (in France on the verge of revolution) and 'now' (in the post-9/11 West). A second doubling is the play between different versions of *The Swing* as icon. Fragonard's young woman in the painting is, even for her times, scandalously exposing herself to a young man and is pushed by a priest into doing so. Shonibare's headless reproduction of her is thus both a little joke for her own history (she will lose her head in the revolution for this), and an opening to our own period of celebrity scandals. A third doubling of identities and blurring of boundaries is the play between Shonibare's own class positions as British-born

Nigerian artist. In Nigeria, his family was regarded as upper-class, and hence he was part of the black bourgeoisie that was complicit with empire, and thus with the ruling class and its excesses, represented in *The Swing*. But

> As a black man living in the UK, I find myself in a position where I am not so-called 'upper-class' . . . And this got me thinking about social and class mobility in the context of the dandy. The dandy can remake himself again and again; he can do that through the image, he can remake his own image and thereafter re-create and remake himself . . . All identity construction is a form of re-enactment . . . The dandy is a figure who not only lives out this fact but is also an insider and an outsider who disrupts such distinctions . . . Historically, the dandy is usually an outsider whose only way in is through his wit and style. Coming from a middle-class background the dandy aspired to aristocratic standing so as to distinguish himself from both lower and middle classes. In this sense, his frivolous lifestyle is a political gesture of sorts, containing within it a form of social mobility.
>
> (Shonibare, cited in Kent, Hobbs and Downey 2008: 42–3)

In his photographic series, *Diary of a Victorian Dandy*, a re-working of Hogarth's *Rake's Progress*, Shonibare frivolously pictures himself in the rake/dandy role, a black, disabled man whose white female servants attend to his every pleasure and need. Shonibare has said, 'Excess is the only legitimate means of subversion . . . Hybridisation is a form of disobedience, a parasitic disobedience on the host of the species, an excessive form of libido, it is joyful sex' (p. 34).

Rachel Kent, curator of Sydney's Museum of Contemporary Art where Shonibare exhibited in 2008, has noted the strong postmodernist influence of Homi Bhabha on Shonibare's work. She emphasizes the artist's shift of post-colonialism from a Said-style representation of the power struggle between self and Other, (as between 'mother culture and alien') to Bhabha's emphasis on

> a strategy of disavowal, [where] the *reference* of discrimination is always to a process of splitting as the condition of subjugation: a discrimination between the mother culture and its bastards, the self and its doubles, where the trace of what is disavowed is not represented but repeated as something *different* – a mutation, a hybrid.
>
> (Bhabha, cited in Kent, Hobbs and Downey 2008: 22)

Both Berger and Shonibare have worked with Gainsborough's painting, *Mr and Mrs Andrews*. Their different responses are symptomatic of their alternative critical realist and constructivist/postmodernist positions.

For Berger, the meticulously crafted oil landscape represents aristocratic ownership of huge and beautiful areas of countryside, in which no peasant dwellings were visible. He might have added that the reason there were no poor people in the picture is that it was customary for landowners to remove their dwelling walls as a blot on the landscape. The cottages were reduced – as in Berger's words on

Palestine, or the image of two boys in Bangladesh – to rubble, and other walls were built around the estate to keep poorer people out.

In 1998, Shonibare produced his sculpture, *Mr and Mrs Andrews Without Their Heads*. They are life-size fibreglass mannequins that, like traditional shop window dummies, have no heads. They are dressed in resplendent Dutch wax printed costumes that are even more exotic to our eyes than the silks in Gainsborough's painting. Mr Andrews also has, as in Gainsborough's painting, his gun and his gun-dog.

Gainsborough painted Mr and Mrs Andrews looking directly into our eyes. It is a glance of class confidence and superiority, marking their indifference to us. But Shonibare's Mr and Mrs Andrews cannot turn their heads to us, because they have none. Hence the sculpture seems de-centred:

> Gainsborough's painting is an anachronism of sorts insofar as a man stands next to his belongings, in this case his wife, dog and gun – in no particular order – and displays the extent of his land ownership in the background . . . This painting is first and foremost a celebration of deference and I want to deflate that somehow. I think I achieve that by beheading them which is an allusion to the French Revolution and the beheading of the French landed gentry and aristocracy.
>
> (Shonibare, cited in Kent, Hobbs and Downey 2008: 40)

We can see that Shonibare's class interpretation of Gainsborough's painting as about ownership is much closer to John Berger's than to Kenneth Clark's. But the de-centring of Shonibare's sculpture is not simply about power and the politics of deference. It is also about the hybridity of the British/African artist re-working Gainsborough's painting. This kind of de-centring is conveyed by the dressing of Mr and Mrs Andrews in 'African' excess, which is itself clothing simulated from nothing really African (because 'African' fabric was originally made in Holland for an Indonesian market and then sent to Africa when that market failed). It is also de-centring in the fact that by removing the characters' heads, there is a removal of eye line and of the interpellated 'claim' for authority, not only by the characters in the art-work but also by the artist himself. Naturalistic 'reality', which Gainsborough strove for in his painting, and which is at the heart of Kenneth Clark's liking of it (Chapter 2), is removed, and the theatricality of spot-lit, headless mannequins takes its place.

Where Berger sees walls enclosing, articulating and enforcing injustice, Shonibare sees shifting borders, doubling, simulation, mirrors and performance. Where Berger's optimism lies in 'becoming', through the agency and interaction of the real world's poor, Shonibare's is in identity change and hybridity between shifting imagistic claims of the 'real'. Their different approaches to *Mr and Mrs Andrews* define the differences not only between Said's and Bhabha's post-colonial theory, but between modernist realism and constructivist post-modernism as theories of interpretation. But it is in the similarities and differences between 'walls' and 'borders', between critical realism and constructivism as, in Irwin's term, 'actively generated co-construction' (2001: 173), that this book's narratives of the iconic play.

We have a political and an ethical reason for this view and it is most clearly stated by Judith Butler. She argues that after 9/11 there developed the perspective in the United States that 'permeability of the border' represented not only a national threat, but one to identity itself:

> Identity, however, is not thinkable without the permeable border, or else without the possibility of relinquishing a boundary. In the first case, one fears invasion, encroachment, and impingement, and makes a territorial claim in the name of self-defence. But in the other case, a boundary is given up or overcome precisely to establish a certain connection beyond the claims of territory.
>
> (Butler 2010: 43–4)

Human beings are social beings; and

> if we are social beings and our survival depends upon a recognition of interdependency (which may or may not depend on the perception of likeness), then it is not as an isolated and bounded being that I survive, but as one whose boundary exposes me to others in ways that are voluntary and involuntary . . . , an exposure that is the condition of sociality and survival alike . . . The boundary of who I am is the boundary of the body, but the boundary of the body never fully belongs to me.
>
> (p. 54)

Likewise identities are hybrid, even at war within themselves. This, as Butler says, is the 'complex and dynamic character of new global subject formations' and the 'migratory constitution of dynamic subject positions that do not reduce to single identities' (p. 161). 'Walls' are actions: they are built to make borders impermeable, as in the case of the Soviet Union in Berlin and Israel in Palestine. But 'walls' are also 'the notion of the subject produced by the recent wars conducted by the US, including its torture operations' (p. 47). It is a notion 'in which the US subject seeks to produce itself as impermeable, to define itself as protected permanently against incursion and as radically invulnerable to attack' (p. 47).

Instead, Butler calls for interdependency which is a move

> toward the recognition of a generalized condition of precariousness. It cannot be that the other is destructible while I am not; nor vice-versa. It can only be that life, conceived as precarious life, is a generalized condition, and that under certain political conditions it becomes radically exacerbated or radically disavowed.
>
> (p. 48)

This is a move towards the hybridity of identities, the co-constitution of bodies. We can think, Butler says:

About demarcating the human body through identifying its boundary . . .
but that is to miss the crucial fact that the body is, in certain ways and even
inevitably, unbound – in its acting, its receptivity, in its speech, desire and
mobility. It is outside itself, in the world of others, in a space and time it does
not control, and it not only exists in the vector of these relations, but as this
very vector. In this sense, the body does not belong to itself.

(pp. 52–3)

This is a move, from 'walls' to permeable 'borders' and to a 'memory without
borders' (Assmann and Conrad 2010: 5) which, we contend, all the thinkers of the
visual we have discussed here foreshadow.

References

Abdul-Ahad, G., Alford, K., Anderson, T. and Leistner, R. (2005) *Unembedded: Four Independent Photojournalists on the War in Iraq*, White River Junction, VT: Chelsea Green Publishing.

Abercrombie, N. and Longhurst, B. (1998) *Audiences: A Sociological Theory of Performance and Imagination*, Thousand Oaks, CA: Sage.

Alam, S. (2011) 'Shahidul Alam: Photographer, writer, curator'. Drik. Online. Available HTTP: http://www.shahidulalam.com/index.php#mi=1&pt=0&pi=32&s=0&p=0&a=0&at=0 (accessed 1 October 2011).

Alam, S. (2008) 'Musings by Shahidul Alam'. Online. Available HTTP: http://shahidul.wordpress.com/2008/02/22/bangladesh-1971 (accessed 8 August 2008).

Alam, S. (2007) 'Conversations with photo-journalist Shahidul Alam'. Online. Available HTTP: http://uprisingradio.org/home/?p=1577 (accessed 1 May 2008).

Alaszewski, A. and Coxon, K. (2008) 'The everyday experience of living with risk and uncertainty', *Health, Risk & Society*, 10(5): 413–20.

Alexander, K. and Hawkesworth, M. (eds) *War and Terror: Feminist Perspectives*, Chicago: University of Chicago Press.

Anam, T. (2008) 'The war that time forgot', *The Guardian G2 Magazine*, 10 April: 12–15.

Apel, D. (2005) 'Torture culture: Lynching photographs and the images of Abu Ghraib', *Art Journal*, 64(2): 89–100.

Appleton, J. (2003) 'Back to Baudrillard', spiked. Online. Available HTTP: http://www.spiked-online.com/index.php/site/article/4909 (accessed 2 September 2011).

Archer, M. (2003) 'The private life of the social agent: What difference does it make?', in J. Cruickshank (ed.) *Critical Realism: The Difference it Makes*, London: Routledge.

Archer, M. (2000) *Being Human: The Problem of Agency*, Cambridge: Cambridge University Press.

Arendt, H. (ed.) (1968) *Illuminations: Walter Benjamin, 1892–1940*, trans. H. Zohn, New York: Schocken Books.

Arquilla, J. and Ronfeldt, D. (2001) *Networks and Netwars: The Future of Terror, Crime and Militancy*, Santa Monica, CA: RAND.

Assmann, A. and Assmann, C. (2010) 'Neda – the career of a global icon', in A. Assmann and C. Assmann (eds) *Memory in a Global Age: Discourses, Practices and Trajectories*, Basingstoke, Hampshire: Palgrave Macmillan.

Assmann, A. and Conrad, S. (2010) 'Introduction', in A. Assmann and C. Assmann (eds) *Memory in a Global Age: Discourses, Practices and Trajectories*, Basingstoke, Hampshire: Palgrave Macmillan.

Australian Transport Security World Conference (2003) 'Workbook', 10–11 November. Sydney: The Westin.

Bacevich, A. (2005) *The New American Militarism: How Americans are Seduced by War*, Oxford: Oxford University Press.

Barthes, R. (1973) *Mythologies*, London: Paladin Books.

Baudrillard, J. (2002) *The Spirit of Terrorism and Requiem for the Twin Towers*, London: Verso.

Baudrillard, J. (1995) *The Gulf War Did Not Take Place*, Sydney: Power Publications.

Baudrillard, J. (1994) *The Illusion of the End*, trans. C. Turner, Stanford, CA: Stanford University Press.

Baudrillard, J. (1993) *Baudrillard Live*, M. Gane (ed.), London: Routledge.

Bayoumi, M. and Rubin, A. (2001) *The Edward Saïd Reader*, London: Granta.

Beck, U. (2009) *World at Risk*, Cambridge: Polity Press.

Beck, U. (1992) *Risk Society: Towards a New Modernity*, trans. M. Ritter, London: Sage.

Benjamin, R. and Khemir, M. (1997) *Orientalism: Delacroix to Klee*, Sydney: Art Gallery of NSW.

Benjamin, W. (1973) *Illuminations Walter Benjamin*, H. Arendt (ed.), trans. H. Zohn, London: Fontana/Collins.

Berger, J. (2007) *Hold Everything Dear: Dispatches on Survival and Resistance*, London: Verso.

Berger, J. (1980) *About Looking*, London: Writers and Readers.

Berger, J. (1972) *Ways of Seeing*, London: BBC and Penguin.

Best, K. (2004) 'Visual imaging technologies, embodied sympathy and control in the 9/11 wars', in D. Grenfell (ed.) *The First International Sources of Insecurity Conference*, Melbourne: RMIT Publishing. Online. Available HTTP: http://search.informit.com.au/fullText;d n=875996970699395;res=IELHSS;type=html (accessed 7 May 2005).

Bhabha, H. (1998) 'The location of culture', in J. Rivkin and M. Ryan (eds), *Literary Theory: An Anthology*, Oxford: Blackwell.

Bhaskar, R. (1979) *The Possibility of Naturalism: A Philosophical Critique of Contemporary Human Sciences*, Brighton, UK: Harvester Press.

Bideleux, R. and Jefferies, I. (2007) *The Balkans: A Post-Communist History*, London: Routledge.

Bird, C. (1999) 'The village that died, when the butchers came at dawn', *The Observer*, 17 January: 1.

Blair, T. (1999) 'Doctrine of the international community'. Speech to the Economic Club, 24 April. Online. Available HTTP: http://keeptonyblairforpm.wordpress.com/blair-speech-transcripts-from-1997-2007/ (accessed 17 June 2009).

Boholm, Å (2009) 'Speaking of risk: matters of context', *Environmental Communication*, 3(2): 335–54.

Boholm, Å (2008) 'Visual images and risk messages: commemorating Chernobyl', *Risk Decision Policy* 3(2): 125–43.

Boholm, Å (2005) '"Greater good" in transit: The unwieldy career of a Swedish rail tunnel project', *Focaal, European Journal of Anthropology*, 46: 21–35.

Burston, W.H. and Green, C.W. (1964) *Handbook for History Teachers*, London: Methuen.

Butler, J. (2010) *Frames of War: When is Life Grievable?*, London: Verso.

Cellini, B. (1968) *The Life of Benvenuto Cellini*, trans. J. A. Symonds, London: Heron Books.

Chomsky, N. (1999) *The New Military Humanism. Lessons from Kosovo*, London: Pluto Press.

Clark, K. (1969) *Civilisation* [TV programme] BBC 2, 1969; [DVD] London: BBC.

CNN (2001) 'The unfinished war'. Online. Available HTTP: http://edition.cnn.com/CNN/Programs/presents/index.unfinishedwar.html (accessed 2 May 2008).

Cody, E. (1991) 'Allies claim to bomb Iraqi targets at will', *The Washington Post*, 31 January: A01. Online. Available HTTP: http://www.washingtonpost.com/wp-srv/inatl/long-term/fogofwar/archive/post013091_2.htm (accessed 2 May 2008).

Croft, B.L. (2007) *Culture Warriors: National Indigenous Art Triennial*, Canberra: National Gallery of Australia.

Datta, A. (2008) 'Scattered memories of 1971', Bangladesh watchdog. Online. Available HTTP: http://bangladeshwatchdog.blogspot.com/2008/02/scattered-memories-of1971. html (accessed 2 May 2008).

Dean, M. (1999) 'Risk, calculable and incalculable', in D. Lupton (ed.) *Risk and Sociocultural Theory: New Directions and Perspectives*, Cambridge: Cambridge University Press.

Denov, M. and Gervais, C. (2008) 'Negotiating (in)security: agency, resistance and re-sourcefulness among girls formerly associated with Sierra Leone's Revolutionary United Front', in K. Alexander and M. Hawkesworth (eds) *War and Terror: Feminist Perspectives*, Chicago: University of Chicago Press.

Duffield, M. (2001) *Global Governance and the New Wars: The Merging of Development and Security*, London: Zed Books.

Eccleston, J. (2010) 'Jennifer Eccleston: Fan mail and site feedback'. Online. Available HTTP: http://jennifer-eccleston.com/jennifer_eccleston/jennifer_eccleston_email_005.htm (accessed 14 January 2010).

Erdbrink, T. (2009) 'A martyr emerges from the bloodshed', *The Sydney Morning Herald*, 24 June: 9.

Faas, H. and Fulton, M. (2000) 'How the picture reached the world', *The Digital Journalist*. Online. Available HTTP: http://digitaljournalist.org/issue0008/ng4.htm (accessed 2 May 2008).

Feldman, A. (2004a) 'Deterritorialized wars of public safety', *Social Analysis*, 48(1): 73–80.

Feldman, A. (2004b) 'Abu Ghraib: ceremonies of nostalgia'. Online. Available HTTP: http://www.opendemocracy.net/media-abu_ghraib/article_2163.jsp (accessed 1 August 2011).

Ferreira, C., Boholm, Å. and Löfstedt, R. (2001) 'From vision to catastrophe: A risk event in search of images', in J. Flynn, P. Slovic and H. Kunreuther, H (eds) *Risk, Media and Stigma: Understanding Public Challenges to Modern Science and Technology*, London: Earthscan.

Fiske, J. (1989) *Reading the Popular*, London: Unwin Hyman.

Fox News (2008) 'B-2 bombers lead "shock and awe"'. Online. Available at: http://www.foxnews.com/story/0,2933,82262,00.html (accessed 13 October, 2008).

George W. Bush White House Archives (n.d.) 'Apparatus of lies: crafting tragedy'. Online. Available HTTP: http://georgewbush-whitehouse.archives.gov/ogc/apparatus/craft-ing.html (accessed 13 October 2008).

Griffiths, P. (2005) 'Forward', in G. Abdul-Ahad , K. Alford, T. Anderson and R. Leistner (eds) *Unembedded: Four Independent Photojournalists on the War in Iraq*, White River Junction, VT: Chelsea Green Publishing.

Grusin, R. (2011) 'Affect, mediality and Abu Ghraib', Detriot: Wayne State University. Online. Available HTTP: http://eng7007.pbworks.com/f/GrusinAffectMediality.pdf (accessed 1 September 2011).

Grusin, R. (2004) 'Premediation', Detriot: Wayne State University Press. Online. Available HTTP: http://muse.jhu.edu/journals/criticism/v046/46.1grusin.html (accessed 1 September 2011).

Hall, J.R., Stimson, B. and Tamiris Becker, L. (2005) *Visual Worlds*, London: Taylor & Francis.

Hall, S. (2001) 'New world disorder', in S. Hall, D. Massey and M. Rustin (eds) *Soundings*, London: Lawrence & Wishart.

Hammond, P. (2007) *Media, War and Postmodernity*, London: Routledge.

Hanningan, J. (1995) *Environmental Sociology: A Social Constructionist Perspective*, London: Routledge.

Hariman, R. and Lucaites, J.L. (2007) *No Caption Needed: Iconic Photographs, Public Culture, and Liberal Democracy*, Chicago: University of Chicago Press.

Harris, R. (2001–07) Rolf on Art [TV Programme] BBC 1, London: BBC.

Harvey, D. (2005) *A Brief History of Neoliberalism*, Oxford: Oxford University Press.

Hawkesworth, M. (2008) 'War as a mode of production and reproduction: Feminist analytics', in K. Alexander and M. Hawkesworth (eds) *War and Terror: Feminist Perspectives*, Chicago: University of Chicago Press.

Higgins, J. (2003) 'He spoke the truth to power', *The Times Higher Education Supplement*, 10 October: 2.

Hoskins, A. (2004) *Televising War: From Vietnam to Iraq*, London: Continuum International Publishing.

Hoskins, A. and O'Loughlin, B. (2010) *War and Media: The Emergence of Diffused War*, Cambridge: Polity Press.

Humphrey, M. (2005) 'Reconciliation and the therapeutic state', *Journal of Intercultural Studies*, 26(3): 203–20.

Humphrey, M. (2004) 'Postmodern wars: Terrorism, the therapeutic state and public safety', in D. Grenfell (ed.) *The First International Sources of Insecurity Conference*, Melbourne: RMIT Publishing. Online. Available HTTP: http://search.informit.com.au/fullText;dn=875996970699395;res=IELHSS;type=html (accessed 7 May 2005).

Ignatieff, M. (2000) *Virtual War: Kosovo and Beyond*, London: Chatto & Windus.

Irwin, A. (2001) *Sociology and the Environment*, Cambridge: Polity Press.

Jackson, R. (2005) *Writing the War on Terrorism: Language, Politics and Counter-terrorism*, Manchester: Manchester University Press.

Jarvis, L. (2008) 'Times of terror: Writing temporality into the war on terror', *Critical Studies on Terrorism*, 1(2): 245–62.

Junod, T. (2003) 'The falling man', *The Observer Review*, 7 September: 1–2. Reprinted from *Esquire*, September 2003, 140(3): 177–83. Online. Available HTTP: http://www.esquire.com/features/ESQ0903-SEP_FALLINGMAN (accessed 1 August 2011).

Kabbani, R. (2008) 'Regarding orientalism today', in N. Tromans (ed.) *The Lure of the East: British Orientalist Painting*. London: Tate Britain.

Kaldor, M. (1999a) 'Bombs away! But to save civilians we must get in some soldiers too', *The Guardian*, 25 March: 18.

Kaldor, M. (1999b) *New and Old Wars: Organized Violence in a Global Era*, Cambridge: Polity Press.

Kavoori, N. and Fraley, T. (eds) (2006) *Media, Terrorism and Theory*, London: Rowman & Littlefield.

Kellner, D. (2005) 'Baudrillard, globalization and terrorism: Some comments on recent adventures of the image and spectacle on the occasion of Baudrillard's 75th birthday', *International Journal of Baudrillard Studies*, 2(1). Online. Available HTTP: http://www.ubishops.ca/baudrillardstudies/vol2_1/kellner.htm (accessed 2 September 2009).

Kellner, D. (2003a) 'September 11, spectacles of terror, and media manipulation: A critique of Jihadist and Bush media politics', Logosonline. Available HTTP: http://logosonline.home.igc.org/kellner_media.htm (accessed 2 September 2009).

Kellner, D. (2003b) *Media Spectacle*, London: Routledge.

Kellner, D. (1994) 'Introduction: Jean Baudrillard in the fin-de-millennium', in D. Kellner (ed.) *Baudrillard: A Critical Reader*, Oxford: Blackwell

Kellner, D. (1992) *The Persian Gulf TV War*, Boulder, CO: Westview Press.

Kellner, D. (1989) 'Boundaries and borderlines: Reflections on Jean Baudrillard and critical theory'. Online. Available HTTP: http://www.uta.edu/huma/illuminations/kell2.htm (accessed 2 September 2010).

Kent, R., Hobbs, R.C. and Downey, A. (2008) *Yinka Shonibare MBE*, London: Prestel.

Klein, N. (2007a) *The Shock Doctrine: The Rise of Disaster Capitalism*, Toronto, Canada: Alfred A. Knopf.

Klein, N. (2007b) 'The erasing of Iraq', *The Guardian*, 11 September 2007. Online. Available HTTP: http://www.guardian.co.uk/world/2007/sep/11/iraq.features11 (accessed 5 May 2008).

Kolhatkar, S. (2007) 'Conversation with photo-journalist Shahidul Alam'. Online. Available HTTP: http://uprisingradio.org/home/?p=1577 (accessed 8 August 2008)

Lau, R. (2004) 'Critical realism and news production', *Media, Culture and Society*, 26 (5): 693–711.

leander37 (2010) 'Gulf war 1 smart bomb'. Video uploaded to YouTube. Online. Available HTTP: http://www.youtube.com/watch?v=YvIl9wNsNLs (accessed 2 September 2008).

Livingstone, S. (1990) *Making Sense of Television*, London: Pergamon.

Lovell, T. (1980) *Pictures of Reality: Aesthetics, Politics, Pleasure*, London: British Film Institute.

Lowry, J. (2009) *Between the Hallucinatory and the Real*. MA Photography, University of Brighton.

Lupton, D. (ed.) (1999) *Risk and Sociological Theory*, Cambridge: Cambridge University Press.

Lyons, J. (2009) 'Death on video grips world', *The Australian*, 24 June: 1.

Malcolm, N. (1998) *Kosovo: A Short History*, New York: New York University Press.

Mekhennet, S. (2010) 'Mistaken as Iranian martyr, then hounded', *New York Times*, 1 August: A1.

Mernissi, F. (2008) 'Seduced by "Samar", or how British orientalist painters learned to stop worrying and love the darkness', in N. Tromans (ed.) *The Lure of the East: British Orientalist Painting*. London: Tate Britain.

Merrin, W. (2005) *Baudrillard and the Media: A Critical Introduction*, Cambridge: Polity Press.

Mitchell, W.J.T. (2011) *Cloning Terror: The War of Images, 9/11 to the Present*, Chicago: University of Chicago Press.

Mitchell, W.J.T. (2008) 'Cloning terror: The war of images 2001–04', in D. Costello and D. Willsdon (eds) *The Life and Death of Images: Ethics and Aesthetics*, London: Tate Publishing.

Morley, D. (1980) *The 'Nationwide' Audience*, London: The British Film Institute.

Morrison, W. (2006) *Criminology, Civilisation and the New World Order*, London: Routledge-Cavendish.

Naaman, D. (2008) 'Brides of Palestine / angels of death: Media, gender, and performance in the case of the Palestinian female suicide bombers', in K. Alexander and M. Hawkesworth (eds) *War and Terror: Feminist Perspectives*, Chicago: University of Chicago Press.

National Commission on Terrorist Attacks upon the United States (2004) *The 9/11 Commission Report*, New York: W. W. Norton & Co.

O'Hagan, S. (2005) 'A radical returns', *The Observer Review*, 3 April: 1–2.

O'Malley, P. (2008) 'Governmentality and risk', in J. Zinn (ed.) *Social Theories of Risk and Uncertainty*, Oxford: Blackwell.

Oventile, R. (2003) 'Review of *Art and Fear* (2003) by Paul Virilio', Culture Machine. Online. Available HTTP: http://www.culturemachine.net/index.php/cm/article/view/211/192 (accessed 2 October 2010).

Parker, R. and Pollock, G. (1981) *Old Mistresses: Women, Art and Ideology*, London: Routledge.

Patrick, G. and Busfield, A. (1999) 'Kosovan boy tells of horrors', *The Sun*, 27 March: 2–3.

Philipose, L. (2008) 'The politics of pain and the uses of torture', in K. Alexander and M. Hawkesworth (eds) *War and Terror: Feminist Perspectives*, Chicago: University of Chicago Press.

Philo, G. (1990) *Seeing and Believing: The Influence of Television*, London: Routledge.

Pollard, J. (2011) 'Seen, seared and sealed: Trauma and the visual presentation of September 11', *Health, Risk and Society*, 1(13): 81–101.

Pollock, G. (2008) 'Responses to W.J.T. Mitchell', in D. Costello and D. Willsdon (eds) *The Life and Death of Images: Ethics and Aesthetics*, London: Tate Publishing.

Radway, J. (1987) *Reading the Romance: Women, Patriarchy and Popular Literature*, London: Verso.

Rectenwald, M. (2003) 'Gulf war II: The new "real"'. Citizens for Legitimate Government. Online. Available HTTP: http://www.legitgov.org/mike_essay_the_new_real4_031103.html (accessed 2 September 2009).

Rich Mix programme (2008) 'Bangladesh Film Festival 1–27 April', Rich Mix. Online. Available HTTP: http://www.richmix.org.uk/prelive/downloads/press/spring08/RM_PR_Banglade sh%20Fiilm%20Festival.pdf (accessed 20 November 2008).

Rudd, K. (2009) 'The global financial crisis', *The Monthly* (42): 20–9.

Rutherford, P. (2004) *Weapons of Mass Persuasion: Marketing the War against Iraq*, Toronto: University of Toronto Press.

Sadowski, W. (2009) 'William Sadowski', Faculty of Arts, University of Brighton. Online. Available HTTP: http://arts.brighton.ac.uk/study/pmis/photography-ma/student-work/william-sadowski (accessed 2 October 2010).

Saïd, E. (1978) *Orientalism*, London: Pantheon Books.

Schama, S. (2008) *The American Future: A History* [TV programme] BBC 2, London: BBC.

Schama, S. (2006) *The Power of Art* [TV programme] BBC 2, [DVD] London: BBC.

Schama, S. (1999) *Rembrandt's Eyes*, London: Allen Lane.

Shafique, T. (2008) 'The people's war', Life as is IsBlog. Online. Available HTTP: http://tahminashafique.wordpress.com/2008/05/01/the-peoples-war (accessed 2 September 2008).

Shotter, J. (1993) *Cultural Politics of Everyday Life: Social Constructionism, Rhetoric and Knowing of the Third Kind*, London: Open University Press.

Sinco, L. (2007) 'Two lives blurred together by a photo', Los Angeles Times, 11 November. Online. Available HTTP: http://articles.latimes.com/2007/nov/11/nation/na-marlboro11 (accessed 2 September 2009).

Sontag, S. (2004a) 'The photos are US', *The Guardian G2 Magazine*, 24 May: 1.

Sontag, S. (2004b) 'Regarding the torture of others', *The New York Times Magazine*, 23 May: 25.

Sontag, S. (2003) *Regarding the Pain of Others*, New York: Farrar, Straus and Giroux.

Sontag, S. (1977) *On Photography*, New York: Farrar, Straus and Giroux.

Stallabrass, J. (2008) 'The power and impotence of images, Brighton Photo Biennial 2008, catalogue, Brighton, Photoworks: 4–9.

Stephens, C. (2001). 'Art and war', Direct Art. Online. Available HTTP: http://www.slowart.com/articles/war.htm (accessed 1 May 2008).

Strydom, P. (2002) *Risk, Environment, and Society: Ongoing Debates, Current Issues and Future Prospects*, London: Open University Press.

Terzieff, J. (1999) 'Kosovo Serbs massacre 45 villagers', *The Sunday Times*, 17 January: 2.

The Australian (2009) 'A fight for democracy', Editorial. 24 June: 13.

The Canberra Times (2009) 'Dying Neda icon of Iran unrest', 24 June: 8.

The Guardian (2009) 'The Berlin wall had to fall, but today's world is no fairer', 31 October: 35.

The Landmark Art Series, BBC 4 (2008) [TV Programme] London: BBC.

The Sun (1999) 'Time to act', Editorial. 24 March: 8.

The Times (2008) 'Has capitialism failed?', Editorial. 14 October: 8.

Toynbee, J. (2008) 'Media making and social reality', in D. Hesmondhalg and J. Toynbee (eds) *The Media and Social Theory*, Oxford: Routledge.

Tromans, N. (2008) 'Introduction: British orientalist painting', in N. Tromans (ed.) *The Lure of the East: British Orientalist Painting*. London: Tate Britain.

Tromans, N. (ed.) (2008) *The Lure of the East: British Orientalist Painting*, London: Tate Britain.

Tulloch, J. (2008a) 'Risk and subjectivity: Experiencing terror'. *Health, Risk & Society*, 10(5): 451–65.

Tulloch, J. (2008b) 'Culture and risk', in J. Zinn (ed.) *Social Theories of Risk and Uncertainty*, Oxford: Blackwell.

Tulloch, J. (2006) *One Day in July: Experiencing 7/7*, London: Little, Brown.

Tulloch, J. (2000) *Watching Television Audiences: Cultural Theories and Methods*, London: Arnold.

Tulloch, J. (1999) 'Fear of crime: Sociological theories of risk', in D. Lupton (ed.) *Risk and Sociological Theory*, Cambridge: Cambridge University Press.

Tulloch, J. (1982) *Australian Cinema: Industry, Narrative and Meaning*, Sydney: Allen & Unwin.

Tulloch, J. (1981) *Legends on the Screen: The Australian Narrative Cinema, 1919–1929*, Sydney: Currency Press/Australian Film Institute.

Tulloch, J. and Blood, R.W. (2010) 'Iconic photojournalism and absent images: Democratization and memories of terror', in S. Allan (ed.) *The Routledge Companion to News and Journalism*, Abingdon, Oxon: Routledge.

Tulloch, J. and Lupton, D. (eds) (2003) *Risk and Everyday Life*, London: Sage.

Urry, J. (2010) 'Consuming the planet to excess', *Theory, Culture and Society*, 27(2–3): 191–212.

Virilio, P. (2002) *Ground Zero*, trans. C. Turner, London: Verso.

Visual Statistics Studio (n.d.) 'Ethical canons of war, Amiriyah shelter'. Online. Available HTTP: http://www.visualstatistics.net/east-west/Amiriyah/Amiriyah.htm (accessed 1 October 2009).

Weeks, E. (2008) 'Cultures crossed: John Frederick Lewis and the art of orientalist painting', in N. Tromans (ed.) *The Lure of the East: British Orientalist Painting*. London: Tate Britain.

Wilkinson, I. (2006) 'Health, risk and "social suffering"', *Health, Risk & Society*, 8(1): 1–8.

Wright, K. (2011) 'Reality without scare quotes: Developing the case for critical realism in journalism research', *Journalism Studies*, 12(2): 156–71.

Wynne, B. (1996) 'May the sheep safely graze? A reflexive view of the expert-lay knowledge divide, in S. Lash, B. Szerzynski and B. Wynne (eds) *Risk, Environment and Modernity: Towards a New Ecology*, London: Sage.

Young, A. (2007) 'Images in the aftermath of trauma: Responding to September 11th', *Crime, Media, Culture*, 3(1): 30–48.

Young, A. (2005) *Judging the Image: Art, Value, Law*, London: Routledge.

Zelizer, B. and Allan, S. (eds) (2002) *Journalism After September 11*, London: Routledge.

Žižek, S. (2004) *Iraq: The Borrowed Kettle*, London: Verso.

Žižek, S. (2002) *Welcome to the Desert of the Real! Five Essays on September 11 and Related Dates*, London: Verso.

Index

Page numbers in *italics* refer to an illustration. Individual works are indexed under the name of the author/artist/presenter.